Local family history in England

Colin D. Rogers and John H. Smith

Local family history in England

1538–1914

 Manchester University Press
Manchester and New York

distributed exclusively in the USA and Canada by St. Martin's Press

Published by Manchester University Press
Oxford Road, Manchester M13 9PL, England
and Room 400, 175 Fifth Avenue, New York, NY 10010, USA

Distributed exclusively in the USA and Canada
by St. Martin's Press, Inc., 175 Fifth Avenue, New York, NY 10010, USA

A catalogue record for this book is available from the British Library

Library of Congress cataloging in publication data
Rogers, Colin Darlington.
     Local family history in England, 1538–1914 / Colin D. Rogers and
John Smith.
          p.   cm.
     Includes bibliographical references (p.   ) and index.
     ISBN 0–7190–3200–8 (cloth), — ISBN 0–7190–3201–6 (paper)
     1. England—Genealogy. 2. England—History, Local. I. Smith,
John Henry. II. Title.
     CS414.R534   1991
     929'.2'0942—dc20   91–17939

ISBN 0 7190 3200 8 hardback
     0 7190 3201 6 paperback

Photoset in Linotron Joanna
by Northern Phototypesetting Company Limited, Bolton
Printed in Great Britain
by Bell & Bain Limited, Glasgow

Contents

Acknowledgements   *page* vi
Introduction   1

Part I THE HISTORY OF THE FAMILY, 1538–1914

Introduction   12
Historical background   12
   The early modern period   12
   Industrialisation   19
The English family   28
   Marriage in the early modern period   30
   Marriage in the age of industrialisation   41
   Children in the early modern period   60
   Children in the industrial age   68
   Solitaries, the widowed and the aged: the early modern period   74
   Solitaries, the widowed and the aged: the industrial age   78

Part II THE EXPLOITATION OF SOURCE MATERIAL

Introduction   82
Lists   86
Listings   95
Censuses and community reconstitution   102
Aggregative analysis   113
   Marriage   119
   An excursion into mobility   122
   Birth and baptism   126
   Death and burial   129
Family and total reconstitution   132

Part III A FAMILY HISTORY RESEARCH AGENDA

Organisation   146
What to investigate   150
Making it public   170

Appendices
1 Hearth Tax return for Tintwistle, Cheshire, 1664   173
2 Population pyramid constructed from the list of inhabitants of
   Ealing, Essex, 1599   176
3 A listing of inhabitants of Ringmore, Devon, 1698   178
4 1801 census 'return' for Croston, Lancashire   181
5 Aggregative histogram of parish register entries for Billinge,
   Lancashire, 1772–1812   195
6 List of family reconstitutions held by the Cambridge Group for
   the History of Population and Social Structure   197
Resource reading list   201
Index   213

Acknowledgements

We are indebted to the following for permission to reproduce material: Appendix 1, the Controller of Her Majesty's Stationery Office (Crown Copyright); Appendix 3, the British Library; Appendix 4, the Rev R. J. Brunswick, Rector of the parish church of St Michael, Croston, Lancashire; Appendix 6, the Cambridge Group for the History of Population and Social Structure.

Dr Kevin Schurer was helpful enough to allow us to see the text of his forthcoming book (with Tom Arkell), and we have also benefited from a discussion with him at 27 Trumpington Street, Cambridge.

We would also like to express our thanks to those transbinary guinea pigs, the students in the earliest cohorts of the course on which this book is based.

Introduction

This is an unashamedly evangelical book, aimed at those who are already genealogists or local historians as well as at students of economic and social history. It is based on the proposition that both disciplines are currently defective in an important respect, and suggests ways by which that defect, if accepted as such, can be remedied.

Genealogists in particular may be offended by the suggestion that their normal objectives and methods of research may be significantly inadequate. To many, 'genealogy' and 'family history' are virtually synonymous, the latter term being used in order to convey either a more up-to-date image, or the impression that there is an interest in researching the social circumstances of those ancestors already uncovered by strictly genealogical research. Hence, family history is thought to move outwards from specific individuals, related genetically to the researcher, into the penumbra of local history, sometimes social or economic, often merely antiquarian.

We believe that, in reality, this distinction is a myth. Associations or societies round the world name themselves, one might suppose, in the light of their own specific aim. Those which include 'heraldry' in their title (the Birmingham and Midland Society for Genealogy and Heraldry, or the Lancashire Family History and Heraldry Society, for example) give a bias in the appropriate direction. However, we believe that differences between 'genealogy' and 'family history' societies are negligible. A study of the lecture programmes or the contents of their respective journals supports our contention that there appears to be little significance in the phrase 'family history' as it is currently used, distinct from 'genealogy'. The journal of the Institute of Heraldic and Genealogical Studies in Canterbury is called *Family History*; and most 'genealogical' societies, in England and Wales at least, are affiliated to the Federation of Family History Societies (FFHS).

Well, what's in a name? Does it really matter that these appellations are used almost interchangeably? Surely, if such societies are offering their members a menu which is satisfying their needs, not to say cravings, as their often huge memberships suggest, the name should be taken as little more than an advertising guide, or a collective, generic title.

We suggest, however, that there are two consequences of the present state of the art which are far more serious than any uncertainty about the interpretation of title. One stems from a failure of many of its practitioners to realise that genealogy is not a branch of history at all – at best it is only one of the tools which a few historians use. History itself is about causes, consequences and generalisations concerning the past; genealogy is normally the discovery of the identity (however defined) of individuals with whom the researchers, or their clients, happen to be genetically related. Family history, as presently understood, is merely the subsequent acquisition of data about those individuals, whether that be about their place of work, wages, housing conditions, taxation payments, or any of a large range of information linked only because they relate to the specific individuals concerned. It is what genealogists world-wide understand by 'putting flesh on the bones'.

Genealogy is a fascinating, not to say obsessive hobby. It has given pleasure to hundreds of thousands of people, each of whom has to fight a series of stumbling blocks and frustrations which are unique to the individual researcher. It requires relatively little historical understanding or knowledge, yet it sets the researcher into his or her individual place in history which is impossible to achieve through any normal historical enquiry. It requires a knowledge of archives, their content, location, and accessibility, as extensive as that used by most local historians (to such an extent that we have not felt it necessary to give long introductions to the many sources of information about family history used in the book); but that knowledge is only a means to an end – and that end, however absorbing, however exciting, is *essentially personal*.

Everyone, in England and Wales at least, who has tried to trace a family tree will have encountered the phenomenon of the unsympathetic archivist or librarian. It is not uncommon to find in correspondence columns complaints about short shrift being given to genealogists in one Record Office or another despite the fact that this group now form a substantial proportion (in some a clear majority) of clients. Without genealogists, certain Record Offices would have very few visitors indeed.

If the suspicions of archivists' and librarians' offhandedness are accurate, wherein lies the cause? Some of them deride beginners who know too little of the sources, or of the techniques, or of the historical background required for the research; yet, even in understaffed estab-lishments, education is one of the functions of the professions con-cerned. Others will quote horror stories of vandalism; yet, compared with other users, such offences are relatively rare, and, in any case, tarring all with the same brush is hardly the act of rational beings. We believe that behind much of the unease felt by many archivists towards genealogists is the feeling that their research is too self-centred (the 'train-spotting syndrome'); that only the researcher (or client) reaps the rewards, in contrast to the historian who aims to publish for the benefit of society's understanding of its own past. However, we have not developed the thesis behind this book merely in order to change an image, but to change a reality. We are fully behind Rosalin Barker (1985), who wrote: 'Don't stop being genealogists. Just become responsible genealogists. Become family historians.'

We believe that there is an area of genuine historical research, as closely allied to genealogy as many of the current activities of the societies, which we have called for the purpose of this book 'local family history' – that is, 'family history' in the sense widely used outside genealogical circles but in its local setting. The Resource Reading List will show that it is a modern study, but by no means a new one. It adopts and adapts the techniques and advantages of three different disciplines.

Genealogy develops a great concern for the minutiae and accuracy of establishing genetic relationships between identifiable individuals, by painstaking research motivated largely by the fascination of knowing that your genes are the ones in question. It leads to an interest in historical characters as individuals with feelings, motives, joys and sorrows, whether they are of the realities of moving house, of being widowed, or of child labour.

Demography is the study of the history of population and population change, so ostensibly there should be a close liaison between this and genealogy, especially as they are using substantially the same source material – parish registers, civil registration, census and taxation returns, and so on. There are two main reasons, however, why demography has scarcely touched the average genealogist. First, its concerns are about people on a large scale, often without the necessity to identify individuals; in some relatively elementary exercises, as we shall see, gaps in records can even be filled by the creation of mythical people in order to achieve a meaningful result. (If genealogists could do that, the family tree industry would collapse overnight!) The individual disappears from view, and it is always with individuals that genealogists are concerned. Second, demographers have developed a battery of statistical and modelling techniques (such as back projection, a statistical method of establishing the base populations of individual parishes before 1801 which we have excluded from Part II) which are enough in themselves to convince most genealogists that the study is far too academic and remote to be of relevance to their needs. We hope to show that, in this attitude, there is a grave danger of throwing out the baby with the bathwater, and that there are several demographic methods which can and should be used by the local family historian and even the genealogist.

However, it must be recognised that facts uncovered by a demographic approach will still be open to non-demographic interpretation. As John Demos wrote (Laslett 1972, p. 569): 'Demographic results, on the other hand, are arid – and sometimes quite meaningless – without a level of "qualitative" insight', and Edward Shorter (1975) went further (we believe too far), seeing changes in the personal relationships within families as the key to a major revolution in the place of the family within western society in the last 300 years. Suppose, for example, that your research leads you to find that bridegrooms in 'your' parish were on average three years older than their brides in the first half of the eighteenth century. Why did this particular difference exist? We are at once in the realms of biology, social psychology, and economic history, though the demographer might continue to have something to say about variations in time, space and social class, about the availability for marriage of different sex cohorts, and the implications of the three-year difference for population growth. We believe that family historians will be just as interested in the exceptions – in the motives and consequences for marrying across widely differing ages.

Local History is the black hole of amateur historical studies, an area into which it is all too easy to fall, and from which it is virtually impossible to escape. Second only to genealogy in its ability to attract large numbers of devotees, it lures the unwary who enter its territory for innocent, often specialist purposes; but whether it be for the history of schools or sewers, telephones or toll roads, the researcher quickly acquires an interest in the general history of the geographical area concerned, and genealogists are no exception. The communities in which our ancestors lived were essentially local, and these communities become the subject of study, often at the peril of the main objective. Those who are tempted to sample the local family history described in this book must be warned that, whereas they will be using genealogical and demographic techniques, it is local history which is the likeliest source of distraction. The family history project, in short, can rapidly dissolve into local history unless you keep a very firm grip on it. This is a pity because, to us at least, one of the deficiencies of local history is the very stuff of genealogy – an interest in individuals and what motivated their lives.

Local history begins with place, with an identifiable unit that may range from a hamlet to a city. The object of study is to explore its history, to understand its modern form and topography, its changing character over the centuries and the lives that have been lived in it. It is therefore to local historians that we look for detailed and painstaking reconstruction of the growth or decline of population, changes in the local economy or society and the physical appearance of the place. Their results provide the framework within which we can attempt to examine the family in general or specific families which were located within the place described. It also enables us to ask questions that will relate our families of the past, and those around them, to the times in which they lived.

In the past, antiquarians and local historians were principally interested in the genealogy of great or gentry families which dominated local manors or estates. Later they turned with equal interest to the descent and characters of local merchants and industrialists or those of humbler origins who had made some national mark, whether good or ill. More recently the lives of ordinary people have come into focus through the exploitation of such sources as parish registers, probate records and the parliamentary censuses. Both local historians, and genealogists in search of their genetic roots, have mined these rich seams but they have brought to them their own preoccupations. For the local historian the place is paramount; individuals create and inhabit it, but it is the sum total of their activities that attracts attention. Individuals or families may feature as exceptions or examples, but it is their group affiliations that merit most attention and normally set the agenda. Thus, the questions that arise for local historians are those that have to do with social order or class, with occupation, with religious and political affiliation, with urban rise or decay, with educational, cultural, and leisure interests. The family as such has rarely featured in their work, though it is now beginning to emerge.

From our own schooldays, and from the media, we all inherit and assimilate a series of truths and myths, lessons and legends about our ancestors, their families, and the way they lived. Some of these myths were exploded years ago, but nevertheless persist among those for whom research is 'academic' and therefore seemingly irrelevant. In Part I, our historical sketch of the way the British family has changed and developed will refer to commonly held views which do not accord with the results of modern research. For the 'family history' of this book is basically (though often not only) the history of the family, to be studied in a way which sets our own ancestors in their immediate context and provides new perspectives for our understanding of them. You will even learn things about them which they did not know themselves.

Take, for one small but not insignificant example to which we shall return several times, illegitimacy, which is regarded by genealogists with a combination of frustration and fascination, and whose cases, as Wrightson observes (1982, p. 84), provide 'one of our few opportunities to investigate the courtships of the poor'. Did it run in families? If so, which families, from which social strata? Were they likely to be in rural or urban communities? Were illegitimate children born to younger mothers or older? Were the patterns of illegitimacy in Newcastle the same as those in Exeter? Were such families outcasts, or accepted and supported by their communities? How did the answers to these and a host of other related questions change over time?

A number of different disciplines could be at work on this problem. The demographer would be interested in illegitimacy rates and their geographical and chronological variations, and how illegitimacy related to bridal pregnancy; the historical sociologist will be concerned with the social status of the mothers, and of the illegitimate children and adults, as well as with establishing the causes for any endemic undercurrent of illegitimacy. The social psychologist will wish to study attitudes towards extra-marital sex and the raising of illegitimate children, from such sources as plays, diaries and autobiographies. The comparative sociologist could puzzle over why, apparently, Paris had one of the highest rates in pre-industrial France, yet London had one of the lowest rates in England.

The genealogist and local historian can call on all of these techniques in an effort to set particular families into significant context, whereas most academics tend to concentrate on only one discipline. A general and very enlightening introduction to the methods, scope, and disadvantages of looking at family history is Michael Anderson's *Approaches to the history of the western family, 1500–1914* (1980) which provides an analysis to enable the general reader to fit writers and approaches into their (albeit modern) traditions and assumptions, and Anderson himself (1971) demonstrates the great effectiveness of supporting statistical research by reference to contemporary observations.

In terms of its general aims and the way it uses source material, genealogy has scarcely changed in a century or more, despite the enormous growth in its popularity. In contrast there has been a rapid development of, and growth in the publication of books concerned with family history in the last twenty years, especially since the appearance of Peter Laslett's *The world we have lost* in 1965 and E. A. Wrigley's *An introduction to English historical demography* a year later.

As in the case of local history, family history has been undertaken by a spectrum of interested individuals and groups, from evening-class projects and undergraduate programmes (notably those of the Open University) to the professionals in CAMPOP, the Cambridge Group for the History of Population and Social Structure. Indeed the writing is now so substantial, covering many different directions, that we can hardly claim that this book is more than an introduction to it. Nevertheless, considerable research continues to be undertaken outside the immediate sphere of academic establishments. The support literature from the Open University is very instructive about sources and methods for projects and project assessment, and the journal *Local Population Studies*, originally inspired and still supported by CAMPOP, forms a very useful bridge between the professional and amateur researcher in family history.

On the whole, genealogists have not benefited from all this writing and research, though there have been some notable exceptions. A section of the Yorkshire Archaeological Society is for 'Family and Population Studies'; articles on mobility, age at marriage, and similar subjects appear occasionally in the genealogical journals; and there is an interesting attempt by Prideaux (1986) to apply demographic techniques to the history of his own family name. However, these are exceptions. The present authors started a course in family history for genealogists in Manchester during 1987. We visited the very good genealogical library of one of the local family history societies, and found not one book from the course's extensive family history reading list. This is a symptom of the second consequence of a failure, referred to earlier, to have an adequate definition of the phrase.

That course, and this book, are attempts to bridge that gap; to demonstrate to genealogists in particular that there are whole worlds of investigation to open up concerning the very people in whom they are already interested – their own ancestors. These involve looking in new ways at all the sources with which they are already familiar – Hearth Tax returns, wills, or marriage allegations, for example, as well as the obvious parish registers and census returns, in order to derive the maximum benefit from them. Much of the research, therefore, has involved some ingenuity in exploiting the source material – the Aladdin's cave contains a remarkable rearrangement of the jewels rather than a wholly untapped treasure.

That is by no means all. We are confident that research into local family history, when undertaken by those with a genealogical rather than a demographic interest, will be a two-way exercise, and our purpose is in consequence twofold. Not only should genealogists learn the lessons from family history for an enlightened understanding of their own ancestors; we also believe that family history has a lot to gain from genealogists, especially in those many questions which remain in need of detailed and numerous local investigations, and genealogists as well as local historians are ideally placed to identify locally surviving records which may be of considerable importance to family history, once the features of such records are recognised.

There is also the question of interpretation of data, and of the consequences of social situations being as they appear from the source material. This should include the use of autobiographies and diaries, largely untouched in our methodological section (Part II) below. (For useful lists of many which were published before those dates, see Matthews 1950 and 1955.) Discovering that migrants have more children than the average for the host community, for example, is relatively easy compared with establishing the reasons; the consequences of a wife taking in, as opposed to going to live with a mother or mother-in-law are also worthy of investigation, again only when the facts and statistics have been established. There are several quite different reasons why this should be so. We have already touched on one – the passionate interest in individuals, and the impact of social and economic circumstances on their lives. Second, the majority of genealogists are female, whereas the majority of writers on family history, including ourselves, are male. The fact alters neither the source material nor (probably) the techniques, of course – but it might well affect the sort of questions which are asked when the research is being designed, and the nature of the interpretation placed on the resulting data. This may be particularly true for those who accept the view that the family is the key institution to understanding the oppression of women in our society over hundreds of years. (See, for example, Tilly 1987 for a discussion of this issue.)

Third, genealogists are already mobilised on a permanent basis in a way which does not apply to any other similar group. The total member-ship of societies in England and Wales affiliated to the Federation is about 70,000, and (even allowing for dual and overseas members) there is thus a veritable army of knowledgeable and industrious volunteers, many already involved in individual projects and potentially available to help with large-scale ones; societies can also organise plenty of advice on how to develop them. See, e.g., Johnston 1971b and Rogers 1977.

We make no apology for presenting a rather large 'resource reading list' on p. 201. This is not only a convenient way to present the works referred to in the text of the book; it is mainly intended as a resource for those readers, hopefully the great majority, who will not be satisfied with merely reading it but will feel the urge to start research themselves. For them, the reading list is a point of reference in order to discover who has undertaken the main published research of the same kind before.

Perhaps we should also add that we have deliberately restricted the reading, and indeed the book, to local family history in England, and that, arising from the nature of our own researches, many of the examples we use come from the north-west of the country. Since the 1960s demo-graphy has become increasingly international, or comparative, as well as more mathematical; neither approach, however valid or enlightening, is the most appropriate starting-point for those whose principal interests and essential motivations are (in the neutral sense) amateur and parochial.

Finally, we are tempted to offer, on the basis of our own students' evaluation, an authors' two fold guarantee to genealogists. You will find that your own research, individual but especially collective, supplementing the methods and findings of this book, will enhance your understanding and enjoyment of your own ancestry. You can also be sure, therefore, that local family history will not dilute your passion for genealogy. As you read Part I, think to yourself how facts and opinions might have been arrived at; as you read Part II, consider the possible application of the methods discussed to that part of the country or that aspect of family history which is of particular interest to you.

Part I

The history
of the family

1538–1914

Introduction

Although we are all aware that families must have economic foundations in order to survive, it is only in comparatively recent years that historians have begun to explore what that means. They have found that it is a far from simple matter. Families were, of course, influenced by economic conditions which might encourage or discourage marriage, for example, but the ways in which families were formed and behaved had their own consequences for society in general. Private decisions on when to marry and on the number of children deemed desirable helped to determine population growth or decline. Laws and customs that governed the ownership of property in families and the ways in which it could be inherited could concentrate or disperse capital. The treatment of children could encourage dependence or stimulate mobility and ambition. The family was not only responsive to but was in part responsible for the economic context in which it was set. It is that complex relationship that we first wish to explore.

Historical background

The early modern period

The England that we know and remember is very different from that which our forefathers knew and the stages by which one became transmuted into the other are still the subject of historical enquiry. What is certain is that we have changed from a rural and largely traditional people living and working in small communities and surrounded by powerful and ill-understood forces of nature to one accustomed to large and complex systems which appear to dominate not only us but the natural world which contains us. What follows is a necessarily brief introduction to some of the major stages in that great change.

In the early sixteenth century the people of England were

predominantly rural: only 5.5 per cent of them lived in urban areas with populations of over 5,000. By 1700 this had doubled and 11 per cent lived in London and the thirty towns with over 5,000 people, seven of which had over 10,000 inhabitants (Wrightson 1982, p. 129). By 1800 this proportion had grown to 25 per cent, some 2,380,000 people in all (Levine 1987, p. 81). In the nineteenth century this modest definition of urban life changed. By 1851 about half of the population lived in towns of 20,000 or more (Levine 1987, p. 144). By 1931 only 20 per cent of the population of England and Wales were rural, 40 per cent living in towns with fewer than 100,000 inhabitants and the remaining 40 per cent living in fifty-one towns with over 100,000 inhabitants. Manchester, Sheffield and Liverpool had populations over 500,000, Birmingham over one million, Greater London over 8 million (Mowat 1964, p. 227). Increasing numbers of people were living in increasingly large towns, and working, not at home or in its vicinity, but in the larger, more distant and impersonal factories, workshops and mines created by industrialisation.

The old society that changed so radically, above all during that series of events we call the Industrial Revolution, was in many ways traditional and hierarchical, but it was far from static or unchanging. Although no longer feudal in a military sense, even in the sixteenth century, the countryside was dominated by the aristocracy and gentry, though there was a market in land, and yeomen and others were able to buy freehold cottages, lands and estates. The towns rose like islands in this 'manorial' sea with their craftsmen and shopkeepers governed by mayors, aldermen and common councilmen. The church, too, was powerful and acted in concert with the landed orders in maintaining a stable society and regulating conduct. This was, then, a society of orders and ranks; the monarch above all, the aristocracy governing the nation under the Crown and the gentry of the countryside ruling their counties and manors with the assistance of the clergy and the substantial yeomen and tenants.

This organisation and control extended to every aspect of life. The ranks below the gentry were excluded from power, and superior authority attempted to regulate where and how they should live and the extent to which they should be educated. Though manorial control was no longer able to tie tenants and cottagers to their native soil, the machinery of the Poor Law of 1601–03 and the Settlement Act of 1662 was introduced to try to prevent them from wandering. Many of their homes and lands were held under the manorial courts which laid down how they passed from generation to generation. In the open-field villages their agricultural calendar and practices were determined by their lord and fellow-tenants in the courts leet. They sought, or were subject to justice in law courts administered either by the manor or the gentry Justices of the Peace or the great law lords of the realm. But they were not fixed and immobile on their land. They could escape, through education (for the fortunate), by apprenticeship to trades or by service in another household or on another farm. Some wandered the country, in defiance of the constables and overseers of the poor, picking up a living however and wherever they could.

For those in towns the guilds and common councils exercised similar control over economic and social life. The aspiring boy hoped to rise from apprentice through the ranks of the wage-earning journeymen to independent master, to become a fellow or warden of his guild, a councilman perhaps, even alderman, mayor or Justice of the Peace. His life would be as regulated as that of the husbandmen of the countryside but he could hope to rise far higher. The labourer outside the guild suffered no such restrictions but his prospects were far less bright. The religious and social character of the whole community was that laid down by the church and its courts, the Establishment in its clerical role, moderated only slightly by local or regional customs and traditions. The church also took responsibility for the legal and moral aspects of family life: the records it generated provide the most important early source material for the study of genealogy and family history.

But of course society was not static before the onset of industrialisation. Population was increasing. Wrigley and Schofield suggest that in 1541 England, excluding Monmouth, had some 2.7 million inhabitants, rising to 3 million in 1551, 4.1 million in 1601 and 5.2 million in 1651. The latter half of the seventeenth century saw a fall to 5 million in 1701 before growth resumed to produce a population of 5.7 million in 1751 (Wrigley & Schofield 1981, pp. 208–9). This growth was not even over time, nor was it evenly distributed: not all places could grow by natural increase, and in many of those where natural increase took place the local economy could not support it. Economic growth took place at different speeds in different regions, and population ebbed and flowed with the movements of local agriculture or trades.

During the late sixteenth century, as population grew faster than the means to support it, there was a growth in the number of landless people, many of whom turned to vagrancy and appeared to pose a threat to social order. The Poor Law was meant both to regulate and to ameliorate the condition of this pauper class but in the seventeenth century, despite legislation that forbade the erection of new cottages without land, the number of those without property who depended upon wage labour appears to have increased. It is impossible to quantify this change. The first attempt to measure the economic and social classes and assess their income was made by Gregory King in 1696 for the year 1688 when his calculations suggest that over 950,000 of the 1,390,000 families were of the lower orders of society, with little hope of inheritance. Not all of these people were wage-earners in the modern sense; perhaps some 45 per cent of all families depended upon skills or labour that would bring in earnings compared with about 20 per cent who owned or leased land, 10 per cent who needed significant capital and the 24 per cent who were cottagers, paupers or vagrants. (For discussion of Gregory King's table see Perkin 1969, pp. 20–5, and the revised figures in Lindert & Williamson 1982.)

In the arable countryside, enclosure, often for conversion from the growing of corn with its heavy demand for labour to sheep-grazing, produced a reduction in the number of separate holdings and deprived many commoners of the means of making a living. Meanwhile in the pastoral, less densely settled regions of the moors, fens and forests, sub-division or the taking-in of new land was encouraging a growth of independent smallholders. Many of these areas were also rich in the raw materials that were needed as wood, now growing more scarce in some areas, gave way to coal for fuel and to brick and stone for building. In general landowners and yeomen improved their position, husbandmen did not thrive so well and there was a great growth in the number of the poor. Extractive and industrial occupations were growing outside the boroughs, offering a lifeline for many and, for some, the road to prosperity.

Thus the population of the weaving areas of Norfolk, Suffolk, Essex, Wiltshire and Somerset increased, along with that in the Forest of Dean which had mining, wood and iron trades. The coal trade fostered prosperity in the Tyne valley, and in north-west England and the West Riding of Yorkshire plentiful, if poor land encouraged the spread of holdings which were supported as much by coal, textiles or other local trades as by agriculture. London, which housed the Court, the growing national administration and the central courts of law as well as being a great port and manufacturing centre, grew in population from 50,000 to 575,000 between the 1520s and 1700 (Wrightson 1982, p. 128).

The country suffered a devastating inflationary crisis between 1590 and 1630 resulting largely from increased demand by the rising population; frequent dislocations of industry and bad harvests often pushed the landless into want, sometimes into vagrancy. Nevertheless this class of people who supplemented or replaced work on the land with an industrial occupation grew steadily. As early as 1591 the Stockport weaver Alexander Daniel left his property between his five sons, at least four of whom were weaving in his house where he had five looms. His list of debts suggests strongly that he was paying them wages (Phillips & Smith 1985, pp. 6–7). During the seventeenth and eighteenth centuries there were more and more families whose incomes were derived partly from industry and the proportions of their income thus derived also grew.

Industry was spreading into the countryside but it was also encouraging the growth of towns. During the early modern period the towns outside London were small: York's population was 12,000 in the 1660s and Chester had 8,700 inhabitants in 1728 (Hey 1986, p. 181; Aldridge 1986, p. 36). The towns were also unhealthy and none could maintain their populations by natural increase until after the mid-eighteenth century, but most people still lived in rural areas and could produce a surplus of births to supply the urban centres. It is estimated that half of the country's excess of births was needed to produce the growth of London in the sixteenth and seventeenth centuries (Levine 1987, p. 80–1).

The communities in which most people lived were small and

parochial, inward-looking and more concerned with their own and their neighbours' affairs than great matters of state. This does not mean that their inhabitants were completely immobile. The aristocracy and gentry, of course, took all England in their stride both for business and pleasure, but those in the lower ranks of society also travelled, not only on short visits and journeys, but over considerable distances, and often emigrated in search of a better life. Necessary trips to markets and fairs, pleasure rambles to do with courting, hunting, coursing or fishing took ordinary people into adjacent townships, and visits to relatives could take them further afield. Attendance at the Quarter Sessions Courts involved not only the local men of substance such as churchwardens and jurymen but prosecutors, defendants and witnesses of all degrees in journeys to their county and sessions towns. Those cited in church causes or unfortunate enough to be executors in difficult probate cases had to attend church courts, while military service opened up further avenues of travel for young men. At times of crisis ordinary people could make great journeys. The tenants of the Talbots in Glossopdale in Derbyshire, for example, went to London to protest to the Privy Council about changes in their tenancies in April and again in November 1579, in March 1580, in April 1581 and finally, when they were told not to come any more in a body but to send one or two, in September 1581. In May 1579 the Ashford tenants from the same county were also in London complaining about their tenancies (Talbot & Shrewsbury Papers 1971, passim).

Such crises were rare, but migration was common. Richard Gough's survey of the parish of Myddle in Shropshire in 1701 portrays not the settled and static community we might expect but a shifting kaleidoscope in which families appear and dis-appear, prosper and climb the social ladder or fall into ruin and decay (Gough 1981, passim). The aristocracy and gentry sought by various legal devices to secure continued family possession of their estates but even they moved across country, buying and selling manors and setting down new roots as opportunity offered. The great Derbyshire stronghold of the Cavendishes owed its existence to Elizabeth Cavendish's desire to return to her native county, but it was only made possible by her husband's willingness to sell his own estates. The yeomanry appear to have been more settled on their lands than those below them who looked more for economic opportunity in their tenancies or short leases than for long continuity on the same ground (Wrightson 1982, pp. 42–3). Sentimental attachment to the ancestral home and acres was often secondary to the attractions of better land, easier terms and rents or the rich pickings that might be found in the towns. Those with skills looked for the best openings, wherever they might be, and landless families moved for seasonal work while the vagrant poor were endlessly restless, the bane of sixteenth- and seventeenth-century local administration. In 1688 61.8 per cent of the people living in Clayworth parish in Nottinghamshire had not been there in 1676 and 50 per cent of those in 1628 at Cogenhoe in Northampton had not been there in 1618 (Laslett 1965, p. 147). In Part II, we examine the means by which such conclusions can be drawn about local mobility.

There were political, social and religious changes as well as those that affected the economy. After 1540 England had to come to terms with the consequences of the Reformation which not only changed the nature and forms of religious belief and worship but introduced new political and social views that reflected increasing religious diversity. In the sixteenth century it was proper to believe that the state should countenance only one religion, but by the end of the seventeenth century toleration was tacitly extended to all Christian denominations, except in times of crisis, though there was suspicion of those who did not conform to the Church of England and penalties or restrictions were imposed on them. The Reformation also affected the ownership of property as religious houses and granges with great swathes of land passed into secular hands, often disturbing terms of tenure that had operated for many years.

In the seventeenth century the civil wars and Interregnum produced another series of shifts in landownership, in the organisation of church and state and in the fortunes of families. Not everything was restored at the Restoration: some landowners could never regain lost lands or money expended, neither could the Crown nor the church recover all they had lost, and the Glorious Revolution of 1688 put relations between Crown and Parliament on a new footing.

Industrialisation

From roughly the middle of the eighteenth century population growth in England was of a new order (see Table 1).

Table 1 The population of England, 1541–1921 (excluding Monmouth)

Year	Millions
1541	2.7
1551	3.0
1601	4.1
1651	5.2
1701	5.0
1751	5.7
1801	8.6
1851	16.7
1901	32.2
1921	37.3

Source: 1541–1851, Wrigley & Schofield 1981; 1901–1921, parliamentary census.

This increase could have arisen only from net immigration, an increased birth rate, a decreased death rate or a combination of these factors. Immigration was light in the eighteenth century coming mainly from Scotland and Ireland, and it was more than matched by emigration from England, principally to the Americas. It did not become substantial until the 1840s, when the acceleration in population had already taken place. Modern research suggests strongly that about three-quarters of the acceleration in the growth rate of the late eighteenth and early nineteenth centuries was brought about by increased fertility, the other quarter by changes in mortality. What lay behind these developments will be explored in the later sections of this book, but by 1798 the growth itself caused T. R. Malthus to publish his *Essay on population* with revised editions produced in the early nineteenth century.

Malthus viewed the growth in population with great anxiety. His researches led him to believe that the relationship between population and resources was such that births could not exceed deaths except where there were large new areas of virgin land to develop. Without controls or checks, population would grow

geometrically, but food production could only increase arith-
metically, so that it always provided a barrier beyond which
populations could not be sustained. When numbers of people
began to press closely against this barrier the result was misery,
starvation and a breakdown in social order. It was possible for
societies to foresee and prevent this growth, but if they failed then
'positive checks' would come into play. Thus high death rates
caused by unhealthy occupations, extreme poverty and severe
labour, excesses, diseases and epidemics, wars, plagues and
famines were not fortuitous but could be attributed, in part at
least, to the failure of society to control its own population
growth. The 'preventive checks' he advocated were designed to
restrict fertility and thus depended on deferment of marriage and
on changes in any social policies that encouraged people to marry
without economic independence. Malthus saw the family in a
national economic and social context: the most intimate and
personal affairs of humanity were also those that had the greatest
public consequences (Malthus 1973, *passim*).

The research carried out by E. A. Wrigley, R. S. Schofield and
others through the application of statistical techniques to parish
register data has given us the population estimates summarised in
Table 1 (see Part II). It has also set Malthus in his period and
outlines a population history of England that explores the
economic and demographic concerns he expressed.

Whatever growth took place had to be economically
sustainable if population was to be maintained and there were
periods in the late seventeenth and early eighteenth centuries
when growth was not sustained and the population fell. It was not
simply that population pressure produced dearth or famine
which produced more deaths. Wrigley and Schofield suggest that
up to the mid-eighteenth century fertility and mortality were of
roughly equal importance in determining the level of population.
However, high real wages did not necessarily reduce the number
of deaths. Indeed it is possible that they could draw people into
towns where they were subject to the high risks of urban living.
Economic prosperity or depression, always linked to good or bad
harvests, did largely determine the course of population growth
or decline but the link was principally through fertility rather than
mortality. Changes in real wages had only a limited and uncertain

impact on death rates but much more strongly affected people's ability to marry and the number of children subsequently born. People were more or less inclined to marry as real wages rose or fell during the period. They were also more likely to marry during the year following a year of population crisis.

What underlay this behaviour was the necessity for couples considering marriage to have access to economic opportunity that would offer a sufficient degree of security – a home, land, capital, skills or the expectation of wages. A rise in economic activity and real wages that increased such opportunities or recent deaths that left vacant places encouraged marriage; depression, dearth, or the uncertainty caused by current epidemics or other crises discouraged it (see Howson 1961). Long-term changes in real wages were slower to take effect, operating mainly through the age at which people married; views on the right age to marry changed only slowly as each generation came to terms with the experience of their parents' lives. Wrigley and Schofield describe this linkage of economic factors with marriage as a 'low-pressure system' which, on the whole, kept population at a level in which there was a balance between the population and the resources needed to sustain it.

It was this system that Malthus advocated in the late eighteenth century as the major bulwark against the evils that would arise from population outstripping its means of subsistence. As he wrote, however, it was giving way to a new situation in which the productive capacity of English agriculture and manufacture was growing so rapidly as to break the link between rising population and a rise in prices. Population growth after 1780 was higher and more sustained than ever before, but unlike the growth of the sixteenth century it did not promote higher prices, even before imported food became significant in the 1830s. This improved economic base stimulated population less by its reduction of mortality (the expectation of life at birth was 37.11 years in 1701 and it did not rise above 40 until the late 1820s) than by its encouragement of marriage. Not only were more people able to marry, they married earlier and produced more children until a rise in the age at marriage and the growing control of fertility within marriage produced a downturn in family size after the 1870s (Wrigley & Schofield 1981, *passim*).

Whatever the level of population, the people had to be fed and housed. Famines had brought high death rates in many parts of the country in 1597 and 1623 but later harvest failures, though severe, did not have the same consequences. From the 1680s to the 1720s the population was static or growing more slowly and agricultural improvement brought lower grain prices and better crop balances (Wrightson 1982, pp. 146–7). Transport was expensive, especially by land, and bulky cargoes such as grain were better carried by water, either on coastal vessels or by boats using navigable rivers wherever possible until turnpike roads, first introduced in 1663, became widespread after the mid-eighteenth century. Canals, pioneered by the Sankey navigation in 1755, also reduced the cost of inland carriage.

The improvements in transport that enabled food to be carried more effectively also brought down the cost of carriage for coal and other raw materials and for manufactured goods. They did not, of themselves, change the economic basis of life but from the mid-eighteenth century they opened up sources of raw materials and markets that could be exploited by the new industrialists of the period.

Both agriculture and manufacture underwent great changes during the eighteenth and early nineteenth centuries. It is now accepted that agricultural improvement began before the eighteenth century and after 1660 enclosure of common fields and pasture went ahead in great waves. During the second half of the eighteenth century enclosure became simpler and cheaper, using machinery laid down by Parliament for private acts. After 1760 there were about 5,400 acts covering 7 million acres, some one-fifth of the total area of England. Even before this period the number of small farmers and owner–occupiers had begun to decline and, though enclosure itself did not drive masses of people off the land, it did strengthen that tendency and reduce the opportunities for smallholders and cottagers to improve their position by gradual stages (see Tate 1967 and Mingay 1968). By 1800 agricultural practice was largely dictated by market demands and the cottagers who could not find work locally on farms or in extractive or manufacturing industries were obliged to look elsewhere.

Industrial changes were even greater. Before the eighteenth

century the scale of industrial enterprise was usually small, although there were exceptions such as shipbuilding, iron-working, London brewing and the coal industry of north-east England. Most manufacturing was carried on in people's homes or in small workshops attached to them, coal-mines were generally small and worked by family groups; outside the greater towns many families kept one foot on the land, deriving their income partly from trade or industry, partly from agriculture. In 1702, however, Thomas Cotchett built Britain's first silk mill at Derby. This water-powered mill has been overshadowed by the larger and more successful silk-throwing mill of the Lombes, also at Derby, built between 1717 and 1720, which was of five storeys and had 300 employees operating its intricate water-powered machinery (Nixon 1969, pp. 120, 180–3). The example set at Derby was followed at Stockport and later at Congleton and Macclesfield where silk throwing and spinning also took root.

An even greater change was the application of machinery to the equally exotic cotton industry, first, from the 1730s, by the flying shuttle and the hand-powered spinning-jenny, which left the industry in people's homes, then in 1769 by Richard Arkwright's water-frame which applied water power to the spinning process and took it into the mill. Arkwright's first water-powered mill at Cromford and the mule-spinning mills of Samuel Crompton, introduced a little later, revolutionised spinning while, pro-gressively, from about 1810, the power-loom took weaving into powered mills. The use of mechanical power absorbed the spinning of cotton between 1769 and 1800 and the weaving of most cotton cloth from about 1812 to 1860. It also spread into the spinning and weaving of wool, linen and silk and its example brought the mechanisation of the hatting, clothing and shoemaking trades after mid-century.

In the late eighteenth century the demands made by entre-preneurs on the millwrights, carpenters, clockmakers and smiths who had graduated to machine making produced the engi-neering trade, with its concentrations of workers in large engi-neering shops. The use of power brought innovations in water-wheels, then the introduction of steam, which again expanded the engineering trade but also stimulated a great growth of coal mining, with large mines employing hundreds of workers.

Mobility, too, was much easier, with better roads and canals, and after 1830 the railway, which enabled young people to seek their fortunes in any corner of the land. The new industrial centres offered many prospects. Commerce and trade, regular work and wages brought people from all over the British Isles and later from abroad to the industrialising areas and as mills and mines, houses, shops and chapels spread across the fields more and more people lived urban as opposed to rural lives.

The nineteenth century brought further economic change. In transport the Stockton–Darlington railway, and still more that from Liverpool to Manchester, set an example that revolutionised the carriage of goods and people, encouraged the development of new suburbs and stimulated the growth of new towns, as at Swindon and Crewe. As industrialisation spread in the early nineteenth century, working people were obliged to adapt to the disciplines and uncertainties of wage labour in larger units as well as to the strains and stresses of living in unplanned, insanitary and overcrowded urban concentrations. It is hardly surprising that the dislocations of their lives brought industrial and political unrest. It was in these new industrial districts that observers forecast the ruin of society and the family alike.

The domestic system in industry which utilised the labour of all the family under one roof enabled children, once married to stay close to the family home. The factory system had different effects. The mills required hands – men, women or children as their machines dictated; men to work mules in spinning, women as throstle spinners or power-loom weavers, children to work on the water-frames and on later machines as piecers, doffers or scavengers. Families were no longer working units; each member might go to work in a different direction and to a different trade. Their homes became temporary as renting for periods as short as a week replaced leasing for longer periods, and they moved house frequently. Population growth in the industrial districts led to worse problems – boarding or lodging in other people's houses, so evident in nineteenth-century censuses, living in dank cellars, low attics or tiny back-to-backs without ventilation or sanitation. Even the nuclear family of parents and children was overcrowded and there was little space, though other relatives were often squeezed in. Part II explores ways in which this overcrowding in the nineteenth century can be assessed.

From the late eighteenth century there is a chorus of criticism of the factory system's effects on human life. In the early 1790s Dr Ferriar's report to the Manchester police committee listed damp cellars, uncovered privies, lodging-houses, fevers and night working in mills for some children (Aiken 1795, pp. 193–6). The children started work young, were overworked both in hours and tasks, cruelly treated by overlookers, received no education and had their health ruined by premature physical exertion and a lack of proper food and rest. They were perhaps fortunate to have reached working age, for infant and child mortality were high, some half of the children born in Manchester, for example, dying under the age of five in the 1780s in social conditions worsened by the developing factory system (Percival & Heberden 1973, p. 7).

As the factory system developed there were other complaints. Both Friedrich Engels and Benjamin Disraeli in the 1840s forecast the breaking-up of families through industrialisation, though they viewed it from very different perspectives. For Engels it was the employment of women, particularly married women, that was destroying the family. In his view women and children, who were cheap and malleable, were replacing men in manufacturing industry with the consequence that married men were increasingly unable to find work and depended upon the earnings of their wives and children. In Engels's own words: 'The employment of the wife dissolves the family utterly and of necessity, and this dissolution, in our present society, which is based upon the family, brings the most demoralizing consequences for parents as well as children' (Engels 1969 ed, p. 172). Engels's evidence includes an account of an unemployed man, formerly a hard worker, found by a visitor mending his wife's stockings in their cellar in St Helens while she worked long hours in the mill. This can be far from typical; St Helens had almost no occupied cellars and very few male jobs that could be done by women (see Engels 1969 ed, pp. 173–4; Barker & Harris 1959, p. 321), but there were many married women and mothers of families employed elsewhere in the mills. There was a further consequence of this increasing child labour. Young people could easily find themselves supporting their fathers and resenting the patriarchal discipline they still tried to enforce. Escape was easy since they became financially independent early on in life and could leave home for lodgings, abandoning their parents, perhaps to the mercies of the Poor Law with its threat of the workhouse after 1834. Disraeli too was struck by this ability of young people to leave home and parental authority at an early age; like Engels he saw in it the seeds of the dissolution of the family (Disraeli 1845, Bk2, chs. 9–13, Bk3, ch.9). But the two contemporaries differed over the nature of the family; for Engels the traditional family was a means whereby the father exploited his wife and children while Disraeli saw it as the foundation of a civilised life. Both were pessimistic about its future.

The early years of the factory system from 1790 to 1850 seem therefore to have been marked by a breakdown in the family which matches the general disorder in a society beset by strikes, riots and disturbances. Religion was at a low ebb and with it regard for marriage and the sanctity of family life. Life expectancy was low, especially in the manufacturing districts, the manners and behaviour of many classes of people in both town and country were drunken, coarse and brutal and children were treated with particular severity and cruelty. High illegitimacy led to many abortions and infanticide was common. The children that survived infancy were far from safe; the ill-treatment meted out to mill children by overseers was hardly greater than that suffered by middle-class young boys in the public schools. Nor were children at home immune; beatings were frequent and severe and there were even cases of parents killing their children for their burial money (Stockport Advertiser, 16 May 1851). The breaking-up of the family from outside seemed to be paralleled by decay from within. The accepted patriarchal discipline of the past appeared to have broken down, to be replaced by open exploitation and brute force. It is hardly surprising that contemporaries feared for the future of the family; it is only with the benefit of hindsight that we can view it more optimistically.

Behind the disorder of the first half of the nineteenth century lay a three-cornered struggle between the old landed families, the entrepreneurial class of merchants and millowners and the continually recruiting body of wage-earners. By the second half of the century the landed had conceded a share in power to the middle classes through the advances of the 1830s, the Reform Act, the Poor Law Amendment Act and the Municipal Corporations Act. They had also suffered an outright defeat in the repeal of the Corn Laws in 1846 which did not in the short term damage English agriculture, as had been feared, but did open the doors to cheap food which seemed to contradict the gloomy forebodings of Malthus.

Luddism, Chartism, Owenite socialism and trade unionism had failed to transform society for working people but after the middle of the century their condition began to improve. Technical changes could still sweep over industries but none affected such a large proportion of the population as those that transformed the spinning and weaving of cotton between 1780 and 1850. Violent trade unionism slowly moderated into bargaining that brought steady improvements in wages. There was a continual growth in technical, supervisory and clerical jobs that produced new opportunities. Working people also benefited from the improvement of towns brought about by new municipal corporations, by the better conditions that followed the Factory Acts and, later in the century, workmen's compensation and the implementation of compulsory schooling. They also progressively won the parliamentary franchise in 1867 and 1884 to realise part of the Chartist dream and in 1918, when women over thirty were also enfranchised. Poverty remained, to be rediscovered in the 1890s, and the country farmers and labourers underwent a great crisis from the 1870s but, in general, the period from 1860 to the end of the century was marked more by harmony than discord in political and industrial life. At the beginning of the twentieth century this period of greater consensus began to break down but the Liberal government of 1906 began a movement towards state intervention in matters of welfare with old-age pensions and health insurance before the outbreak of war turned attention elsewhere.

Thus by the early twentieth century the industrial economy and society had reached a level of maturity, though increasing competition at home and abroad was producing stresses and a return to radical analysis. Administratively the local associations and mechanisms of the sixteenth century, in employment and government, welfare and education, health and security were giving way to national organisation. England was absorbing the powers and functions of townships, manors and counties and was in the process of becoming one village.

The English family

We now turn to consider the role and place of the family in the development of English economy and society. First we shall offer some general observations on family life, then go on to consider the major events in the lives of families – courtship and marriage, the arrival and upbringing of children, widowhood, old age and death. We shall also look at those who never married, at illegitimacy, at wider kin, at older and younger sons, at the situation of women as girls, spinsters and wives. At each point we shall attempt to relate what was happening in the family to those factors in the wider world which influenced it and which it, in turn, affected. We should stress, however, that the 'family' was not a single entity, and that English families differed from each other quite markedly according to time, place and class. We will normally be concentrating on those modest ranks, orders and classes in society below the aristocracy and gentry.

It has already been suggested that people before indus-trialisation were far from fixed and immobile. Indeed, mobility was built into society. The family functioned as an economic unit, but not in the simple and straightforward way we are tempted to assume, with most children staying at home to assist their parents on the family farm or business in the hope of eventually inheriting or sharing in the inheritance of it. Between 1574 and 1821 some 60 per cent of the population aged between fifteen and twenty-four left home to serve in someone else's home or farm, to follow an apprenticeship or work and live in another household as a journeyman (Macfarlane 1986, pp. 82–3). Others were educated away from home. This diaspora ranged across the social classes, except for the very poorest, for whom home must have been at best a nebulous concept. According to Gregory King, in 1688 almost half the families were unable or scarcely able to pay their way and modern revision of his figures suggests that 40 per cent of the population were close to poverty or actually poor (estimate based on Lindert & Williamson 1982). For the youth of the aristocracy and gentry, service in another household was an introduction to a wider world and offered them opportunities. The pinnacle of this service was at Court, where the fortunate youth or maiden might find notice and rise to dizzy heights. The children of the yeomanry or the poorer relatives of the gentry served in gentry households, indoors or out, again, learning superior manners and meeting a new stratum of people. Below this degree the children of the husbandry found work in other households, and there were also apprenticeships with varying levels of premium that would take boys into craft or mercantile occupations that guaranteed their futures.

The family of these times was therefore not the close nest of parents and siblings that we might imagine but one that included servants working in house, farm or business and replacing the children who had departed. This system must have worked well economically; perhaps the children of strangers cost less to keep and were more easily disciplined than the householder's own. Further, it is suggested that these servants rarely returned home to live after entering service and most married, not from their own homes, but from the houses where they served (Macfarlane 1986). There was therefore a high degree of movement inherent in this pattern of education and training which enabled young people not only to experience life in other parishes and regions but widened their choice of possible marriage partners and ways of life.

This dispersal of children was made easier by the structure of property-holding and the ways in which property descended from generation to generation. Had English land and property been held in common by the family or been shared out equally between children on the parents' death then it seems reasonable to assume that children would have stayed close to home. In general, however, most property in England was held by individuals and its descent, though strongly influenced by law and custom, especially in the case of copyhold lands, was governed by the parents and, in particular, the father. He decided what he could afford for his children's education, how much he could pay for an apprenticeship or what 'portion' or dowry he could give a child who was marrying. After 1754 he could refuse permission to marry to children under twenty-one. Throughout life, the prudent father had to have an eye to his old age and that of his wife: there were no effective legal or customary arrangements that would guarantee support from his children. The wise man kept as much of his property as possible until death; King Lear was an extreme example of impotence arising from abdication of control. The family was a network of relationships of all kinds but most of its crucial decisions arose from the need to safeguard its economic life and future.

Marriage in the early modern period

Enough has probably been said to suggest that people did not marry in order to produce many children who would support them in their old age. Nevertheless, children usually followed marriage as night follows day in an age without effective contraception, and the couple marrying had to take account of that fact. Macfarlane suggests that the procreation of children was secondary to the desire of individuals to find mutual comfort in life with a partner of their choice. Marriage was also a remedy against fornication and sin, but this was subsidiary to more personal concerns.

Under common law, marriage was legal at fourteen for boys and twelve for girls (though requiring parental consent after 1754), but since marriage normally resulted in the setting-up of a separate new household the age at which most married was considerably higher, determined by the age at which they were economically independent (Laslett 1965, p. 90). Thus a sample of twelve parishes from 1600 to 1649 shows men marrying at a mean age of 28, women at 26, the means falling to 26.4 and 24.9 respectively by 1750 to 1799 (Wrigley & Schofield 1981, p. 255). Among the aristocracy and upper gentry the age was lower, 21 for men and 20 for women in the sixteenth century, rising to between 27 and 29 for men and 24 to 27 for women in the early eighteenth century (Stone 1977, p. 46–8). The economic independence that enabled couples to marry differed according to degree; for the aristocracy and gentry it was almost entirely through parental settlement, but for the middle ranks it was a combination of the child's portions and dower and the savings of many years of service. These were likely to accumulate with age and strengthen the tendency to marry late. The dowry as such is now long departed for most families, but we still offer to help out with our children's marriages even if only through continuing the custom of paying for our daughters' weddings.

Marriage was a matter for the contracting couple. Neither church nor state laid down whom one could marry, except for the prohibited degrees of siblings, parents, aunts, uncles, nephews and nieces after 1540 (see Rogers 1989). Nor was the consent of church and state, lord of the manor or parents or kin legally necessary. Indeed, given the poor life expectancy, between two-fifths and two-thirds of all brides had lost their fathers in the sixteenth and seventeenth centuries though fathers, in their wills, appointed overseers to watch their daughters' conduct (Gillis 1985, p. 21). Great people commonly arranged marriages to safeguard succession, cement alliances or consolidate estates but children were normally consulted and had a veto before 1700, and were later more likely to take the initiative (Stone 1977, pp. 270–3). Among middle ranks the economic advantages of listening to parents was clear, but if children were fixed in their intentions the fathers could not prevent the match though they could deny the couple the help they needed. Without parental help prospects were dim and many during these years were never in a position to offer or accept marriage.

Nor was marriage essentially a religious or state institution. Until 1540 marriage in church was a sacrament, after it a rite, but secular marriage by individual contract, known as espousal or betrothal, was equally valid in law. Couples could promise to marry and proceed to sexual intercourse without setting up house, though when the bride became pregnant they usually proceeded to a church wedding and the setting-up of a household (Gillis 1985, pp. 38–52). Up to 1700 some 10 per cent of brides were pregnant when they married, a proportion that later increased, and the church made them do penance for fornication even if they had been betrothed (Macfarlane 1986, pp. 305–6).

Late marriage restricted fertility and limited family size. It thus regulated population increase to levels that could be supported by the country's resources in normal times and, it is claimed, allowed capital accumulation which underpinned economic progress (Macfarlane 1986, p. 27). Our concern is with the family itself. What were the resources our ancestors needed in order to marry, and how did they acquire them? First they needed somewhere to live and the evidence is that normally they founded a new and independent household (Laslett 1965, pp. 1–21). The very poorest may have been put to all kinds of shifts and were sometimes discouraged from marrying by the Poor Law authorities (as with certain institutionalised individuals today). Above the level of the poorest, it was the groom who provided the house and land or skills or labour that would be needed to support the family. The bride for her part brought in cash and furnishings. Both might have their own savings but what their parents could provide was vital. Boys received a notional share of their father's personal estate when they entered a trade as apprentice or needed money for a lease or stock on marriage. Girls normally received a dowry or marriage portion and the bride's parents would also pay for the wedding which could cost up to £5 for a labourer, £25 for a husbandman, £50 for a yeoman or merchant and £200 for the gentry. Marriage portions were substantial. In the seventeenth century brides from the upper gentry could expect £4,000 to £10,000, from the yeomanry £200 to £500; these sums were equivalent to three years' income for their fathers. The husbandman's daughter would get £10 to £50, the labourers' between £1 and £5 but these represented one to two years' income (Macfarlane 1986, pp. 264,271). There were also gifts from friends and kin as there are today and in the early part of the period there were charitable bequests to provide dowries for poor girls.

Although both partners contributed to the capital of the new family it was owned and controlled entirely by the husband. On her first marriage a woman merely changed masters, from her father, if he was alive, to her husband. A married woman had no legal personality separate from that of her husband and could not enter into contracts, own property or even claim the income derived from property held for her by trustees. Her dowry was absorbed into the family stock and she could do nothing to restrain a drunken or spendthrift husband from dissipating it. The family was, in theory, patriarchal and the husband had all authority. There were, however, legal and customary safeguards. The dowry entitled the wife to a jointure, an annual payment or pension usually equivalent to one-tenth of the dowry, when her husband died. Wives without jointure agreements were entitled to one-third of the husband's freehold estate for life and all widows received a part of their husband's personal estate, one-third in the Province of York, which they retained for life and could leave by will. Wives retained their own apparel and ornaments and their former freeholds and credits reverted to them on their husband's death. If the husband held land under copyhold in a manor or by burgage tenure in a borough there was usually 'free bench', the retention of the holding, for the widow but the terms of this varied. In some manors she might lose it on remarriage or imputation of unchastity; in others she might retain it until death even if she remarried. Joint tenancies in copyholds were one device by which married couples ensured continuation on the holding if the husband died. Some married women made wills, leaving personal estate and sometimes their 'thirds' under common law, with the consent of their husbands. In the seventeenth century they could not will real estate under common law but in the eighteenth century, as a consequence of changes in equity, the situation became less clear though few wives could dispose of land (Pollock & Maitland 1898, II, p. 428; Jenks 1928, pp. 226–9).

This legal subjection of wives accommodated a range of relationships which included not only the wretch who ruined his wife but the couple who worked together in loving harmony on the land or in a trade or handicraft. The Puritans did not invent equal sharing of responsibility and mutual respect within marriage but their concentration on the household as the basis of Puritan organisation greatly enhanced the role of women. Puritan men held to patriarchal authority but they regarded women as spiritually equal, able to catechise their children and servants (Richardson 1972, pp. 91–108). Not only that, but their general suspicion of secular feasts and festivities and their desire to keep their dependents close to home so as to avoid the temptations of the world must have increased the intimacy of marriage and with it the influence of the wife. The Quakers perhaps went furthest in acknowledging the equality of women.

On the land, husbands and wives had their own spheres of activity and both partners were equally essential. Thomas Tusser's *Five hundred points of good husbandry* of 1580 allocates to the housewife not only the cleaning of the house and yards, washing and cooking for the family, baking and brewing, the fetching of fuel, candle making and the endless mending of clothing but the supervision of carding and spinning, malt grinding and the salting of meat, the feeding of the cattle, pigs and poultry, the work of the dairy and the maintenance of hedges. She is first up in the morning to rouse the servants to their work and at night she is the last to retire after making sure that all is secure and locked away. Her summer day begins at 4 a.m. and ends at 10 p.m.; in winter it lasts from 5 a.m. to 9 p.m. (Tusser 1984, pp. 154–83). During the Civil War, but not only then, many gentry wives ran their husbands' estates and tradesmen often depended on the acumen and judgement of their wives in their business affairs. The diaries of Samuel Pepys even indicate that some wives were not above furthering their husband's careers by the granting of sexual favours. Clark suggests that the participation of wives in trades, commerce and estate management began to decline in the late seventeenth century when wives began to lose their employments (Clark 1968, *passim*). Samuel Pepys was engaged in professional pursuits his wife could not share. In the 1660s, when he bought her some jewellery, his comment was revealing – 'it is fit the wretch should have something to content herself with.' (Pepys 1976, IX, p. 89). It was only the upper and middle ranks that were treading this path; those lower in society were still maintaining their working partnerships.

The wills of many husbands offer testimony to harmonious relations with their wives. Expressions such as 'my loving wife' may be the words of the scribe or empty forms but many husbands made additional provision for their wives. Sometimes they left them a bay of the house with fire, bed and cooking utensils or accommodation for life in the family home. Often there is an alternative if the widow finds co-residence with a son or daughter not to her liking. Additional bequests are common or the widow's maintenance is laid on a member of the family. But husbands were torn between generosity to their wives and care for their children. Commonly, extra bequests in wills are for life and usually only to be retained 'so long as she keep herself sole and unmarried and of chaste conversation'. The companionship that men sought for themselves was not always extended to their widows.

In the early modern period a wedding was a significant occasion not only for the families involved but for the whole local community. The setting-up of a new household marked the entry into adult responsibility of the new couple. It also entailed a new claim on local resources, and though many families had engaged in careful negotiations intended to give the new couple the right start, others were not in a position to do so. These poorer families needed the help of the community and if it viewed the marriage favourably it could assist in a variety of ways. Bequests for dowries have already been mentioned, and bride ales to raise money for the wedding and contributory weddings where neighbours brought gifts were also common. The lord of the manor could help in many ways, such as the granting of a lease for land or a cottage; some provided wedding houses where the feast took place and the bride and groom were bedded. The only wedding house that we know to survive is situated by the parish church at Matching in Essex, said to be 500 years old (*Country Life*, 30 March 1989).

Not all poor couples met with kindness. After the Poor Law of 1601 and 1603 the parishes or townships became responsible for the poor, and overseers and churchwardens would sometimes try to prevent the marriage of the poorest people, fearful that they would produce broods of children dependent on the poor rate (Wrightson 1982, p. 78). It is also suggested that the Puritans did not favour these poor marriages so that during the seventeenth century community help at weddings declined or disappeared (Gillis 1985, pp. 85–8). Much depended on the lord of the manor and the degree of control he exercised over his tenants. The tightly controlled 'closed' villages of the corn arable were likely to be less hospitable than the 'open' villages of the wood, moor and fen.

The 'big wedding' was accompanied by feasting, by regional rites and rituals, charms and symbols. At the service the ring and coins were blessed, symbolising the dower. Mock fights between the groom's and bride's parties were common, gloves and ribbons were given, steps scrubbed, shoes thrown, garters seized, lych-gates and church doors barred. There were bedding ceremonies and threshold rites on entering the new home. The parents were minor figures; they did not usually attend the service and it was the peer group that accompanied the couple to church, with friends and siblings acting as witnesses as they still do today.It was the couple, too, that played the part of benefactors. Childhood and adolescence had ended for bride and groom, and legally they were now adults even if under twenty-one years of age. They still owed respect to their parents but they were now responsible for their own lives (Gillis 1985, pp. 59–75).

The marriage thus entered upon was for life. Divorce, with remarriage of the innocent party, was possible from 1552 to 1602 but from 1603 to 1837 marriage was almost indissoluble. There were only two ways out, either by judicial separation or, from the late seventeenth century, by divorce by private act of Parliament. Both were expensive and there were only 200 divorces granted by private act up to 1857, only six at the suit of women (Macfarlane 1986, p. 225). Desertion was a much more common course and the husband who had run away leaving his wife and children chargeable to the rates is a recurring figure in Poor Law records.

It was, of course, possible to evade the complications of law by never entering a formal marriage through the church service and register entry. 'Common-law' wives retained control over their own persons, property and income though it is likely that few who took this route had much property or income to control. They lost, however, any right to dower or customary 'bench' rights and would have to depend on specific bequests in their husbands' wills. It is far from clear how their children stood. Were they legitimate and, if the husband deserted his family, would the Poor Law authorities try to bring him back? Could the children make claims on the father's estate? What surname did they use? Does the 'alias' that family historians often find in documents sometimes indicate common-law marriage? Whatever the problems associated with these 'informal' marriages it is estimated that by the early eighteenth century the church was losing from one-quarter to one-third of all marriages to 'irregular unions

of one kind or another' (Gillis 1985, p. 84). We know less about the
very poor, those most likely to enter into these marriages, than
about the more comfortable and respectable sections of society.
They are an army of extras whose fleeting appearances reveal little
of their lives unless they were brought before the church courts.

Although marriage was for life its average duration was not very
extended. At the age of twenty-five average life expectancy was
about a further thirty years for both sexes, but one marriage in
three was broken by death before the end of the wife's period of
fecundity (Levine 1987, pp. 78–80). Remarriage was common,
especially for widowers left with children (Wrightson 1982,
p. 103). The widowed might need help in the rearing of children,
in farming the land or carrying on a trade. They also looked for a
renewal of companionship and emotional satisfactions but not all
such second marriages turned out well. We shall discuss later the
sources we can use in trying to understand the inwardness of
relationships; diaries and autobiographies are the most revealing
but they do not survive in vast numbers. In the seventeenth
century Widow Langford of Newton at Myddle took Thomas
Hodgkins as her second husband but he drank away her farm,
cattle, corn and goods 'even to the Wainscott': 'and thus shee that
was descended of good Parentage, shee that had lived in a plentiful condition in her first Husband's time, shee who maintained
the best Hospitality and good housekeeping of anyone in Myddle
Parish; shee I say dyed in a poore cottage in great poverty and
want, if not for want' (Gough 1981, pp. 191–2).

In 1765 the Sussex shopkeeper Thomas Turner, a widower
since 1761, confided his motives for remarriage to his diary.
Despite his own stormy relationship with his wife, it was, he
wrote, 'a state agreeable to nature, reason and religion and in
some manner the indispensable duty of Christians'. His own
immediate situation was more down to earth. His house was not
at all regular, there was no family devotion in a serious manner
and he had no friend to whom he could trust the management of
his affairs nor any agreeable companion. His second marriage
appears to have proved happy, companionable and prosperous
(Turner 1979, pp. 318–19).

Not all marriages were successful. Gough's History of Myddle gives
many instances of drunkenness, not only on the part of husbands,

of wife beating and of infidelity by both partners. Sometimes the tensions within marriages provoked fatal violence. In August 1733 Dr James Clegg of Chapel-en-le-Frith went to Macclesfield to investigate the death of Robert Carrington. His diary records his findings:

'There are violent suspicions and strong presumptions that his wife destroyed him by giving him cantherides but we could not find sufficient strong proofs' (Clegg 1978, p. 177). But where some faltered, many marriages clearly followed an even and pleasant tenor or jogged along in the manner described by Henry Newcome in 1652:

'I was exceedingly perplexed about my wife. God knows what I should do. These four years have I now lived with her, and do not know how to humour her. When she is angry, I do aggravate her passion by saying anything . . . When she is patient, peace is so sweet to me that I dare not speak lest I should lose it' (quoted in Wrightson 1982, p. 95) This was far from the respect that, tradi-tionally wives, should yield to their husbands. Samuel Clarke, who married in 1625, found a paragon. His wife was 'singular and very exemplary in that reverence and obedience which she yielded to her husband both in words and deeds. She never rose from the table, even when they were alone, but she made curtsy. She never drank to him without bowing. His word was a law unto her' (quoted in Richardson 1972, p. 108)

This formality, however, contributes to the split between historians concerning the nature of early modern marriage. Stone suggested in his work on the upper classes in society that there were very low levels of affection in such families until the later seventeenth century. The family, which contained many non-family retainers and servants, was large and lacking in privacy. It had been formed at the behest of parents and kin and the spouses were as tied to kin, friends, neighbours and institutions outside the home as they were to their immediate family. Shorter, looking at western European experience, also takes the view that marriage was an austere economic contract in the seventeenth and eighteenth centuries. He suggests that the general level of sexuality was low, producing little sexual experience before marriage and marriages which had very low levels of passion, affection and companionship. Once again it is the peer group outside the home that dominates private lives (Shorter 1975, *passim*).

One English county, Somerset, investigated in detail by Quaife gives a very different picture of sexual and amatory conduct. There, men and women formed attachments on the grounds of personal attraction and sometimes married despite parental prohibition. They were sexually active before marriage and after, contraception was not unknown and abortion was practised. Unlike Shorter's women who were, in the main, sexual victims, Quaife found a good deal of evidence that some women were as independent and initiatory as men in their love affairs. The people of Somerset were far removed from the apathetic and bloodless villagers of Shorter (Quaife 1979, *passim*). Gough's people of Myddle support this view. Some courted intemperately and many married unwisely but there is no doubting the romance of John Vaughan and his wife who, 'when they were married were so yong, that they could not make passing thirty years betweene them, and yett neither of them were constrained by parents to marry, butt they going to schoole togeather fell in love with one another, and soe married. They live lovingly togeather, and have many children' (Gough 1981, p. 169). Similar evidence of strong emotions and binding affection in marriages in all social classes can be found for the seventeenth and eighteenth centuries alike. Economic and social concerns could both encourage and constrain marriage and limit the choice of marriage partners and there were, no doubt, fortune-hunters who married with only property in mind. Perhaps motives for marriage and behaviour within it were not so very different from those we know today. What is certain is that the consequences of a wrong choice or foolish behaviour could be even more disastrous so that courtship was more prolonged and entailed much anxious negotiation.

Marriage was not only a private relationship but a public institution and failure in it reflected on the community values that it embodied. The people of the seventeenth and early eighteenth centuries were, on the whole, reluctant to trouble the law, preferring to settle disputes between themselves, especially where they had a communal bearing. Marital disputes and cases of adultery that threatened the peace were often dealt with in the lord of the manor's courts, the ducking stool and scold's bridle being used in support of patriarchal dignity, but as the authority of the courts declined in the seventeenth century village communities took matters into their own hands. There was particular abhorrence of women who overturned the proper order and abused, beat or cuckolded their husbands and the village charivari, rough music or 'stang riding', each of them a community demonstration, was visited on them. Men too who went beyond what were thought to be reasonable bounds in disciplining their wives or engaged in philandering could be subjected to the same humiliation (Gillis 1985, pp. 78–80). For the most blatant offenders there were the strictures of the church courts, though the sanctions were ecclesiastical and as William Tyler, an energetic lecher of Myddle demonstrates, ineffective with the most hardened sinners. Dr James Clegg's diary for October 1734 provides another, though Presbyterian example:

Peter Wood came up to consult what to do about his wife. Divine providence hath at last discovered that she has for some years livd in adultery with a wicked wretch calld Will Fox, who had before debauchd Ellen Ward. . . . she formerly behavd well, was catechizd and admitted to the Lords supper and I had good hopes of her, but I fear the Love of strong liquors hath ruined her. (Clegg 1978–81, p. 210)

Fox was carried before the magistrates and named by Clegg at the next chapel service as a person to be avoided. Alice Wood was named at the same service and suspended from the Lord's Table until it could be accepted that her repentance was sincere. Her maid Priscilla was also reproved for knowledge of the affair. In March 1735 Dr Clegg was still discoursing Alice Wood and testing her repentance.

For most couples children were an inevitable consequence of marriage. It is estimated that before 1700 up to 10 per cent of English brides were pregnant at marriage, more in the north-west of the country. A sample of four parishes has suggested that one-third of wives bore their first child within the first twelve months of marriage and two-thirds to four-fifths within two years of marriage (Wrightson 1982, p. 104). The intervals between conceptions were lengthened by long lactation for, in middling and poorer society, infants were fed on demand until weaning at between one and three years old. Coitus interruptus was also practised. A recent commentator on the family, Levine, directs his research more to demography than families as such and he recognises that there were great variations in the rates at which families reproduced. Nevertheless his 'peasant demography' model offers an average that could be tested out against specific parishes. If, he suggests, the wife married at 26 she would then have, on average, 14 years of child bearing. In the first 5 years she would bear 2.25 children, 1.5 in the second 5 years and 1.0 in the final 4 years to give a total of 4.75 live births. Adjustments for the early death of spouses bring this down to 3.8 children, of whom two-thirds might be expected to survive into their mid-20s, some of them to marry and continue the family (Levine 1987, pp. 79–80).

Marriage in the age of industrialisation

As has been indicated above, the population of England began to grow more rapidly and consistently after the mid-eighteenth century. Until then fertility and mortality had been of roughly equal importance in determining population size, but after 1751 it was the growth in fertility associated with earlier and more frequent marriage that was the strongest influence (Wrigley & Schofield 1981, p. 244).

There was a marked increase in the proportion of people who married. In the second half of the seventeenth century some 20 per cent of people between 40 and 44 remained unmarried but this fell to 10 per cent and below from the 1750s, only rising above 10 per cent again in the late 1840s (Wrigley & Schofield 1981, p. 260). Also the mean age at which women married fell by about 3 years, from 26 to 23 by the early 1800s, increasing their span of fertility within marriage and, simultaneously and paradoxically, illegitimate fertility rose as the marriage age fell (Wrigley & Schofield 1981, p. 255).

This apparently small drop in marriage age was of great significance. Levine calculates that a model population of 100 in which women married at 26 would grow to 300 over a period of 300 years, while one with a female marriage age of 23 would grow to 6,000 over the same period of time (Levine 1987, p. 88). He describes this latter regime as the 'proletarian model' in contrast to the slow-growing 'peasant model' and illustrates the growth of the landless, his 'proletarians', by suggesting a ratio of 33 proletarians to every 100 employers in the 1520s with 450 proletarians to every 100 employers in 1851 (Levine 1987, p. 40). Patrick Colquhoun's table of income distribution for 1803, published in 1806, offers some grounds for crude comparison with King's figures of 1688 and perhaps some hints on how far this process had gone by 1803. Families dependent on land and capital remain at about 20 per cent and 10 per cent respectively but the paupers, cottagers and vagrants have fallen from some 24 per cent to 20 per cent and wage earners have risen from 45 per cent to 50 per cent. The large numbers of men serving in the army and navy obviously affected these figures and some may have been drawn from landowning, farming or merchant families but there appears to be a clear if not massive rise in Levine's 'proletarians'. (Estimates based on Perkin 1969, pp. 20–1, with revisions from Lindert & Williamson 1982.)

Clearly had the 'proletarian model' that Levine offers been in place from the 1520s then the population of England would have reached astronomical levels. However, the change did not become marked until the late eighteenth century and fertility began to fall in the 1870s. Additionally there was a high level of emigration from the seventeenth century. Perhaps 850,000 people, mainly young men, left England for America and the West Indies between 1630 and 1699 with a similar number departing in the eighteenth century (Levine 1987, p. 82). Wrigley and Schofield's estimates of emigration from England from 1551 to 1851 total almost 2.4 million (Wrigley & Schofield 1981, p. 219).

The fall in the age at marriage reflected economic changes. We have already seen how Alexander Daniel kept his weaver sons at home in Stockport in 1591 and the spread of unapprenticed 'country' industry encouraged others to do likewise in the seventeenth and eighteenth centuries. These family economies were part industrial, part agricultural but as manufacture became more profitable the agricultural element was progressively reduced. The fixed capital required for domestic industry was low compared with that needed for agriculture, and credit networks for the purchase of raw materials were well established by the eighteenth century. Indeed in the fustian and cotton branches of textiles and in felt hatting, many of the domestic workers became wage-earners rather than independent producers during the early eighteenth century. They drew the raw materials from the masters and received their wages on returning the finished work. (See Wadsworth & Mann 1931 for developments in the textile trades.)

Low capital needs were matched by easy entry into the trades. Much of textiles appears to have lost any apprenticeship requirement early in country areas though the more skilled branches and the class of merchants in towns kept it into the late eighteenth century. As early as 1633 the shoemakers, skinners, whittawers and 'glasiers' of the Lancashire incorporated towns were complaining of interlopers who had never been bound. In hatting, where apprenticeship persisted, countrymen apprenticed their own sons, unlike the London men who were subject to tight restrictions. After the Restoration country trades in general had become very much more free of regulation (Wadsworth & Mann 1931, pp. 55–63, 333). It was not necessary for young people engaged in such occupations to serve a long apprenticeship, to wait for a large portion from their parents or to save for many years before contemplating marriage. Nor was it necessary to leave home for service in others' households. The weaver's loom, the hatter's plank, the coal-pit and the forge could keep more of them at home and promise work to support them when they married.

Other developments in the countryside diminished the restrictions on early marriage. Parliamentary enclosure did not of itself drastically reduce the number of landholders but it did make life difficult for the smallest, while the enclosure of commons ended the possibilities of that way of life that combined a tiny holding of land with heavy dependence on the common. During the late eighteenth and early nineteenth centuries the number of landholders did decline as the smaller ones failed to compete with the market strengths of the larger and more competitive (see Tate 1967 and Mingay 1968).

The pattern of the farming household, like that of its industrial counterpart, was also changing. In commerce and industry the household was becoming more private as apprentices, journeymen and trade servants were no longer boarded with the family. According to John Aiken, the Manchester drapers' apprentices of the 1690s lived in their masters' houses over the cloth rooms and dipped their spoons into the same porridge pot. By the 1760s they had their own parlours but later, as the merchants themselves moved away from their warehouses, they ceased to board with them and found private lodgings (Aiken 1795, pp. 183–4). The same shift to privacy combined with economy progressively transformed the resident farm servant, hired for the year and boarding in his master's house, into the labourer paid by the day or week. He now had to find his own board and lodging out of his wage, which not only reduced the restraint on marriage but could positively encourage it by its promise of greater comfort and permanence in his own home.

It was these forces that lay behind the reduction in the age at which people married in the late eighteenth and early nineteenth centuries. The coming of the factories merely strengthened them. The spinning-mills that followed Arkwright's pioneering Cromford Mill of 1769, especially after the expiry of his patents in the early 1780s, provided work for women and children, while Crompton's mule of the same period gave work to men. From the 1820s the vast expansion of power-loom weaving greatly increased work for women and young people, though at the expense of the hand-loom weavers, and the cotton industry became the greatest employer of women outside domestic service. These millworkers lost all contact with the land. The proprietors of country mills might still provide gardens attached to their workers' cottages but in towns the price of land discouraged millowners and, even more, speculative builders, from providing such amenities. In any case the emergence of weekly renting for houses as opposed to the longer leases of earlier times encouraged mobility rather than permanence. And the millworkers were highly mobile, changing home and job frequently, flitting from street to street in response to economic or social factors (as we know from genealogical research). Nor did they have time to follow by-occupations; they worked very long days in the mill and most had neither time nor energy for any other sustained activity until the Factory Acts began to reduce hours for children in the 1830s and adults after 1850.

Where silk and cotton had shown the way other industries followed. Engineering grew alongside the textile trades, developing from independent machine makers and millwrights to vast workshops manufacturing for the mills, the mines and the railways. After the middle of the nineteenth century tailoring, shoemaking and the hatting trades followed cotton into powered mills; chemicals, pharmaceuticals, glassmaking, paper and food processing, furniture and the metal trades, all increased in scale and the domestic trades became a backwater often marked by exploitation and underpayment. In coal-mining the small 'family' pits of the eighteenth century grew into large deep mines, recruiting labour where they could find it. Generations became progressively more accustomed to a future as wage earners; they married not on the basis of any property of their own but in the expectation of future wages. The change could be dramatic or stealthy but it was progressive.

Table 2 Mean age at first marriage (years)

Years	Men	Women
1700–1749	27.5	26.2
1750–1799	26.4	24.9
1800–1850	25.3	23.4

Source: Wrigley & Schofield 1981, p. 255.

As marriage became more popular and was entered into earlier the 'big wedding' of earlier times seems to have declined. It was also becoming increasingly a private rather than a community affair, as wage-earning replaced the earlier claims on local resources. The use of licences rather than banns grew, and the church, which had no control over informal marriages, could not even control its own clergy. Peculiars, such as Peak Forest in Derbyshire which 'conducted a great trade between 1720 and 1750', were not within any episcopal jurisdiction and were free from regulation. London had many chapels where marriages were performed without banns or licence and, more seriously, housed a number of unbeneficed clergy such as Parson Gaynam of the Fleet who had personally presided over the marriage of 36,000 persons there when he himself married his servant–maid in 1737 (Burn 1829, p. 154).

Clandestine marriages were highly suspect. They opened the door to unscrupulous fortune-hunters, the enticement of minors and bigamous unions and Lord Hardwicke's Marriage Act of 1753 was meant to put an end to them. Under its provisions, most of which lasted until 1837, only marriage in an Anglican church by banns or licence or by Quaker or Jewish rites was valid in England and Wales. At least one party had to be resident for three weeks in the parish where the wedding was to take place, betrothal became invalid in church courts and parental consent was needed for those aged under twenty-one who were not widows or widowers. Tampering with parish registers was made a capital offence (Gillis 1985, p. 140).

Hardwicke's Act was amended in 1823 (Macfarlane 1986, p. 127; Burn 1862, p. 37). It had put a stop to the clandestine marriages of the Fleet, St James at Duke Place and the other notorious lawless churches of London and the provincial peculiars. It did not stop common-law marriages, the later versions of the old espousals and betrothals, especially in the industrial areas of the North. Here there was a rise in the incidence of pre-nuptial pregnancy and of illegitimacy, the latter probably arising mainly from the breakdown of common-law unions. At Culcheth in Lancashire the illegitimacy rate rose to 30 per cent in the early nineteenth century, largely due to informal marriage, but the arrival of a child was not seen as a disaster where the work of even young children could contribute to the family economy (Gillis 1985, p. 110).

In the rural areas of southern and eastern England there was much more pressure to enter into formal unions. In 1795 the Oxfordshire magistrates, faced with the poverty of the labourers, began to subsidise the wages of those with families to support and in the same year their neighbouring JPs at Speenhamland in Berkshire placed such relief in aid of wages on a regular footing. It now became more economic for farmers to employ married men whose wages were subsidised out of the Poor Rate so that single labourers, placed at a disadvantage, had nothing to lose and something to gain by marrying early (Horn 1980, pp. 48–9, 108). Some one-third of brides in England are said to have been pregnant at marriage in the eighteenth and nineteenth centuries, but failure of the pregnant woman to marry was clearly less disastrous in the industrial areas. There her work and, after a few years, that of her child could contribute to the income of the parental home, but in the low-waged agricultural areas she would be at the mercy of the overseers and justices. Both industry and the Poor Law were encouraging earlier marriage for working people but the propertied maintained the old practice of postponing marriage until there was a prospect of independence (Gillis 1985, pp. 161–4).

Few considered the gloomy views of T. R. Malthus as they lived their emotional lives. Most responded to their own desires with some eye to their economic prospects so that the fall in the average age at marriage conceals differences between the landed and the landless, between those with property and those without, between town and country, between those with expectations and those with nothing to lose. Where the preventive checks of Malthus did not operate his positive checks did, and the teeming back streets and courts of London, Manchester and Liverpool displayed some of the evils he had foretold.

The amendment of Hardwicke's Marriage Act did not end legal regulation of marriage. In 1829 all marriages of children under the age of sixteen were delared void though there is no evidence that the number of child brides had become a scandal (Macfarlane 1986, p. 128). The law also removed the Church of England's near-monopoly of formal marriage in 1837 when civil marriage was instituted and Nonconformist and Roman Catholic chapels were licensed to marry. But marriage itself was under attack. In the 1750s Ann Lee and her 'shaking Quakers' at Bolton reanimated medieval heresies by advocating complete celibacy. After her departure to America in the 1770s a similar view was taken by the followers of Joanna Southcott though her followers at Ashton-under-Lyne, the Christian Israelites, were broken by sexual scandals in the 1820s (Gillis 1985, pp. 220–2; Shaw c.1906). Freethinkers such as William Godwin and Mary Wollstonecraft advocated free love and Thomas Paine and the Owenites wanted to change the economic basis of the family. Paine looked for companionate marriage supported by allowances from the state but the Owenites struck at the root of the nuclear family by their advocacy of easy divorce, communal child-rearing and common property. Later they moderated their views sufficiently to register their Halls of Science for marriages (Gillis 1985, pp. 224–7).

The politicians who were changing the forms of marriage were also looking at the social factors which, in the view of Malthus and others, influenced it. For the propertied, whether of land, trade or apprenticed skill, the old way of marrying only when economic independence was assured generally continued. At the other end of the spectrum the reckless and itinerant, typified by the navvies of the early and mid-nineteenth century, engaged in informal liaisons in their shanty towns, turf huts or village lodgings. Early marriage among the settled rural poor was facilitated by the Poor Law system of outdoor relief though there was usually little work for the resultant children. The Poor Law Amendment Act of 1834 was intended to put a stop to this dismal cycle by restricting outdoor relief for the able-bodied. Paradoxically, in the areas where domestic industry prevailed, it was the very possibility of work for women and children that stimulated early marriage, often of an informal nature, regularised only upon the arrival of children, if at all. These little family units producing fustians or cotton cloth lost spinning to the mills from the 1780s and were broken by the mechanisation of weaving from the 1820s. In the short term these changes were disruptive to family economies but in the longer run they did not reduce the value of the labour of women and children but merely transferred their activities to the powered mills.

For the gentry, industrialisation brought no real change in their patterns of courtship, marriage and family life. In the manufacturing and merchant middle classes, increasing prosperity and the separation of home and work progressively removed the women of the family from participation in working life. This withdrawal of women from involvement in economic affairs which had percolated down from the gentry to the yeomanry and mercantile classes increasingly confined them to the home and family, to a social round among their peers and to charitable works of a respectable kind. The trend reached the working classes where the participation of adult women in paid employment declined in the late nineteenth century (Gillis 1985, p. 242). The family thus became not merely the principal interest of women but their only legitimate theatre of activity, and marriage their only proper career. Gillis has described the period from 1850 to 1960 as the era of mandatory marriage and the social arrangements of the upper and middle classes were meant to ensure that children made the right choices (Gillis 1985, pp. 229–31).

Both the men and women of these classes lived most of their social round within their own class strata but the dominance of the family bore more heavily on women than on men. It was not until the 1870s that the Girls' Public Day Schools Company widened the scope of education for substantial numbers of middle-class girls. The same decade saw women forcing their way into the universities and the professions but these were a minority. Most young women, dominated by their parents, lived the lives appointed for them. They were courted, carefully chaperoned, by suitable young men, married in church after the calling of banns in big weddings which involved nineteenth-century novelties – white gowns and veils, the giving away of the bride, the throwing of rice. Increasingly they went away on honeymoon and returned to the role of angel in the home they had learned from their mothers (Gillis 1985, pp. 285–7). Marriage was preferable to the financial insecurity of spinsterhood. In 1851 there were 24,770 governesses in Britain, many badly paid and ill treated, and there were few other openings for ladies who had only genteel accomplishments (Strachey 1928, p. 97).

Pleasant homes, wealth and servants and a regular social round would seem desirable features of life but there is considerable evidence that many young women of the middle classes found the constraints of the close family unbearable. In the late nine-teenth century Beatrix Potter suffered from the tyrannical insensitivity of her father before she escaped into writing, drawing and an 'unsuitable' marriage. Florence Nightingale, frustrated by the empty family and social rounds of her life, wrote a bitter polemic in 1852 when she was thirty-two years old but never published it. For her both married and single women were victims of the family, unable to live their own lives, seek their own friendships or develop their own talents because of the ceaseless petty demands of conventional family and social life. 'The family uses people, not for what they are, nor for what they are intended to be, but for what it wants them for – its own uses. . . . This system dooms some minds to incurable infancy, others to silent misery' (Strachey 1928, pp. 395–418).

Despite the spread of education and the opening of the universities to women, little had changed by the early years of the twentieth century. Katharine Hopkinson grew up in Alderley

Edge just before the First World War and has described a very happy childhood and youth there. But the family still kept its 'Victorian' character. 'For the men were the money-lords, and since for almost every family the community values were fundamentally economic, it followed that their women were dependents. They existed for their husbands' and fathers' sakes and their lives were shaped to please masculine vanity' (Chorley 1950, p. 150).

For the working classes life was very different, though in general men tried to emulate the middle class in keeping their wives at home. We have seen that in the countryside the poverty of rural labourers led to relief in aid of wages in the 1790s and neither that relief nor its virtual abolition in rural areas after 1834 did much to increase their prosperity. Having no expectations from their parents and living in uncomfortable, crowded and insanitary cottages they either migrated to replenish the industrial areas or married early. Marriage rates rose when bread prices were low, illegitimacy increased when they were high. Malthus's preventive checks had failed (Gillis 1985, pp. 111–16). Their marriages were now very modest affairs, 'walking weddings' with a tea-time meal and cake, the whole conducted in the interval of a working week. Outside the margins of the industrial areas agricultural labourers' wages were low: in 1851 Lancashire had the highest labourer's wages in England at 15s a week, South Wiltshire with its 6s was lowest and outside the coal and cotton counties only Sussex paid as much as 10s a week. Within counties there was the same distinction; in Cheshire wages near the manufacturing towns were 20 per cent higher than elsewhere (Horn 1980, pp. 242–3). The poverty of the rural districts is also demonstrated by their low figures for friendly societies. In 1801 Lancashire had 820 enrolled friendly societies, the West Riding 330, but Somerset only 123 and Wiltshire 30. In 1803 some 16 per cent of the Lancashire population was covered by them, in Wiltshire only 6 per cent and in Norfolk and Suffolk only 5 per cent (Horn 1980, p. 144).

Nor was the work of the labourers' wives and children valuable unless they lived in areas where there were still thriving domestic trades such as straw plaiting in Bedfordshire and Hertfordshire or lace-making in Buckinghamshire. Elsewhere their children were forced to enter domestic service away from home, migrate to the industrial areas or towns or find ill-paid and unpleasant work in the agricultural gangs that grew in the early nineteenth century. In 1843 it was reported that children as young as four or five were walking five to seven miles to work for 3d or 4d a day in the gangs, sometimes being sent back home empty-handed if it rained. The Agricultural Gangs Labour Act of 1867 raised the age to eight, outlawed the mixing of sexes in gangs and made gangmasters subject to licensing by magistrates (Horn 1980, pp. 249–50). By then the children of the mills had been protected by law for over thirty years.

It is difficult to generalise about the position of wives in this rural society. In the 1880s in Oxfordshire, according to Flora Thompson, men gave their wives their weekly wages of half a sovereign, taking back a shilling for spending, but leaving the difficult job of managing to the women (Thompson 1948, pp. 56–7). She has little to say about more intimate relations but John Skinner, a Somerset rector of the 1820s and 1830s, records cases of wife beating, describes adultery as far too common and regularly comments on pre-nuptial pregnancy. Many of his parishioners however were colliers drawn by the increase in mining in the district and they were far less subservient to either rector or lady of the manor than purely agricultural workers. Skinner still held to the old view of marriage. In April 1830 he was asked to marry a couple who proposed to live with the bride's father and advised against it. 'They ought at least to have been as wise as the birds of the air, who made themselves nests before they brought up their young'(Skinner 1984, p. 402).

Francis Kilvert was curate of a much more rural parish in Herefordshire in the early 1870s. The picture he paints is that of a much more settled and respectable community. In April 1870 he was asked if nothing could be done to separate a couple living in concubinage, the woman having borne a child. 'People are very indignant about this affair and think it a great scandal to the parish and rightly so. But what is to be done?' In May his question was answered when the landlord of the couple's farm gave them notice to quit (Kilvert 1974, pp. 23, 39). Even in and around Kilvert's beloved Cliro however there were cases of pre-nuptial pregnancy, illegitimacy and, in June 1871, 'Mrs. Griffiths told me a few days ago a man named Evans kicked his wife to death at Rhulen. He kicked her bosom black and her breasts mortified' (Kilvert 1974, p. 123). Women were not always totally guiltless of offence. In November 1873 'Edward Humphries married a young woman when he was 83 and had a son within the year. "Leastways his wife had", said Mrs. Hall' (Kilvert 1974, p. 228).

Childbirth was dangerous in the country as it was in the town. In July 1830 when a collier's wife bled to death in childbirth Skinner commented on the need for 'a medical person instead of an ignorant female to attend them in difficult cases' (Skinner 1984, p. 413). Babies were at great risk and parents frequently asked him to name them on the day they were born without ceremony or godparents because they feared they would not live until these could be arranged. In 1871 Kilvert suggests other risks, referring to 'the child found dead in the water closet at the Three Cocks Station' (Kilvert 1974, p. 133). Under the 1834 Poor Law there was only the disgrace of the workhouse for unmarried mothers and their babies; infanticide was far from unknown, (see, e.g., Wrightson 1981; Rose 1986).

Country labourers' wives were completely dependent upon their husbands, unlike those of the manufacturing districts who could fall back upon their own earning capacity. This was serious enough in their husbands' lifetime but separation or the death of the husband left them in great difficulty. Divorce was, of course, virtually impossible for them before 1923 when male adultery became a cause for divorce though adultery by the wife had been a cause since 1857. In 1900 only one in 500 marriages ended in divorce and few working people in town or country ever considered it. More common than divorce were desertion, or the sale of wives for which evidence has been found as early as the 1690s, with 387 cases identified up to the late nineteenth century, as another means of separation (Gillis 1985, pp. 211–12; Macfarlane 1986, p. 226; Menefee 1981). This was never legally sanctioned but was popularly believed to be a means of divorce though increasingly frowned upon by the local authorities. According to Higson, writing in 1859, 'in May 1851 a Droylsdenian attempted to sell his wife in Stockport market place – a fellow weaver at Droyslden mills starting the bidding at seven pence, which was soon advanced upon up to ten shillings; but the police dispersed the

competitors ere she was "knocked down" ' (Higson 1859, p. 56).
The symbolism of the wife sale appears to have been deceptive,
for the rope and halter in which she was brought to market, the
passing through a toll gate and the 'auction' sometimes concealed
a prior agreement between the spouses, and there was often a
'second husband' primed to 'buy' the wife. Perhaps such a device
was better than outright desertion, for the deserted labourer's
wife or the widow who had no man to support her was in a
desperate situation. She could look only to her own ability to earn
from unskilled work, to her relations who had little to spare, to
charity and, finally, to the Poor Law.

While the agricultural labourers carried on the declining traditions of their rural way of life in the face of advancing technology
and intensive farming the domestic industries went from prosperity into a decline that ended in virtual annihilation. We shall
concentrate on cotton manufacture, which became the greatest of
the domestic industries and the first to be absorbed into powered
factories, but it was by no means the only domestic trade.
Coalmining in the eighteenth century had a distinct family character, the metal manufacturing trades of the Midlands and south-
west Lancashire, the widespread woollen trades, especially in the
West Riding, hatting, shoemaking and the needle trades, straw
plaiting and lacemaking, stocking knitting and a host of others
shared the family basis of production. All followed cotton into the
powered mills or workshops except for those whose low wages
enabled them to survive in the home as 'sweated trades' up to the
First World War and beyond.

One feature of the domestic trades was their regionality.
Villages of weavers, colliers, stockingers, watchpartmakers or
shoemakers grew in the eighteenth century. They developed
their own individual character and a rough democracy for they
were often only loosely controlled by manorial lords and were
impatient of the authority of the Established Church and inclined
to Dissent and Methodism. These communities were closely knit,
for it was often possible to build cottages for children who stayed
at home when they married and even to find a little land. As late as
1859 at Droylsden on the edge of Manchester John Higson
observed:

The land of the township generally, excepting Clayton Hall, is broken into small sized farmholdings, which consequently are sub-divided into diminutive fields and enclosures. . . . once smaller than now. Before the extension of the cotton business the cottages were far outnumbered by the farmsteads, and the inhabitants were engaged in an admixture of trade and agriculture. The farming department which only supplied milk and butter for the dairy, was considered least remunerative, and, therefore, neglected in favour of the buckhouse, the plank, and the loom. (Higson 1859, p. 71)

The way of life that Higson described was passing as he wrote. Estimates of the number of cotton hand-loom weavers in Great Britain vary but perhaps a figure of 250,000 at their peak in the 1820s falling to 60,000 in the mid-1840s and 10,000 by 1861 may not be wide of the mark (see Kenny 1975, pp. 71, 94; Bythell 1969, pp. 54–7; Wood 1910, p. 123). The great days of prosperity, though not for all, had been before 1815 when they had built new houses, furnished them with clocks and Staffordshire ware and dressed to their fancy; after 1826 the course was generally downward into poverty (Bythell 1969, pp. 94–112).

In the early days weaving was predominantly a male occupation and each weaver required four to six spinners, usually women, to keep him at work before the spread of Kay's flying shuttle in the late eighteenth century increased the number of spinners needed to between six and eight. The labour of children and old people was also valuable in carding the cotton, winding the yarn for the shuttle and other ancillary tasks. Few weavers could find all this assistance in their own homes and they had to scour their neighbourhoods for labour; clearly the more hands at home the less they had to pay in wages outside it. During the 1790s as the mills drew spinning out of the home the labour of these ancillaries lost its value, but in the cotton districts there was compensation in the growth of jobs for some, though not the old, in the mills.

In these villages and hamlets there was still a need for some property as a basis for marriage. A weaver must have a loom and a loom must be housed. Gillis describes the building of 'clay biggins' in Lancashire between the 1790s and 1840 by the couple's friends between dawn and sunset for the wedding night but it is not clear whether these were permanent or for one night only

(Gillis 1985, p. 159). The evidence of the Lancashire and Cheshire 'folds' and those in Saddleworth on the eastern fringe suggests much more a gradual expansion of tiny settlements as landlords or fathers built or allowed the building of new houses and loomshops for children when they married. The prosperity of their trade encouraged this. For those with less capital there developed the terminating building society in which men subscribed to a common fund to build a terrace of cottages, each adapted to the prospective owner's needs, the cottages being allocated by lot as they were finished and the society wound up when all the bills were paid. Increasingly, however, in the nineteenth century working-class couples looked for houses at weekly rents in which to start their married lives.

Gillis suggests that the people of the North-West maintained the old 'big wedding' customs into the nineteenth century, but the evidence of the Collegiate Church at Manchester where the Revd Joshua Brookes married dozens of couples at weekends at mass ceremonies in the early nineteenth century indicates a pattern similar to that of the poor in country areas. The aristocracy and gentry led the way back to big weddings in the nineteenth century with brides in white, retinues of bridesmaids and the honeymoon but it was not until very late in the century that even better-off working people could afford more modest versions of these conspicuous events.

Once married, the bride in an industrial household, whether domestic or factory, found herself, like her country cousins, legally subject to the 'protection' of her husband until the Married Women's Property Acts of 1870 and 1882 gave her control first over her own earnings and then over her own property. It was not until 1891 that the case of *Jackson v. Jackson* established that a husband could not legally detain his wife in his house against her will (Strachey 1928, p. 223). The drunken, dissolute or gambling husband remained a threat but he was losing much of his power. Communal restraints on extreme misbehaviour by spouses or parents probably diminished in the largest towns where anonymity accompanied restless mobility. There was clearly a continuation of old 'village' practices in the smaller industrial districts. In February 1828 there was a 'stang riding' when workpeople at Sidebottom's mill at Haughton Green near Denton discovered that one of the girls there was keeping company with a married man. When she left work she was greeted by a clashing of dinner cans and her workmates pushed her into the mill dam (*Stockport Advertiser*, 14 February 1828).

The newly-wed woman in the industrial districts could usually continue working. In the coalmining townships of Lancashire women worked underground 'hurrying' the tubs of coal for their menfolk until the 1842 Mines Act prohibited it and they continued to work above ground on the pit bank into the twentieth century. In the domestic industries they were usually ancillaries to their husbands in the early eighteenth century, spinning for his weaving, sewing uppers for the shoes he made or trimming the hats he had manufactured. In the textile trades weaving was usually men's work but as early as 1604 the Stockport webster William Haryson left his daughter Jane 'the Lowme she hath bene Accustomed to worke in' (Phillips & Smith 1985, p. 36). In general however it would seem likely that women were principally involved in spinning for it took four to eight spinners to keep a weaver at work before factory yarn became plentiful in the 1780s. By that time there were already numbers of women weaving; Arthur Young found them weaving in half of the Manchester check and fustian trades in 1770. By 1808 with hand-spinning virtually eliminated in cotton half the total number of weavers were said to be women and children and by 1833, when the power-loom was a strong competitor, it is probable that most hand-loom weavers were women and children (Bythell 1969, pp. 60–3).

There are considerable problems in quantifying the work of women before the parliamentary census enquiries of 1851 and subsequent years. Parish registers rarely give the occupations of women whether married or single but it is probable that most of them, certainly in the industrial districts, followed some occupation. There are a few exceptions in so far as registers occasionally give the occupations of the mothers of illegitimate children. At Langho, near Blackburn, 46 of the 79 illegitimate births between 1813 and 1837 were to weavers (one to a servant, the others to 'spinsters'); a clearer picture emerges at Rivington near Bolton where, in the same period, 110 illegitimate children had mothers who were weavers, 6 had specialised jobs within the cotton industry, 13 were servants, 2 were miners, and there were 10 spinsters, a shopkeeper, a dressmaker and a farmer's daughter (see Leech 1990 and Owen n.d.). Only 43 per cent of legitimate births were to male weavers at the same time. We believe that most of these were hand-loom, rather than power-loom weavers.

With the coming of the spinning-mills and, later, the powered weaving-sheds the wife could leave the home to work and earn a wage on her own account. Both were equally shocking to respectable opinion. It was bad enough that single girls should work in mixed company away from home with no one in *loco parentis*, unlike traditional service where the head of household was seen as acting as a surrogate parent. It was infinitely worse that married women should enjoy this dangerous freedom. Nor did it seem right that a wife should earn an independent wage divorced from her husband's trade or occupation, which could plant ideas of independence in her mind. The mill girl endured many years of head-shaking and outright condemnation from the respectable despite the lack of any real evidence that would justify accusations of immorality. The Cotton Famine of the early 1860s restored her to respectability but it probably did no more than correct a long-held misapprehension (Watts 1866, *passim*).

But, of course, the ability of wives to earn and contribute to the family income was a two-edged sword. Little attention was paid to the working lives and domestic arrangements of the wives of hand-loom weavers but the working wives, especially mothers, in the cotton mills attracted great attention at the time and remain a subject of interest today. Critics, reformist like Ashley or revolutionary like Engels, agreed that the practice of married women working outside the home would end family life as it was known (Hewitt 1958, p. 11; Engels, 1969 edn, p. 172). However, it is far from clear how many married women, still less mothers, worked in the cotton mills. It is estimated that of some 65,000 women in the mills in 1833 only 10,721 were married (Strachey 1928, p. 54). By 1841 there were 115,425 women so employed but almost 50,000 were under twenty and in 1851, of 248,000 some 104,000 were also under twenty and generally unlikely to have been married (Clapham 1926–38, Vol. 1, p. 569; Pinchbeck 1981, p. 317). Samples in the major cotton towns of Lancashire in 1851 suggest that 25 per cent of women operatives might have been married, perhaps 62,000 in all, rising to 68,500 in 1901 (Hewitt 1958, pp. 14-16). Lancashire, with 17.54 per cent of married women working, kept the highest proportion of any county until 1911 at least and the range, from 4.11 per cent in predominantly non-textile St. Helens to 44.46 per cent in textile Blackburn, shows the importance of the cotton industry (Meacham 1977, p. 95).

Not all these married operatives had children. At Preston in 1851 26 per cent of all wives living with their husbands worked but only 15 per cent of wives with children worked out of the home. Some 23 per cent of children under ten who had a father and mother co-residing had a working mother, though only half of them were in factory occupations (see Anderson 1971). In the small mill town of Glossop in Derbyshire in the same year 268 out of about 2,000 mothers with children of thirteen and under worked in the cotton and paper mills and print works and they had altogether 417 children out of over 5,000 in the town (Smith 1979, pp. 49, 56).

Despite more recent folk memories few women gave birth by their looms although many may have returned to work too soon after delivery. In the 1830s some were back at work after nine or ten days, others after three weeks or a month. By the 1860s five or six weeks was sometimes taken and the 1891 Factory and Workshop Act laid down four weeks, but it was difficult to monitor and enforce (Hewitt 1958, pp. 123-8).

Mothers who did work in the mill faced a long working day of twelve hours and upwards before the Factory Acts of 1847 and 1850 reduced it to ten and a half on weekdays and a 2 p.m. finish on Saturdays (Hewitt 1958, p. 24). The Saturday half-holiday that freed men for cricket and football merely gave their wives more time for washing and cleaning with a longer Saturday evening for cheap shopping in the local market and, perhaps, a drink with their husbands. By the late nineteenth century wives were tiring of this ceaseless round of work but remained trapped by the adult hours of the mills.

Although women s employment encouraged earlier marriage, people in the cotton towns married rather later than those in mining districts where there was usually little female employment. In 1843 the average age at marriage of all spinsters was 24.3, in 1886 24.6 and in 1884–85 that for spinsters in the textile industry was 24.38, second among the occupational groups to the 24.06 of spinsters in mining communities. By 1911 the textile workers were marrying later than most skilled artisans (Hewitt 1958, p. 45). In 1833 it was claimed that mill work had no effect on the fecundity of the female operatives but by 1851 textile workers returned significantly lower birth rates than any other working-class group and this was sustained into the twentieth century. It is not entirely clear why this was so. Abortifacients such as pennyroyal and garden rue were included in Culpeper's *Herbal* in the seventeenth century and *coitus interruptus* and the condom were both known and written about in the eighteenth century. Factory reports in 1831 and 1833 stated a belief that contraceptive knowledge was spread in factories but W. R. Greg suggested that the low illegitimacy rate in Lancashire was due to abortion. Abortion had been illegal since 1803 but newspaper accounts of the finding of aborted foetuses and the bodies of newly-born babies in the early nineteenth century indicate that it was far from uncommon. The publication of information on birth control grew in the nineteenth century and improvements to the condom by the 1870s and the introduction of the sponge early in the nineteenth century and the diaphragm before 1885 made its adoption easier. Hostility on the part of the medical profession slowed but could not stop this process. It is estimated that 19.5 per cent of women born between 1831 and 1845 tried to or did control their fertility; for those born between 1902 and 1906 that proportion had risen to 72 per cent. (Hewitt 1958, pp. 93–8. For a full discussion of birth control in the nineteenth century and its social and political context see McLaren 1978).

The increasing adoption of birth control allied with a rise in the age at which women married from 25.13 in 1871 to 26.27 in 1901 reduced both family size and population increase as Table 3 demonstrates (Wrigley & Schofield 1981, p. 437).

In the 1930s the fall in the birth rate provoked a great national debate when mean ultimate family size began to sink below the 2.4 needed for replacing the population. The age at marriage had now lost its significance and the decisions about fertility were largely made within marriage. It was no longer the Malthusian fear of population pressing on inadequate resources that stirred

Table 3 Mean ultimate family size

Year of marriage	Wife's age at birth of last child	Mean ultimate family size
1860	41	7
1880	39	6
1900	35	4
1910	33	3.5
1920	31	2.8

Source: HMSO 1971

political and economic commentators but the spectre of a country unable to support its national aspirations because of a shrinking population.

Children in the early modern period

As in the case of marriage, historians are divided on the treatment of children in the early modern period. For Stone, affective individualism, which included the bestowal of more love, time, energy and money on children, did not begin until about 1640 (Stone 1977, pp. 7–8). Aries and Shorter agree that babies were little regarded, were swaddled into immobility, inadequately fed and washed and often put out to wet nurses who had little care for them. Their arrival was greeted with little joy, their departure without much grief. Those that survived the first hazardous years were perceived as small adults, dressed as such and trained for early entry into the world of work or affairs according to their station. There was no perception of childhood as a time of special needs, discipline was harsh and the children, reared without affection, carried a coldness and cruelty into their adult lives and their own marriages (Aries 1965, Shorter 1975, passim). Certainly John Aubrey, writing in 1670, would have subscribed to many of these views: 'for wheras ones child should be ones nearest Friend, and the time of growing up should be most indulged, they were as severe to their children as their schoolmaster; and their Schoolmasters, as masters of the House of correction. The child perfectly loathed the sight of his parents, as the slave his Torturor' (Aubrey 1962, pp. 25–6). This dominance extended throughout

life. Among the respectable classes the child knelt for its parents'
blessing, the married daughter had to stand in her mother's
presence, even in her own home, unless given permission to
kneel. Men too had to stand bareheaded before their parents,
even though '30 or 40 years old [and] fitt for any employment in
the common wealth'. Feelingly Aubrey recalled that there had
been a time 'when the Holy-mawle hung behind the Church
dore, which when the father was seaventie the sonne might fetch
to knock his father in the head, as effoete and of no more use'.

Aubrey's bitterness can be explained by long frustration with
his father, but sometimes the terms in which people mourned
their dead children have an austere ring. So Adam Martindale in
1659 testified that his son John who died of smallpox at the age of
eight was 'so ripe a child for wit, memory, and forwardness in
learning and religion' (quoted in Bagley 1975, p. 47). But James
Clegg's son Ebenezer died at the age of two in 1721 and his
Presbyterian father was plunged into deep grief, believing that he
had brought the affliction on his family. 'I have been too apt to
think my circumstances too strait and my Family too burdensome
and now God hath lessened the number and the charge to my
sorrow' (Clegg 1978, pp. 12–14). It was not only emerging promise that Clegg regretted. He mourned his infant son as any father
200 years later.

Nor do the celebrations that accompanied baptisms suggest a
casual or an emotionally neutral attitude to the arrival of children.
Even the Presbyterian congregation of James Clegg, heirs to the
Puritan tradition that abhorred large gatherings without proper
discipline, clung to old usages and accompanied baptism with
drink and jollity. In June 1743 when he baptised a child at Malcoff,
Clegg wrote in his diary: 'there was a great deal of company and I
fear of excess, I wish we might have no more of such christnings
or meetings, I think proper endeavours should be used that such
customs should be broke and laid aside' (Clegg 1979, p. 490)

But many so welcomed failed to survive. In pre-industrial
England 34.4 per cent of deaths were of children under 10 and
only 6.7 per cent of adults of 80 and over compared with 2.4 per
cent for children and 48.4 per cent for the over-80s in modern
England. Infant and child mortality were high but variable in the
old society. Wrigley and Schofield found that between 1550 and

1750 from 20 per cent to 27 per cent of children did not reach the age of 10 in the 12 parishes they studied (Wrigley & Schofield 1981, p. 249). At Wem, in Shropshire, infant mortality, that is the death of children in their first year, was at its lowest at 120 per 1,000 in the 1670s but reached 300 for a year or two in the 1660s. Crisis years could bring very high rates, as is shown by 5 north-western parishes that suffered the high general mortality of 1623 (Table 4).

Table 4 Infant mortality in five north-western parishes (deaths under 1 per 1,000 births)

Parish	1620	1621	1622	1623
Cockerham	104	97	111	325
Blackburn	112	227	222	432
Prestwich	200	320	163	292
Bury	217	165	206	400
Padiham	294	137	222	318
Average for the five parishes	162	188	192	389

Source: Rogers 1974, p. 21

At Clayworth the 1680s saw rates of 300 to 385, though they fell to 242 between 1689 and 1691 then varied between 117 and 185 in the subsequent period to 1703 (Laslett 1965, pp. 125–6).

The affection and the grief revealed in numerous diaries, journals and letters and the care taken to provide for children born and unborn in fathers' wills offer support to the 'less austere' school of historians. Swaddling was advised by contemporary medical manuals but only for a month or more, while wet nursing, at its height in the late seventeenth and early eighteenth centuries, was used only by a minority of gentry and urban tradesmen or by parish authorities for their unfortunates (Fildes 1988, pp. 79, 115). Wrightson finds many examples of the love that parents felt and the care they took of their children and he believes that corporal punishment in grammar schools and homes (Aubrey also comments on the severity of it at the university) was only occasional, moderate and reluctantly administered. Children were, in Newcome's terms, expected to be 'comforts', to provide emotional satisfactions (Wrightson 1982, pp. 109–14).

The education of children was not perceived as a matter for professional teachers or for schools except for the gentry and for those exceptional children of lower degree who were marked by outstanding early promise. For these children the grammar schools offered a curriculum of Latin, Greek and sometimes Hebrew that opened the doors to the universities and careers in the church and the law. John Aubrey tells the story of George Abbot, Archbishop of Canterbury, whose mother, a poor cloth-worker's wife, dreamt that if she ate a pike before she bore him he would be a great man. A pike duly swam into her pail when she went to collect water in the river, she ate it, and wealthy neigh-bours offered themselves as sponsors of the child. 'This their Poverty accepted joyfully, and three were chosen, who main-tained him at School, and University afterwards, his father not being able. This is generally received for a trueth' (Aubrey 1962, p. 114). Few poor children could hope for such fortune. In the 1620s when there were at least 75 teachers in Lancashire and Cheshire, roughly one for every 2,600 inhabitants, perhaps 90 per cent of childen were not attending school at any one time. By the 1660s there were more teachers, 150 in all, but the proportion of them who were teaching only at elementary level had greatly increased (Rogers 1975, p. 13). Although by then no place in Lancashire was more than ten miles distant from a school, most children had no more than a brief encounter with the most basic reading and writing, and many lacked even that (Jordan 1962, p. 70).

Certainly the period of childhood as we know it seems to have been short. In the sixteenth and seventeenth centuries children had the right to their own earnings and could make testaments and dispose of their own property at fourteen for boys, twelve for girls, and once away from home it appears that they did not usually contribute to the parental income (Macfarlane 1986, p. 81). If they were thrifty their earnings were saved for their own marriage and family; if not, they went to the alehouse or the fair. In agricultural townships most children of working families were at work by the age of seven, earning 2d or 3d a day, and those that did not later leave home for service clearly carried on working at home (Wrightson 1982, p. 113).

There may well have been regional and occupational factors

that affected the proportions of children leaving home for service. In agricultural districts with impartible inheritance and in town trades with limited entry through apprenticeship it might be expected that sons would leave to make a living elsewhere. Where all the children looked for a share in the family holding and in country trades where strict apprenticeship did not apply, more might stay at home. As for tenancies, while smallholders were declining in numbers on the corn–arable land, those in the pastoral regions were increasing, especially where there was supplementary domestic industry. Early in the period people were moving to the weaving areas of East Anglia and the West Country, to mining and iron areas like the Forest of Dean or the rich coal districts of the Tyne (Wrightson 1982, pp. 126–7). The old forest areas of Lancashire show a growth in copyhold parcels; in Rossendale there were 101 in 1527 and 314 in 1662, in Pendle 101 in 1527 and 189 in 1662 and in Trawden 26 in 1527, 35 in 1662 (Pearson 1985, p. 103). Family formation was clearly easier where less land was required and was more easily available and this, no doubt, encouraged more children to stay at home. They do not appear to have worked at home for nothing. The will of the Stockport weaver, Alexander Daniel, lists debts of 3s 6d, 6s and 12s 5d to three of his sons with a fourth debt to a son undecipherable; they look very like wages.

It was not cheap to apprentice a son to a prosperous trade. In 1729 James Clegg of Chinley Chapel paid £22 10s to apprentice his son John in Manchester and in June 1730 twenty guineas to Mr Berry, a Manchester merchant, with a further five to pay at the end of the first of the seven years' apprenticeship of another son, Joseph. In 1731 he was party to the apprenticeship of a Derbyshire neighbour's son that cost £50 for six years. These were sums comparable to the marriage portions he gave his daughters, £50 to Anne and £90 to Elizabeth. They represented a considerable proportion of his annual income. On 1 January 1731 he 'looked back over the accounts of the year past and found the expenses amount to 120 pounds so plentifully hath God provided for us' (Clegg 1978, xvi–xviii, p. 104).

Although children started work early and often away from home they were not regarded as wholly adult. They could take on what were virtually adult responsibilities at work and might have a large measure of physical independence but until they married or were propertied they had no formal role in their communities. It was not until the late eighteenth century that the period between childhood and marriage was perceived as a formative time that merited special attention or education. That group then lost its earlier freedom, a process that began high in society and worked its way down (Musgrove 1964, pp. 33–57). Before this happened there was for most young people a period of well over ten years, usually lasting into their late twenties, during which they lived single at home or in the house where they served. Roger Lowe, for example, a grocer's apprentice in the 1660s and early 1670s, lived alone in the shop that he kept for his master at Ashton-in-Makerfield in Lancashire (Lowe 1938). There is now great interest in this unmarried group. Gillis suggests that with so many young people independent of home it was masters in service, kin, neighbours and, above all the peer group which 'took the most direct and active role in regulating the heterosexuality of young people throughout this period' (Gillis 1985, p. 22). It was, in his view, a period of 'polygamous innocence' marked by group involvement in the annual round of feasts and festivals, rituals and games. Christmas was followed by the New Year celebrations then by Shrove Tuesday, May Day, Easter and Whitsun, the Harvest Festival and so on to Christmas. And there were also the wakes and the rushbearing, hiring and other fairs, the weekly market and the less regular celebrations for elections, local events or national triumphs. Even the events of the farm or estate's life, such as marling (the digging and spreading of lime-rich clay), were occasions for ritual and merrymaking.

All holidays and festivals had a strong communal element and most were the occasion for adult games for the unmarried such as 'kiss in the ring' on St Valentine's day and dancing round the maypole at the May festival. Nicholas Blundell never failed to provide elaborate entertainment when he finished marling with processions of marlers with guns and head-dresses and girls with garlands; pipers and fiddlers played for dancing and there were sword dances around the specially erected maypole. Even the flax-breaking had its own rituals of supper, 'guising' in fantastic dress or masks, garlands and dancing (Blundell 1952, pp. 136–9). Often, too, the celebrations had a strong parochial or township flavour. Villages defended their maypole against their neighbours or decorated their rushcarts so as to outshine adjacent townships. In the spring and summer social life was outdoors and communal for all but the very highest in society. In the winter it gave way to the tales round the fire, the hauntings of Hallowe'en and the indoor games of Christmas. In Gillis's view it was social as opposed to sexual promiscuity and the group restrained the behaviour of the individual (Gillis 1985, pp. 23–30).

Roger Lowe's diary lends some support to this view. From its commencement in 1663 to March 1668 when he married, he engaged in a number of courtships in which he used friends as intermediaries, sought their help and advice or suffered from their interference. He also played the same roles for his own friends. On 4 January 1663, for example, he rode with Thomas Tickle and his wife to Rainford, 'to avince to old Sephon the young couple's mariage. We came thither and the old man seemed to be displeased but it was but a while' (Lowe 1938, p. 13). Lowe found his recreation in the company of his friends of both sexes, for girls enjoyed a surprising degree of freedom in their comings and goings and could be met not only at the well and in the fields but in the alehouse and at the fair. But all ages were sociable and where the aged were so few and the young so many it was natural that the young were most often in each other's company. In 1752, in his old age, that other Presbyterian, Dr Clegg, saw the young people deserting his own congregation for the parish church, commenting: 'many young people fall off and go to church where they are more at liberty to follow their pleasures and few parents or masters take any good care of these children' (Clegg 1981, p. 795).

Courting was then, for the middle ranks, easy to enter upon in a tentative and preliminary way in the absence of chaperones, marriage-brokers and arranged marriages or a prying, prurient clergy. But it was also the first step in taking perhaps the most important decision in a young man or woman's life, with both aware that their reputation and future happiness and prosperity were at stake. The long conversations that Roger Lowe held with a succession of young women who attracted him and with their and his friends testify to a long period of testing out potential partners. Courtships of six months to two years were usual according to Macfarlane and couples clearly not only sounded out emotional and personal attributes but also learned about each other's families and social and economic standing. Passion might well cut short this process, but the prudent couple had cleared the ground before parents were brought in to discuss the details of financial arrangements.

It was however neither family nor peer group, kin or neighbours that finally decided the individual's choice, nor were they always consulted. Two of Adam Martindale's brothers married against parental disapproval in the 1630s and later his son found his own partner in London (Wrightson 1982, p. 75). A hundred years later, in December 1731, James Clegg was observing similar behaviour among his congregation: 'This week another young woman the daughter of Francis Gee of Chinley has married without her mother's consent. It grieves me to see such as I had the greatest hopes of act so undutifully' (Clegg 1978, p. 135). Worse was to follow. In 1735 Clegg's own son John was set on marrying and Clegg's entry shows the limits of even his authority which combined the parental and the ministerial: 'I returnd to my sons and gave John a solemn charge not to marry without my consent and the consent of her father, he promisd to delay it a while and that was all I could bring him to' (Clegg 1978, p. 222).

Whether with or without parental consent and the approval of peers and neighbours, couples eventually arrived at an agreement that they would wed; postponement or cancellation often led to illegitimacy – see Part III. For the middle and lower degrees their partners would usually come from an area within ten miles of their place of residence though this was, of course, not necessarily their birthplace or family home (Macfarlane 1986, pp. 246–54). Nor is there evidence that they generally married cousins, second cousins or other kin; geographical and social mobility widened their field of choice though, usually, they would have most contact with people of roughly their own status and would be most likely to marry within it. (Bramwell, 1939, attempted to quantify the incidence of cousin marriages.)

Fertility was not a shibboleth in English courtship and marriage and there appears to have been no tradition of 'bundling' or intercourse preceding contract being used as a preliminary testing of the fertility of courting couples (Macfarlane 1986, p. 307). Roger

Lowe, in the seventeenth century, sat up all night with a girl discussing their future but this seems to have been a decorous occasion, a further testing-out of their compatibility before they took the decisive step of betrothal which was a contract in its own right. Normally intercourse followed betrothal rather than preceded it: it was a guarantee that the intentions of both were fixed on a permanent relationship.

Betrothals were often witnessed by friends, were the subject of negotiations on portions between parents and were usually short. They were not indissoluble but committed the man to support any consequent children (Gillis 1985, pp. 43–51). The expected outcome of betrothal was marriage, whether formal or informal. When it broke down and the man failed to honour his word to support his child or where pregnancy resulted from casual intimacy the woman could depend only on her parents or poor relief. It was then that the freedom and privacy of adolescent behaviour was subject to intense and persistent pressure as the overseers and churchwardens sought to discover the putative father and relieve the parish or township of the burden of an unsupported mother and child. The bride who gave birth too early following her church wedding had to do penance with her husband before the altar for her sin of fornication: the unwedded mother was pressed, even on the childbed, to give the name of the father (Wrightson 1982, p. 86). If she was unfortunate enough to be out of her parish of settlement she could find herself passed from constable to constable as each tried to remove her before she could burden the parish with a new pauper. But illegitimacy was not a major problem in early modern society; most children were born into, and spent their early years in the nuclear family of parents and children.

Children in the industrial age

The high infant mortality that had characterised the pre-factory era persisted in some areas into the later nineteenth century in spite of municipal reform and sanitary improvements. Infant mortality was high where mothers went out to work as in Lancashire, Staffordshire, Leicestershire and Warwickshire; in heavily urbanised counties, colliery districts and those agri-

Table 5 Infant mortality, England and Wales and highest and lowest
counties (deaths under one per 1,000 births)

	1845–54	1871–80	1881–91	1891–1900	1901–05
Eng. & Wales	145	149	142	153	138
Highest					
Lancs.	193	172	166	179	163
E. Riding	182	162	149	166	152
Staffs.	180	159	156	172	151
Leics.	173	176	164	164	144
Durham	159	166	152	167	157
Warks.	174	159	150	169	152
Lowest					
Surrey	116	115	110	122	105
Wilts.	128	110	103	102	91
Westml.	102	106	100	107	97
Dorset	123	108	96	102	92
Herts.	135	121	108	110	92

Source: Newman 1906, p. 21.

cultural areas where women were employed in heavy field
labour (Newman 1906, passim; Cruikshank 1981, p. 112). It was
unrelated to poverty, as measured by official pauperism, for the
poorest rural areas in general returned far lower rates than the
prosperous industrial counties (Newman 1906, p. 27).

Indeed in the high-wage cotton towns, trade depressions
usually reduced rather than increased child mortality. This
happened in the North-West in the depressed year of 1842 when a
fall in infant mortality was attributed to the increased sobriety of
adults and fewer mothers going to the mill. Between 1862 and
1864 in the misery of the cotton famine the infant death rate in the
cotton area fell from 184 per 1,000 in 1861 to 166 in 1862, rose to
170 in 1863 when there were unrelated epidemics and fell again to
163 in 1864 (see Watts 1866).

Nor did infant mortality respond very quickly to the improvements that were progressively transforming the towns as a consequence of municipal sanitary, health and housing legislation from
1835 on. In 1905 Dr Newman, who had seen infant mortality
reach 447 per 1,000 from 1895 to 1899 in one slum area of
Finsbury where he was Medical Officer, was convinced that
urban squalor was not of itself the major cause. Scottish and Irish

crofters, he wrote, lived in insanitary, damp, dark hovels overcrowded with human beings in close proximity to their animals,
but their average infant mortality was lower than for any county in
England (Newman 1906, pp. 216–17). Even when these same
Scottish and Irish people came to live industrial lives in the less
salubrious parts of England they, with the Jews and Italians, kept
their low levels of infant mortality. In Manchester in 1904 the
division with the lowest infant mortality at 91, half the Manchester
average of 187, was Cheetham, which had a high proportion of
Jewish immigrants. It was, he concluded, neither the factory, poor
urban conditions nor poverty that caused the death of so many
babies, though they were strong underlying factors. The districts
with high infant mortality were characterised by poorer parental
physique caused by heavy or prolonged labour, by higher
illegitimacy, always associated with high infant mortality, by low
literacy, by mothers returning too early to work, by excessive
drinking and by urban overcrowding. Even in these districts it was
the babies of ignorant and negligent parents who most readily
succumbed (Newman 1906, passim).

A major cause of this phenomenon appears to lie in the care
and diet of infants. Where there were no adult female relatives to
look after young children they were often put out to childminders
or looked after at home by ignorant young girls, the 'nurses' so
often found in poorer districts in the 1851 census. In all these
cases a combination of poor care, an irregular diet that included
dirty and adulterated milk and unsuitable solids, and a continuation of the old practice of soothing infants with narcotics
such as Godfrey's Cordial often produced diarrhoea, pining, con-
vulsions and death (Newman 1906, passim; Hewitt 1958, pp.
110–46). As late as 1904 in Salford the death rates for infants rose
from 128.6 per 1,000 births for those who were breast-fed to 163.9
for those fed on cow's milk only and 439.0 for those fed on other
foods such as condensed milk (Hewitt 1958, p. 224). It was principally traditional breast-feeding that enabled the Scots and Irish,
the Italians and Jews to preserve their infants in the industrial
districts where they settled. The English workers in those same
towns had adopted different and disastrous practices. Between
1887 and 1896 seven of the ten worst affected towns were cotton
towns plus Leicester, Liverpool and Wolverhampton. In 1895

Preston returned a rate of 248 per 1,000 against a national average of 161, Blackburn 236 and Stockport 231 (Cruickshank 1981, pp. 110–11). It was not until after the First World War that infant mortality began to yield to the forces of nutrition, medicine, education and social reform.

The changes that affected the industrialising areas in the late eighteenth and early nineteenth centuries were slow to extend into the agricultural countryside. Children were no less likely to be beaten than in earlier years, perhaps even more so as as public morality became stricter and more judgemental. Francis Kilvert, the Herefordshire curate, was a kind and sensitive man and in June 1871 he could describe the whipping of three girls by their father as brutal. In August 1874, however, he visited a little girl, Fanny Strange, whose father had beaten her so severely for lying and stealing that she had to be put to bed. Two days later he visited her again, ill and still confined to bed, recording in his diary: 'the severe chastisement she has undergone may have had a happy effect and broken her self-will and cured her of her faults. Her parents very wisely have not spared her nor the rod' (Kilvert 1974, p. 253).

The days of country childhood were short, for children there quickly entered the world of work, though their assumption of full responsibility as adults had to await marriage or confirmed single status later in life. Flora Thompson describes how in the 1880s girls in her Oxfordshire village were 'pushed out into the world' in domestic service at eleven, twelve or thirteen. They had left school at ten or eleven and there was no work for them to do in the village but they still occupied valuable space in the two-bedroomed cottages and had to be fed and clothed. Boys were encouraged to stay at home; their wages, however small, were vital to the family income (Thompson 1948, pp. 146–7). The girls sent money home from their scanty wages, perhaps a change from earlier times when, it is suggested, they usually kept their earnings for their own marriages. Some still did. In July 1828 when the choleric Somerset rector John Skinner dismissed his servant Betty he commented on her gross ingratitude: 'I took her absolutely a pauper . . . I clothed her, and gave her wages, beginning at £5 and ending at £10 per annum, so that she has saved £14 and has a large stock of clothes' (Skinner 1984, p. 345).

The young people who carried on the old tradition of leaving home for service returned at traditional times. On Mothering Sunday, 18 March 1871, Francis Kilvert recorded: 'And all the world in an upturn going out visiting. Girls and boys going home to see their mothers and taking them cakes, brothers and sisters of middle age are going to see each other' (Kilvert 1974, p. 113). It was on these occasions that many couples carried on their episodic courting, briefly reunited before separating again to conduct their romances by post until they could afford to marry. By the late nineteenth century it would seem that the old courting customs and perhaps some of the laxity of earlier times were under attack. In September 1870 the parents of a young Cliro girl who became pregnant after sitting up all night with a young man who then refused to acknowledge paternity were reprimanded by the vicar's wife (Kilvert 1974, p. 78).

For those children who survived the early, dangerous years, the 1833 Factory Act which banned children under the age of nine from work in textile mills other than silk began a long process of protection by law. In 1842 the ban was extended to underground work in mines, in 1845 children under eight were excluded from calico print works and in 1860 bleach and dye works were brought under the Factory Acts. Protection was then progressively extended to all factories and workshops until all, including domestic workshops, were brought under the Acts in 1878. The mill children's protection was vitiated by the practice of half-time working introduced under the 1844 Act. This allowed children between eight and thirteen to work a maximum of six and a half hours a day, the other half of the day being spent in school. The device offered a minimal schooling at the cost of making the half-timers a separate, unhappy and unregarded element in the schools (Hutchins & Harrison 1911, passim). It was not abolished until 1918. From 1876 the acts laying down compulsory education combined with factory legislation in raising the age at starting work for all children to eleven in 1893, twelve in 1902 and fourteen in 1918.

Working children were easily identified and their situation was progressively remedied by law. It may be that they were less unfortunate than children in towns where there was little work for them to do. The street arabs of London have provided literature with many tiny criminals from Fagin's pickpockets to the unfortunates of Morrison's *Child of the Jago*. Liverpool swarmed with unemployed children from the late eighteenth century through the nineteenth century and they resisted compulsory attendance at school long after the passing of the Education Acts. Voluntary day schools, Sunday schools and ragged schools could do little to bring these children within the scope of education until parents were willing and able to co-operate with the boards or education committees in counteracting the excitements and opportunities of the streets and docks (Cockroft 1974, pp. 153–4). The 1902 and 1918 Education Acts completed the universality of elementary education and the debate then switched to the desirability of secondary education for all, but this was not to be achieved until long after 1920.

The courtship of the working classes during the era of mandatory marriage reflected a variety of circumstances. In the country, matters perhaps proceeded as they had for generations but the towns began to develop new patterns in the later nineteenth century. This was principally characterised by the Friday or Saturday evening 'monkey run' with groups of young men and women parading the principal streets, exchanging witticisms and eyeing each other with a view to asking out. It could be decorous or boisterous, but for those without strong church or chapel affiliations or other venues for meeting prospective partners it provided a means of first introduction. Among the respectable working class parental control of children appears to have grown stronger in the late nineteenth century and this combined with a higher degree of prudery and sexual inhibition to restore group courting. Girls were conscious that their futures lay in marriage and the home, often within a local family network that centred on their mothers and even grandmothers. Boys emulated their fathers in seeking male companionship at work, in the trade union and at the pub or club. After the restriction of hours of work in the 1850s they were also able to use their free Saturday afternoons playing or watching football or cricket. Their leisure was enjoyed largely outside the home but girls were expected to be much more closely involved in domestic affairs.

Solitaries, the widowed and the aged: the early modern period

So far the discussion has followed the family from its formation to childbirth and rearing, adolescence and courtship. We must now consider those who did not marry and those who survived their partners to face the pains of widowhood. Not all could marry. We have seen that in the early modern period up to one-quarter of the population never married, marriage being particularly difficult for many younger sons and daughters of the gentry. In the sixteenth century 10 per cent of gentry daughters were unmarried at 50, 15 per cent in the early sixteenth century and 25 per cent between 1675 and 1799. For younger sons the numbers of unmarried rose from 20 per cent after 1600 to 26 per cent between 1675 and 1799 (Stone 1977, p. 44). Some of the unmarried were independent enough to live alone but Laslett found that in the seventeenth century 27.6 per cent of gentry households contained resident kin against 17 per cent of the yeomen and 7.9 per cent of the poor (Wrightson 1982, p. 44). These figures may reflect the higher marriage aspirations and greater parental influence over choice of partners among the gentry as well as their relative ability to find space and support for unmarried or widowed kin. Bachelors were seen as fit subjects for taxation in the short-lived Act of 1695 that taxed births, marriages and burials and also laid an annual tax on all bachelors over twenty-five as well as widowers without children. The duty on bachelors and widowers was not renewed in 1706. Dowell noted, grimly, that 'It may be noted that the tax on marriages had the pernicious effect of increasing the number of marriages by irresponsible persons unfit for the solemnity' (Dowell 1884, II, pp. 49–50). Presumably it was the tax on bachelors and widowers that caused this unseemly development. Bachelors were again penalised in 1785 when a revision of the 1777 tax on manservants charged the servants of bachelors at a higher rate than those of married men. This higher rate persisted until 1853. The tax on manservants raised over £600,000 in 1819 and £137,000 in 1883, by which time it was confined to domestic servants only. In 1785 a heavily criticised tax was imposed on the employers of female servants but it was repealed in 1792. It had affected only 90,000 families and raised about £31,000. In Dowell's words, it was 'paid by the poorer class of housekeepers', an indication of the lower status of female servants (Dowell 1884, III, pp. 245–8).

If a first marriage was impossible for many people it is clear that those who could marry once had a very good chance of marrying again on the death of their spouse. Where the property on which the first marriage had been founded had been maintained or had grown, both widows and widowers were attractive prospects. Remarriage of the widowed was common, rapid and repeated though the demand for widows tended to fluctuate with the scarcity or otherwise of land, houses and capital (Laslett 1965, p. 100. See Ravensdale in Smith 1984, pp. 215–19 for a discussion of medieval practice). Why widows so often remarried is not entirely clear. The death of their husbands gave them independence and control over resources for the first time in their lives. They could hold land, houses and personal estate, enjoy their jointure or free bench, carry on their late husband's trade or farm, lend money, buy and sell as they chose. Many, of course, had children and may have sought a stepfather who could assist in their upbringing; others may have remarried for assistance in economic affairs or for the security of a man's support in a male-dominated society. Many, perhaps, remarried for that affectionate companionship that had carried them into their first marriages.

In the sixteenth century Elizabeth Hardwick's four marriages took her from the 400-acre estate where she was born to the dizzy heights of Countess of Shrewsbury, builder of great houses and founder of aristocratic dynasties. But her later years were bitter with quarrels over property as she resisted her husband's claim to the control of her estates. The Gaskells at Disley in Cheshire are a more humble example of similar strife. Peter Gaskell died in 1703, leaving his tenement to his brother John on payment of £100 to Peter's widow Elizabeth. In 1731 John Gaskell brought a suit against Elizabeth, now remarried, claiming that she had kept the tenement and had also charged her late husband's account with £40 made up of ten annual payments of £4 under the marriage settlement, which she should have given up in return for the £100 payable for the tenement. Elizabeth's case was simply that she had not received the £100 from John and was entitled to keep the tenement. The £40 marriage settlement presumably indicates that she remarried ten years after her husband's death. Elizabeth appears from the accounts to have benefited to the tune of £448 from her first husband's estate; her brother-in-law, chief beneficiary in the will, had received nothing (CRO, Prob. R., Peter Gaskell 1731).

Whatever their course through life, death came to all. Most died young by modern standards; in the late seventeenth century those aged sixty and over made up only 10.7 per cent of the population (Laslett 1965, p. 103). As always the old saw only a falling away. Thomas Tyndale was born in 1588 and died in 1672 and Aubrey recorded his late reflections: 'You see in me the Ruines of Time. The day is almost at an end with me, and truly I am glad of it: I desire not to live in this corrupt age. It was not so in Queen Elizabeth's time: then youth bare Respect to old Age' (Aubrey 1962, p. 35).

In general the surest safeguard against poverty in old age was to keep control of sufficient property to maintain the home and standard of living. Retirement in the modern sense was unknown, but probate records often indicate that older men employed more capital in moneylending, especially on bond or security, than in their agriculture or trade. Comparatively few people in England appear to have entered into agreements with their children for maintenance in return for giving up their real property, their lands or businesses. They gave their children education, apprenticeship or their portions but usually retained control over their central property until death.

Those without property had not depended entirely on their families even before the Reformation when the manor, the guild, the church and private charity had all played an important part. After it the Poor Law evolved, taking final form in the Act of 1601 and the Settlement Act of 1662 which laid down a national system for collecting and disbursing a poor rate on a parish or township basis. In the late seventeenth century elderly widows could expect poor relief of about £3 per annum compared with average annual incomes of £15 (Smith 1984, fn. p. 74). The Poor Law stated that children should contribute to the support of aged and impotent parents but it seems to have been comparatively rare for overseers or churchwardens to have taken them before the justices for enforcement. This differed from the wide use made of the legal machinery which could bring back runaway husbands or distrain on their property for the support of their wives and children. The Act of Settlement of 1662 similarly returned the poor to their parishes of settlement, but did not seek to find their children and make them responsible (Macfarlane 1986, p. 107). There appeared to be a common acceptance that, though children should and usually would do what they could for their parents, their true obligation was to the coming, rather than the passing generation.

Death meant a rearrangement of affairs for the living. All wills cater for the payment of debts and funeral expenses and, where necessary, for the payment of the heriot to the lord and the mortuary to the church. The wills of married men show care for their wives and children, born and unborn, and usually only in the absence of heirs record bequests to grandchildren, nephews or nieces and remoter kin (Wrightson in Smith 1984, pp. 313–32). After 1600 there is, too, a decline in bequests to godchildren. The testator, having made provision for his dependents, normally reserved his 'own part' for goodwill gifts to his lord or landlord, bequests to servants and friends and benefactions to the poor, to the church or school, for the provision of a library or the maintenance of roads or bridges. The funeral of George Talbot, 6th Earl of Shrewsbury, in 1590 drew 8,000 poor people to Sheffield for the funeral dole and the consequent disorder encouraged other great men to leave their money to trustees or overseers for the support of local poor (Williams 1959, p. 196). Widows made the most detailed wills, remembering all their kin and friends with gifts of money, jewellery and clothing carefully selected as a remembrance of times past.

The will and testament and the funeral were also the last occasions on which testators could make an individual statement. The words in which they delivered their souls into the hands of God were not necessarily their own but they do reflect the general tenor of the times in which they lived. The clergyman called on to preach the funeral sermon was much more a reflection of their own views but it was in the disposition of the body that the testators often opened their hearts. Many sought to return to their family's parish church and to be buried close by their departed spouse or parents. For them the family survived death itself.

Solitaries, the widowed and the aged: the industrial age

Neither urbanisation nor the factory system significantly improved the lot of working people in old age though the expansion of opportunities to make money in the provision of goods and services may have benefited the classes immediately above them. Life held little comfort for the aged rural labourer and his wife until the grant of old-age pensions by the 1906 Liberal government. Richard Cobbold's account of Wortham in Suffolk, where he was Rector in 1860, describes the latter days of many of the labouring people and his attempts to alleviate their poverty by charitable means. He was a convinced opponent of the workhouse and maintained two cottages for the aged poor as an alternative. One of his industrious parishioners, the labourer Thomas Goddard, died as an aged but 'merry and vivacious man', in a miserable hovel which he shared with an old comrade. He always said: 'I love the sight of the face open Ling on which I have cut turf from my boyhood and would rather give up the ghost there than be the tenant of the Union House in my old days' (Cobbold 1977, p. 128).

Those who followed industrial occupations were no better off. Indeed the disappearance of domestic industry as manufacture moved into powered mills robbed those with skills of the opportunity to exercise them and deprived the unskilled of those ancillary tasks which had been their province when the family was the seat of industry. Poor widows and the ageing unmarried, unmarried mothers and the old were forced into casual or unpleasant employments, hovering between marginal jobs, unemployment and the workhouse. Nor could most working-class families offer complete support or a home for aged parents when there was no clear economic role for them. In 1851 at Chilvers Coton in the Midlands, a mining and ribbon-weaving district, 18 per cent of the aged were living in three-generation households of which they were the heads. Over half, however, consisted of a parent, a single child who was unmarried, separated or widowed and a grandchild, most of them 'fragile economies'. By 1901 there were more aged parents living with children but the numbers remained small (Quadagno 1982, pp. 84–9).

The proportion of elderly people remained fairly static in the later nineteenth century. In 1850 those aged sixty-five or over comprised 4.6 per cent of the population and this did not change much for the next sixty or seventy years. (Quadagno 1982, p. 32).

Table 6 Age distribution, England and Wales (%)

Age group	1871	1901	1931
60–64	2.7	2.7	4.1
65–74	3.4	3.3	5.4
75 and over	1.4	1.4	2.0

Source: based on Marsh 1958, p. 29.

In the 1890s 29 per cent of those over sixty-five were paupers, 21 per cent received outdoor relief and 8 per cent were in the workhouse but only 5 per cent of the aged were dependent upon the Poor Law alone. Samples taken by Charles Booth suggested that some 5 per cent of the aged depended upon relations only but relations were also part-contributors to a further 25 per cent often, it may be, only in a minor way but neverthless offering some help. Over one-half of the aged had either earnings or private means which permitted independence but half of this group depended upon earnings which would clearly fall away as age prevented them from working. From 1871 until 1896 the government attacked outdoor relief for the aged by pressing their children for support, even to the extent of prosecution for failure. It also urged the workhouse on paupers over seventy who were living alone (Quadagno 1982, pp. 104–13, 133). A circular of 1896 removed these pressures and in 1908 the Old-Age Pensions Act gave people over seventy with incomes under £26 per annum 5s per week.

But Rowntree had now identified the 'poverty cycle' in which working-class families moved from relative prosperity to poverty as the children were born, recovered it for a few years as the children started work and then fell into final distress when they had left home and the parents could no longer work. Additionally the family could also be plunged into poverty by sickness, unemployment or the death of the breadwinner; drink, gambling or lack of thought could make families poor at any time. The Old-Age Pensions Act attempted to ameliorate the condition of those at the end of the cycle. The National Insurance Act of 1911 for workers earning under £160 per annum aimed at protection from the accidents of family life – sickness, disability and unemployment – and it also introduced maternity benefit (Baugh 1985, pp. 16–17). The state had, since the seventeenth century, tried to ensure that help was available for those in poverty and old-age pensions can be seen as an extension of that aim. National Insurance can similarly be seen as a centralised way of encouraging the working-class drive to self-help that had produced friendly and building societies in the late eighteenth and nineteenth centuries. What was new was the direct role of the government in assisting working families to insure not only against the accidents of family life but against the happier and more expected contingency of childbirth. It was a small initial step but one with great potential to change the whole economic basis on which family life was built.

Part II

The exploitation
of source material

Introduction

The research during the last thirty years on which Part I is largely based has changed our views on the size and composition of the family and household, on the ages and rates involved in birth, marriage, death and illegitimacy, and on the relationship of all to the local economy (see, e.g., Chambers 1957 and Levine 1977). It is important to recognise the ways in which this has been done, for three main reasons – first, to realise how far national conclusions have been drawn from relatively few and (as a cursory examination of the Resource Reading List will show) often local studies; second, to establish at a more detailed level the relationship between this research and the particular interests of genealogy and local history; and third, to be completed only in Part III, to suggest an agenda for genealogists and local historians to influence some of the ways in which family history can be undertaken in future, ways which would appear more meaningful to their needs and interests.

Source material for learning about the history of the family in Britain is very similar to that required to trace family trees, so that a genealogist approaching what we call family history seems to be on very familiar ground, being used to dealing with parish registers, wills, census and tax returns, and so on. However, what is needed is a new way of looking at these sources so that, instead of following an individual pedigree, like a single thread through a complex tapestry, the whole pattern of family history can be seen, and for the first time the place of those individual threads within it.

Every so often, you read a book which takes your breath away, which arouses in you a whirlwind of ideas for action, and even envy of the author for having written it. One such book was surely Peter Laslett's The world we have lost (1965) which has had an enormous influence on a whole generation of historians, and was a prime mover in the development of a new genre of historical research. Yet it was not acceptable, even as a gift, to the librarian of Laslett's own college, Trinity, Cambridge, because it did not seem scholarly enough. This short-sighted view, still held in some quarters, failed to recognise the nature of the revolution about to commence, though it had been evident on the continent of Europe for some years.

That revolution was the result of bringing together several hitherto disparate methods and sources in order to re-examine the nature of family history over some hundreds of years. Those sources were essentially local in character, and the statistically-minded quickly developed an idea of what 'local' must mean in terms of population size in order to draw meaningful conclusions. The sources were already well known – no new ones became available, though the growth of the County Record Office system facilitated access. The real skill was to look at the familiar in a new way, in order to exploit the same material much more fully than before. In the case of *The world we have lost*, this included an analysis of the *Rector's Book of Clayworth*, Nottinghamshire, which had been published as long ago as 1910. The fact that it had been available to historians for half a century was no guarantee that the lists of people which it contains would have been seen with a family historian's eyes. As time went on, analysis of data by computer became available for this, as for much other historical research; but that facility still depends for its outcome on what sort of questions are being asked – and it was the questions which began to change.

Since the 1960s, however, as Anderson (1980) shows, other writers began to demonstrate some inadequacies in a purely demographic approach to the history of the family, and it is now recognised that many questions deserve a multidisciplinary answer. The basis of the methodology, however, remains demographic in this book for several reasons. One is our belief that, in order to make people count, you have first to count people. Another is that the source material for demography is close to the experience of genealogists and local historians, and is often easy to access. Thirdly, we are both male, and there is the possibility that this approach may be more attractive to the male mind – whatever that is. Whichever approach, or combination of approaches, you choose to make, it is worth remembering that there are always three questions relating to the history of the family which should not be confused – what was said ought to happen, what was said to happen, and what did happen ? Sometimes three different answers emerge, but the third, which we take to be the most important, must initially be answered by using demographic (including genealogical) techniques.

Broadly speaking, sources for demographic-type local and family history research are of two kinds. There are those from which individuals can be traced over a period of time, but these are very limited in number. Only from 1939, with the creation of the National Register, which was taken over by the National Health Service in 1952, has central government attempted to maintain a file on all (or virtually all) citizens from birth until death (see Rogers 1986). Before then, there are series of records in which the same individuals can be found, records of birth, marriage and death, for example, but the fact that different entries relate to the same individual is not recorded. Some ingenuity is therefore required when their life patterns need to be traced, particularly those who have a relatively common name. Until 1939, names are always the single most important identifier for any individual.

Secondly, there are records which purport to be a 'snapshot' of a community at a point in time. The census is the most familiar example, but there are many others, some of which, such as electoral registers, are still with us, and freely accessible (Gibson & Rogers 1990). This type of source also exhibits deficiencies which are especially serious before the nineteenth century. Identification of individuals is often inadequate, and it is sometimes impossible to determine who is missing from such lists, with the result that conclusions drawn from their study are always subject to qualification.

The two types of data, the chronological and the snapshot, need not be used independently of each other. Indeed, as we shall soon see, it is usually advisable to employ more than one source in collaboration. Additionally, if the frequency of 'snapshots' is sufficiently high, a picture can be made to move, however slowly and haltingly, rather like an early movie. Genealogists are used to looking at the same family in nineteenth-century censuses ten years apart; annual Land Tax returns are even better, in order to study change over time. Nevertheless, it will be useful to treat the two types of source separately for the purpose of understanding the methodologies involved in their preliminary analysis.

We begin with lists of individuals living in the same locality at the same time, and will follow a convention of referring to them as 'lists', 'listings', or 'censuses' (see below). The best known, the national census, began in England and Wales only in 1801, and until 1841 the original returns showing the names of individuals are not available. (Local copies, sometimes more complete than the official returns, do occasionally survive, however; see below, p. 103, and Appendix 4.) Earlier listings, though sometimes called 'censuses' at the time, are only local, and it is doubtful in some cases whether their claims to completeness can be substantiated. Most lists before 1801 did not aim for universal coverage: some listed men only, or adults only, or the poor only, according to their purpose, which was very rarely if ever an attempt to list people for demographic purposes.

Omissions from these lists will present problems when you try to draw conclusions about communities in which our ancestors lived. It is bad enough even if you can discover who, or how many are missing; and unless you can work this out, some demographers would argue that the lists should not be used for the purpose of analysis. We think that view is too constricting, and that there is much which can be gleaned from them, beyond the elementary data for which the lists had been compiled in the first place.

We will try to describe the analysis and exploitation of sources, from the simplest to the most complicated rather than in a chronological sequence. We hope to relate these analyses to the purposes for which they have been used, through individual studies, to shed light on family history. First, we would like to emphasise the difference between the way we shall use the three words 'list', 'listing', and 'census'. 'Lists' are simply that – lists of names of people, drawn up for a variety of purposes, and usually giving other information about each individual – how much tax they paid, which candidate they voted for, or where they sat in church, for example; a 'listing' purports to be a complete list of people who lived in one place, be it a township, parish, or larger area (see Appendix 3); and a 'census' is such a complete listing, but on a national scale. The first in England and Wales was effectively that of 1841, so locally surviving originals from 1801 to 1831 can more properly be described as lists for our purpose (see

Appendix 4). There is no certainty that these distinctions are universally applied in the books and articles in the Resource Reading List, incidentally.

Lists

Genealogists use lists for two main reasons – to establish a distribution of surnames at a particular point in time in order to learn something of the history of a particular surname, or to locate places where their ancestors might be found in other records; and to learn more about the lives of their individual forebears once they have located them. We suggest, however, that there is much more to be gleaned from a list than that, but it has to be manipulated in order to extract the maximum family or local history benefit from it. This should be considered in three main ways:

1. We need to extract not only the obviously stated information, largely relating to the purpose for which the list was drawn up in the first place, but also to read between the lines, to compare various parts of the list with other parts, and to notice things which seem to be absent from the list. Always remember to ask yourself why the list was drawn up with that particular sequence of names, for there is always a reason, and that reason, once discovered, may then be used to extract more information from the document.

2. We should try to compare the list with those in the same series for neighbouring areas, similar or contrasting in nature, as well as with any estimates from further afield.

3. We should refer to other, contemporary sources to see what light they can throw on the list and its meaning. Often, what can be gleaned from merging the data from two sources turns out to be far more than the sum of the parts. This process is called 'record linkage'.

Let's start with a familiar example, a Hearth Tax return, on which much has already been written – see particularly Schurer & Arkell (1991), who give some interesting legislative and administrative background as well as new research on the subject, and the introduction to published versions, especially Webster (1988). These returns are available for most parts of the country between 1662 and 1666, and 1669 and 1675, after which they survive only rarely until the abolition of the tax in 1689. Original returns are in the Public Record Office, but some have been published, and many more are locally available on microfilm. (See Gibson (c).) Most genealogists and local historians consult them sooner or later, either to see in which parishes and townships families of specific surnames were living at the time, to learn the size of the house (via the number of fireplaces) in which their ancestors lived, which may give a rough indication of their relative wealth, or to pinpoint a date when their ancestors moved or died. Tax was collected at the rate of 1s every six months for each fireplace in the house occupied by each taxpayer. Of course, the number of hearths is not necessarily directly proportional to the number of rooms in the house, especially after some had been bricked up to avoid the tax. Nor, incidentally, does payment of the tax imply ownership of the property, only occupation as householder.

Appendix 1 is from our own home patch, the 1664 Hearth Tax return for the township of Tintwistle in the parish of Mottram-in-Longdendale, north-east Cheshire, copied from microfilm. We will look at this list, like so many other sources, on three levels. First there is the information which the compiler of the document meant to record, and we can try to read between the lines in order to uncover what was either taken for granted at the time, or what was meant to be concealed. Secondly we can compare this document with those for other areas. Thirdly, the results can be collated with information from other sources in order to reveal even more.

There is nothing uncharacteristic about the Tintwistle Hearth Tax given as Appendix 1. It is in two parts, the latter including those who, paying neither church nor poor rates, and dwelling in houses deemed to be worth less than £1 per annum, were exempt from paying the tax (as were certain others who earned their living through a fire of some kind – bakers or blacksmiths, for example, though this seems to have caused some confusion among the collectors). Typically, the house of the average non-chargeable had fewer fireplaces than that of the average taxpayer, but in the countryside this difference was usually slight, as the majority in each group had only one.

The list distinguishes between men and women, and possibly between widows and other women. (We say 'possibly' because there is no guarantee that Jane Heaward, for example, in the non-chargeable list, was a spinster rather than a widow, and a genealogical search would have to be undertaken in order to find out.) It does seem, however, that this particular tax official deliberately specified widows as such. Women number only three of the fifty-five people paying tax, and all three are widows. Yet of the sixteen exemptions, six were women, of whom four may not have been widows. The significance of this observation would once again need to be tested against similar figures for other places. It does suggest that a single woman could live independently in the mid-seventeenth century, but that her income was likely to be very small. Later, we shall explore the means by which the number of adult spinsters in the township might be estimated – but the skewing of males/females in the 1664 list certainly seems significant. For the economic place of widows in pre-industrial England, see B. A. Holderness (in Smith 1984, Ch. 13), Wall (1983) Ch. 16); cf. Anderson (1984). The percentage of households headed by women, especially widows, declined during the eighteenth century from the evidence of lists, with a complementary rise in the proportion of households headed by unmarried men. The family history of women in a Quaker community might be a revealing exercise in order to see how far their belief in the equality of the sexes could overcome the considerable prejudices of the time (see Appendix 6).

There are several reasons why the names on lists might be presented in a particular sequence. This one is not in alphabetical order, as are the heads of household in the famous Clayworth listing of 1676, so 'avoiding envy', but it might be the geographical order in which the taxman collected the money (and it is known that collectors of the Hearth Tax in 1684 were ordered to use this method of recording because other systems had proved less efficient (see Schurer & Arkell 1991)). Does Appendix 1 show the sequence in which the inhabitants of Tintwistle came to pay the Hearth Tax? Original poll books were drawn up not in the alphabetical sequence which characterises most printed versions, but in the chronological sequence, virtually at random, in which they arrived at the hustings to vote. If that were the case in the Tintwistle Hearth Tax, how were the non-chargeables arranged? Brown (1971) noted that different parts of the parish of Aldenham were usually listed in the same sequence from year to year in the overseers' assessments of Hertfordshire. Perhaps the Tintwistle list was copied from an earlier list, written for another purpose – but we need to solve the problem for that earlier list. It might be entirely random, as the tax collector assembled scraps of notes on individual payments. It might be in order of social status, as so many of the early lists and listing were – pew holders, for example – (see Laslett 1965) and it has been noted that the Lord of the Manor, followed by the parson, was often the first on a Hearth Tax list (Webster 1988, pp. xxxvii– xxxviii).

Of these possibilities, we can eliminate only social status from the evidence of the data in the list itself, as there is the occasional householder with up to four hearths part-way down. The other explanations must be teased out through record linkage. Reference to a Tintwistle Hearth Tax return immediately before or after this one would confirm or eliminate the random theory (and indeed, while some names change, enough are found in the same part of the list as in 1664 to abandon randomness as an explanation). Note, however, that had it not been eliminated, it would not have been proved – the next tax official might have gathered the money or made the assessment using a different route, for example, giving the appearance of being random. Checking for a geographical explanation needs a source to dis- cover where these individuals lived within the township, and there are no contemporary maps available to show this level of detail. However, the local parish register sometimes locates individuals in small hamlets, and wills indicating hamlets can be found in sufficient numbers to test the theory, sometimes with confirmation of identity through an associated inventory which lists property room by room, providing at the same time an interesting tangential exercise which links appraised wealth with the number of hearths.

Once that is done, the explanation becomes clear. When the

dwellings of enough householders can be identified, the list is seen to show the route taken by the tax collector from the head of the valley down to the little township of Tintwistle proper and finally into the hamlet of Arnfield. When he arrived at each little group of houses, he visited the largest first. Not only have we solved this problem – we now know something about those who left no will, and whose place of dwelling cannot be found in a parish register, manor court roll, or other source.

Webster (1988) has published two Nottinghamshire Hearth Taxes ten years apart, and much of the introduction concerns problems in comparing the two. When Laxton is examined in detail, it does seem as though the same pattern emerges, each section of the parish being taken in the same sequence ten years later, and though houses are not always visited on the same route (e.g. in Moorhouse) the fact that up to eight consecutively are so treated suggests houses along a street.

It is not all good news, however. The method cannot be applied to the non-chargeables, only one of whom (Hugh Lawton of Tintwistle) can be located in the probate records. Until another source is used, it is largely a matter of surmise that their sequence also follows the track of the tax collector as he trudged down the valley.

Those readers who have any responsibility for publishing original documents should note that, had this Hearth Tax return been resequenced in the printed form (in alphabetical order of surname, for genealogical convenience, for example), it would not have been possible to make this discovery. All documents should be printed as close to their original form as possible, though with adequate indexes where appropriate.

We can look a bit deeper into the list, and learn more about the community and something of the family history of the area. In addition to the number of houses with more than one hearth, the proportion of chargeable occupiers is interesting – over 77 per cent, compared with a national average for rural England of about two-thirds. Apparently, this township was able to maintain an economic buoyancy which is surprising in a sparse Pennine valley, whose houses stand at heights above sea level from 500 to 1,000 feet. Perhaps more of the poor were lodgers, if the area was short of living accommodation; lodgers, boarders or servants would not show up as householders. Perhaps some householders were omitted, as was clearly the case in Glossop, only three miles away, where only three non-chargeable houses appear against a list of forty-four chargeables. In 1662 indeed, it was not required that non-chargeables be listed at all. (Webster 1988, p. xvii. See also Wrightson 1982, p. 148, and Schurer & Arkell 1991 for comments about varying degrees of exemption in Hearth Tax documents, which ranged from under 20 to over 80 per cent.) The exempt were of three kinds – those too poor to pay, those whose income or property was below a certain level, and those who had exemption for occupational hearths; not all on the lists of exemptions seem to have included all three categories (Patten 1971). Some houses had no fireplaces, in the conventional sense; we have never seen a return showing zero in the assessment column, though occasionally householders are given no number at all. Some other source would need to be used in order to check these theories. We cannot, however, jump to the conclusion that this little village was comparatively wealthy, because other factors might be influencing the outcome – the omission of some remote, poorer dwellings; or numbers living in dwellings which were not provided with a formal fireplace, though they would not survive long in that climate,

It has also been found that, although most individual people – especially wives, children, lodgers and vagrants – were not listed by the tax assessors or collectors, the number of names on the Hearth Tax return can be used as a basis for estimating the total population of the area through the use of a multiplier. Such multipliers vary according to the nature of the source document – it would be different in the case of the Poll Tax or Protestation returns, for example, but the figure used for the Hearth Tax is normally 4.75 (see Laslett 1972). Multiplying the 70 residents of Tintwistle (not the 79 fireplaces) by 4.75 gives an approximate population of some 330.

However, the use of such multipliers in isolation, without corroborative evidence, is not advisable. There is an unavoidable degree of arbitrariness – it still seems odd that we know better than the most notable demographer of the time, Gregory King, whose multiplier for the Hearth Tax was 4.03! Webster (1988, p. xxi) suggests 4.25 for Nottinghamshire, but we feel that would be significantly low for the urban areas. We can be more confident in

D

these multipliers when we have another source of information about the actual population from a different source, and use that to calibrate the multiplier being used for neighbouring parishes. More importantly, Laslett (1965, Ch. 4) shows that the figure for the mean household size varied from one community to another (and one social class to another) at the same period. London and other cities were particularly high, probably over 7, partly because their houses were larger (Gregory King suggesting 30 residents for houses of 20 hearths), and partly through pressure of urban in-migration on the housing stock. Country districts, on the other hand, varied from parish to parish, some being lower than 3.7, which would bring the Tintwistle population in 1664 down to 260. As Schurer & Arkell (1991) note when discussing Marriage Duty Act returns, immediate localities rather then regions of the country show considerable variations. Calculations from Richard Price's aggregated data in eighteenth-century England indicate a family size of 5; but there were 21,263 families living in only 15,439 houses in those places in which the number of each had been counted (Ashton-under-Lyne, Liverpool, Maidstone, Manchester, Nottingham, Salford, St Michael's Chester, Tatton and Waverton). The large urban centres show the greatest number of families per house, as might be expected, and the position had worsened by 1803 despite the fact that the average family size in these places had gone down (Price 1803, Vol. 2, pp. 70–3).

Whatever the multiplier used, however, it does seem as though it remained fairly constant across a long period of time, perhaps from the Middle Ages until the end of the nineteenth century, even if not across space. That in turn implies that there was no major change in whether, for example, the elderly lived on their own or with their married children. Wall (in Laslett 1972, Ch. 5) found a significant increase in household size only in Cheshire and Lancashire in the second half of the eighteenth century, despite the overall national growth in population. A related, but as yet unresolved problem is how to analyse the relative availability of housing to population trends in specific localities.

For further details of these multipliers, and the concepts behind them, see Laslett 1972, especially Ch. 4, Wrigley 1966 and Arkell 1982. In the meantime, it should be remarked that when family historians talk of 'mean household size' they do not mean average family size in the genetic sense of the word. In the same house, there might be two unrelated families, each with seven members and two servants; the average family size would be seven, the average household size would be nine and the 'houseful' size would be eighteen. The 'extended family' of pre-industrial England and Wales was the nuclear family with servants, not only with relatives; each might vary in size from one year to another, and indeed from one part of a year to another. Gregory King's 'family' was the household, if not the houseful, temporal lords having an average family of forty persons. (King's famous 'scheme of the income & expence of the several families of England' can be found in several works, e.g. Laslett 1965, 1983; his figures have come under strong criticism in recent decades.)

The study of mobility through surname distribution is another subject close to the heart of genealogists, and is surely one which family history societies could well undertake as a collaborative venture. The place-name origin of many of them can be taken as a first anchor, and it is clear to those who know the area how few appear in these lists whose geographical origins, some hundreds of years earlier, were more than twenty miles away. An interesting attempt by a genealogist to use a variety of sources for the history of his own surname is that by Roy Prideaux (1986), but we have some doubts as to how far conclusions should be drawn from studying only one surname in this way.

Surnames, however, are one of the features of Hearth Tax returns which should not be studied in isolation, and we move into the third and most important method of looking at any list, listing or census – the linking of data with information gleaned about the same individuals (or record linkage) from other sources. We have looked in detail at only one example here, but it should be assumed that any analysis of such returns can benefit from a similar treatment. It is not always obvious, of course, which other sources can shed light on the individuals in such a list until experiment and experience show the better sources for individual circumstances.

Record linkage can also provide a simple measure of mobility during the two centuries before censuses become available. Once again, Clayworth provides the classic study, which can be followed by many other listings and even lists. Comparison of the

individuals in consecutive Hearth Tax returns will identify outgoers and incomers, though care has to be taken to ensure that the
same name means the same person – the Land Tax returns are
therefore a better source, because they include reference to
individual plots of occupied land identifiable by size, rather than a
simple '1 hearth'. If local burial registers, wills and monumental
inscriptions are then used in order to remove the dead from the
outgoers, you are left with an indication of geographical mobility
– but only among the class of persons concerned in a list – in this
case, taxpayers.

We have concentrated on the Hearth Tax, but this is only one of
many lists of named people which are commonly available at
parish level between the Middle Ages and the nineteenth century.
We should also make passing reference to Views of Frankpledge
(see Champion 1988), Easter Books (Wright 1989), lay subsidies,
muster rolls (see Gibson & Dell 1991), the Protestation of 1642, the
thinly surviving Poll Tax returns from 1641 to 1702 (from which
about a quarter of eligible taxpayers escaped, but on which
Gregory King seems to have largely based his table of the income
and expenditure of various families in 1688), the Compton census
of 1676 for a few places (Whiteman 1986), the Association Oath
rolls of 1696, the much more satisfactory listings under the
Marriage Duty Act, 1695–1705 (see Hindson 1983), the Window
Tax (1695–1852), though the returns are difficult to interpret for
individual houses because of changing definitions of, and rates for
a window; and of course the Land Tax records which are available
on an annual basis, normally from 1780 to 1832. Each source can
be exploited in a slightly different way to give a better picture of a
locality than merely reading the surface appearance, or the names
thereon. See Schurer & Arkell 1991 for considerable information
and research on the Hearth Tax, the Poll Tax, the Compton
census, and the Marriage Duty Acts; Gibson (c) for the location of
several later seventeenth-century tax lists; and Gibson & Mills
1987 for Land Tax records. Peter Park (of the Society of
Genealogists and Cumbria FHS) informs us that several parishes
in west Cumberland provide details of family structure in the
Protestation Returns.

Listings

Once we move from lists into the 'complete' listing as a source, we can be more extensive in the conclusions drawn, and more confident of their validity. It was from such listings that the belief in the extended family as the common basis for household structure in pre-industrial England was challenged and demolished by Laslett (1965).

The earliest known listing giving ages is that of Ealing in 1599 (though a few earlier lists of communicants also include non-communicant children), whose text can be found in an article by Allison (1963). In this case, each member of the household (not just the family) is given, with their relationship to the head of the household, their ages and occupations. (See Laslett 1972, Introduction and Knodel 1979 for ways in which this particular listing can be analysed.) The arrangement is clearly in order of social importance, though how households of equal rank are arranged is unclear. A useful first indicator of the completeness of a listing is to represent the inhabitants in a population pyramid, arranged according to age (see Appendix 2). Convention puts males on the left of the pyramid and the youngest at the bottom. Keys can be built into such a pyramid so that particular features can become immediately apparent – in this case, the few heads of household under the age of twenty-six; the gradual disappearance of the male adult who was not the head of a household by the age of fifty; the increasing frequency of widowhood in householders from the age of thirty. We could have added many other features – for example, whether single mothers with illegitimate children lived 'at home' or on their own; whether widowers lived alone or were taken care of by their younger relations. With this sort of analysis, a great deal can be gleaned about the way people lived in those days, and if you are lucky enough to have ancestors in a parish where such a listing has survived, they can be set into their immediate context of neighbours and social organisation.

One of the main differences between this sort of pyramid and one for our own day is the proportion of inhabitants who are under twenty-one. Before the twentieth century, children normally formed a substantial proportion – at least half – of the population, as they still do in many developing countries; and a sure sign that one of these 'listings' is incomplete would be a failure to include large numbers of children. You should always beware of listings which are published if you do not have access to the original – read the small print to discover whether it purports to be a complete roll of inhabitants, to ensure that all the entries have been included, and that it appears in the same sequence as in the original. For example, Appendix 3 is a listing, believed to have been taken by no less than Gregory King, purporting to be 'A list of all men, women and children in ye parish taken Sept 14 1698' at Ringmore, Devon. A cursory glance at the age structure suggests under-registration, even allowing for the relatively high pro-portion of women well above childbearing age, as there are only eleven, out of a population of 187, under the age of five, while there are nineteen others under ten. The Cardington survey of 1782 omitted some inhabitants, especially servants from outside the parish, and children from the households of farmers and gentry, while including some children who are known to have already left the parish (Baker 1973, p. 5).

Not all such listings offer the same facility, as they vary con-siderably in the amount of detail provided. Ages are found in about 15 per cent of the listings in Law 1969; ages as well as some names are lacking in the 'Hayes census' of 1790 (Silverthorne 1986), and there is the clear suspicion that not all inhabitants have been included. 'Lord Lewisham's House' is listed as such, without residents – perhaps the Rector, who compiled the listing, felt that the family details of the Lord of the Manor should not be, or need not be displayed. Listings can, of course, be analysed in the same way as the lists such as the Hearth Tax, treated above; the same principles apply, but in the case of a listing, there should be far more to analyse, and you should be more confident about a meaningful result.

Clayworth had two listings (taken twelve years apart) and the 'turnover' of individuals was therefore much more significant to measure, as all classes, occupations and ages could be included. Listings are, of course, far fewer in number than lists, but there are nevertheless more of them than we once supposed. Interest in listings has been considerable, following publication of *The world we have lost* in 1965, and pre-1801 listings can be found identified in

Law 1969, particularly for urban areas, and Laslett 1972 (Chs. 4, 5), as well as in a number of issues of *Local Population Studies*, Vols. 20–37. There is as yet no single, comprehensive published list of listings, as new material is being discovered as a result of local history research and Record Office diligence. Some 2,000 will be contained in a forthcoming guide by Gibson and Medlycott. Laslett (1972, pp. 86–9) also provides an analysis of these listings, and conventions have evolved for interpreting their contents: see Wrigley 1966 (Ch. 5), Smith 1969 and Laslett 1972, pp. 86–7. According to Wall (1983), no place is known to have a listing from both the seventeenth and eighteenth centuries, but there are many from the eighteenth which can be compared with the censuses of 1841 or 1851.

It would be a very useful project for any family history or local history society to publish, verbatim, listings for their area; again, everything should be included, in its original sequence. Hopefully, analyses could be provided, as we are now reaching documents which can yield far more detail of family history than 'mere' tax returns. One of the most significant discoveries was that the normal household consisted of the nuclear family (i.e. parents and children, rather than multigenerational or sibling-related, even in old age) occupying a main dwelling. This has implications for the acquisition of enough wealth to set up independent households, and is in contrast with societies in other parts of the world where multigenerational family structures are common. However, it should not blind us to the fact that there are many other factors, including psychological relationships within the family, involved in each individual decision. Perhaps we should ask married readers to list the pressures which caused them to marry when they did, The nuclear family was the norm, but it was not universal, and there were circumstances in which extended families would co-reside. Howlett (1983) found, for example, that prolonged absences of those with seafaring occupations in Appledore, Devon, made those families come together so that 'they could mutually overcome the problems which faced all families and individuals'. The main discussion concerning the structure of families, discovered through such analyses, is by Laslett (in Wrigley 1966a, pp. 189–91, and in Laslett 1972 and 1977, with summaries in 1983, Table 17).

We should distinguish between the meanings of 'household' and 'family', the former being (expressed simply) all those who live in the same building who have an economic relationship with each other, the latter being those who also have a genetic connection with each other. Thus, the household would include servants, boarders (who ate with the family) and lodgers (who did not). The family and household sizes, which must not be confused with each other, can then be related to occupation or social status and, in some cases, even to the size of buildings (see below, p. 110). As indicated in the very first chapter of *The world we have lost*, however, the seventeenth-century 'family' as they used the word *was* the household, the 'co-resident domestic group', though Chambers (1972, p. 37) believed that this largely affected social classes from the gentry upwards. See Laslett 1972, Introduction for a full discussion of these and associated terms. Wall, in the same volume (p. 160), observes that the earliest census of 1801 used the same terminology. Who took in the boarders and lodgers (as opposed to servants), the rich with the space, or the poor with the need? Laslett observes that it was the poorest in the 1850s and 1860s (1983, p. 96) in contrast with a couple of centuries earlier. Anderson's study of Preston showed the same phenomenon.

The size of families, and the size of households can be obtained, and related to the social status of the head of household. Do richer people have more children, as well as more servants ? Are they 'richer' partly because they have fewer children? Bear in mind, however, that the word 'child' can imply either age or a genetic relationship, and you will have to be clear in what sense you are using it. In some analyses, 'child' is also used as meaning 'unmarried resident offspring' because the fact of marriage carries with it connotations which are psychological as well as economic and legal. How many children were at home, and therefore by inference at what ages they left home, sheds light on the ways in which children were treated – see Wall 1983 for an investigation into unmarried children leaving home. Can orphans be identified? If so, where are they located in the community of families?

The proportion of heads of household who had a wife living can also be discovered from such listings (as indeed it can from many Poll Tax returns). In Clayworth, an indication is even given as to whether a remarriage had taken place. In the Ealing example, only 70 per cent of households were headed by a married couple, and 66 per cent at Ringmore (Appendices 2 and 3), compared with some 90 per cent in colonial America, with clear implications for the reproductive rate of the community. Families, and indeed households, would normally be expected to be headed by a man and his wife, and the extent to which this is not true in any community is said to be a measure of its structural instability. Poll Tax returns from the latter half of the seventeenth century often provide the basis for measuring this feature, though persons taxed on wealth rather than paying the flat-rate charge did not normally submit details of their wives (Lawton 1979, p. 16). Clayworth even provided marital status and information about remarriage – this is not found in most listings, but could be added editorially following genealogical investigation.

Another feature of family structure just as pertinent today is the number of generations of the same family which live together. The popular myth of more than two being commonly found in pre-industrial households was explored, and exploded, by Laslett, but the question of what does happen to those who are widowed, and how independent were unmarried siblings, especially sisters, is still of considerable interest – see Wall 1983. Where there was no wife or husband, for whatever reason, there seems to be an increasing likelihood that other relatives will co-reside. Do the widowed guard against a lonely old age by remarrying, by going to live with their married children, or by having their children (or others) come to live with them ? What makes them choose one course of action rather than another ? Do the solutions of widows differ from those of widowers ? What are the consequences for family life of taking one course rather than another ? Anderson (in Wrigley 1972) found that Preston had a far higher than average (16 instead of 6 per cent) number of young couples living with parents during the mid-nineteenth century, but suggests that this relates to the availability of housing rather than any desire for living as an extended family. (He also gives a statistical method of estimating the number of over-65s living alone who had children who could have cared for them (p. 64ff)).

This last question, of course, carries us far from answers which can be gleaned from the listings themselves, and we have by no means exhausted the ways in which they can be used. Some include the ages of the individuals, while once again genealogical research could add this item of information to others. Appendix 2 provides an age 'population pyramid' for Ealing in 1599. However, we have already seen that a normal population pyramid can be made much more revealing by coding in other features about the same individuals. Here, for example, we have added 'head of household' as an element, occupation, marital status, and so on. (Some 10 per cent of the listings in Law 1969 include marital status.) A glance will tell you that it was by about the age of twenty-eight that a majority of men became independent as the head of a family, and that the few women who were able (or who were forced by circumstance) to do so were much older. Look at the number of children in the community, taking us back to Laslett's memorable observation that 'in the pre-industrial world there were children everywhere' (1965, p. 104).

Some listings include occupations, which are interesting not only in themselves, but in the way they can be 'tabled' to vital events, rather like two axes on a graph – occupations and age of marriage, occupations and numbers of offspring, and so on. The fact that occupations are sometimes included in listings of inhabitants means that we can see who were resident servants, and how the number of servants relates to the status of the head of the household. Domestic service was, for both sexes, an important factor in geographical mobility until the twentieth century. The Cardington survey of 1782 (Baker 1973) reveals that boys in particular went away from home in their mid- to late teens. It is not only the number of households having servants which can come as a surprise to the late twentieth-century researcher, Laslett (1977) suggesting that a notional 10 per cent of the whole population at any one time was in service in Stuart England; it is also the number of servants in any one household, though we would be exaggerating to suggest that the Earl of Lonsdale was typical in this respect, having a household consisting of himself and forty-nine servants! About one-third of the families at Ealing had servants, reminding us of Laslett's suggestion (1983 pp. 15–16) that up to a third of households and up to a third of children between puberty and marriage would be involved in service. Lawton (1979, p. 18) found that over a quarter of the population of Cheshire in 1660 over the age of fifteen, were servants, and in a rare display of detail the Protestation return for Hockerton, Nottinghamshire, shows the same figure (Webster 1980, p. 93). There was a higher percentage of servants, and indeed lodgers, in urban areas, especially London, than in rural ones (see Schurer & Arkell 1991). What is difficult but intriguing to ascertain is how far family relationships played a part in locating individual servants in a household. Was a fifteen-year-old second cousin once removed, from an adjoining village, a relative or a servant ? Clearly both in practice, but only the latter in the listings. At Ealing, only four of the servants were also stated to be relatives of the head of household.

When the earliest census of 1801 was generated, therefore, the practice of listing all the inhabitants of a geographical area was by no means unknown, but even for the period 1801–31, the original census returns (surviving in only unofficial draft form and for relatively few areas) must normally be treated as lists, not even listings, except in one respect. When you are considering one of these returns (which is a bit of a misnomer, as they were never 'returned') you may be able to compare a local community with the national picture, as well as with some other areas, because the results were analysed statistically and the national results, with some regional breakdowns, published.

Lodgers significantly increased in number after the Industrial Revolution. Like servants, they tended to be transitory, and therefore relatively 'invisible' in parish registers. Who took them in – the poor with small houses, or the rich with space but no motivation ?

Service was a common reason for leaving home and family, but by no means the only one. Those leaving home unmarried have been studied in listings by Wall (1983), who found that this was one of the main reasons why there are apparently few three-generation families in the seventeenth-century communities. Solitary men and women, either wanderers or residents, have always been a feature of our society, but only the latter normally appear in listings. To live alone is often, though not always, a deliberate act, and rarer without modern state support. Nevertheless, single men appear as head of households, Wrigley and Schofield (1981) estimating that between a quarter and a fifth of adults in the early seventeenth century never married; the proportion varied with the rise or fall in the age of marriage.

Institutions begin to appear in listings much more commonly into the eighteenth century. Those which include details of individual residents are particularly interesting, though many simply list their number, just as the nineteenth-century censuses often anonymised the inmates by supplying only their initials.

Finally, the occasional listing gives an indication of geographical mobility, the best known (indeed perhaps the only one to come to light) being that of Cardington. Schofield 1970c and Baker 1973 contain analyses of the directions from which, and to which, migrants moved. The birthplaces of 357 inhabitants show 161 having been born in, or within five miles of, Cardington, and 95 beyond; (the information was not available for the other 101). This mobility can be assessed in relation to age and to occupation, though it is limited by reliance on the 'snapshot' basis which incorporates only one such move. When children left home, a quarter stayed in the parish, and a further quarter left Bedfordshire altogether. Boys particularly were likely to have left by the age of fifteen. Needless to say, this sort of study is very enlightening to the genealogist who would otherwise be faced with solving mobility problems without any sort of probability guidance. The expert use of the International Genealogical Index (IGI), almost unknown even yet outside genealogical circles, could considerably increase our knowledge of mobility when applied to these listings, as the place of baptism of children before arriving in the parish concerned can often be identified.

Censuses and community reconstitution

It will be clear from the above that when the national census was introduced in 1801, it did not come as something entirely novel; indeed, some of the earlier listings are fuller than any census in the nineteenth century. What set 1801 apart was its compulsory nature, and its universal application in England and Wales. It is therefore doubly annoying that the official returns have not survived from before 1841, and that until then we are reliant on the haphazard survival of some 750 local copies – often the raw data from which the official return was made. Because these were 'unofficial', the content can be rather idiosyncratic (Higgs 1989, p. 25), though we have seen none more so than that now reproduced as Appendix 4. (For an incomplete list of those which are known to have survived, see Gibson (a).)

When the full census returns do finally become available from 1841, the analyses already described are all applicable to them. There is, however, a different dimension, which results from the fact that the available returns are now on a national scale. The sheer volume of information is a problem to handle, but once that is overcome by project design, the extent to which we can study the settings in which our ancestors lived and breathed is enormously extended.

The government required only the numbers chiefly employed in agriculture; in trade, manufacture, handicraft; and in neither of the other two categories (see Higgs 1989, pp. 5–7, 22–6). Appendix 4 is a transcription of the Croston census of 1801, one of the rare survivors of manuscript records compiled to provide the data for the official government returns. It will be seen that it is not even a listing within the definition we are using, naming only householders and those in the workhouse, and it was only in the late nineteenth century that there was a significant advance on the amount of data provided by Cardington or many of the earlier listings. Just as the features of the Croston return will be recognised as forming part of a continuum from earlier listings, so the methods which can be employed to analyse them are broadly similar, with one major difference. Although the official returns were destroyed, summaries based on those returns are easily available in large public libraries because the statistics produced have been published each decade since the 1801 census was taken. Thus, there is a chance that major conclusions which you draw from analysing a census fragment from 1801 to 1831 (and indeed beyond) can be compared with details published for regions and for the whole country immediately afterwards.

The advantages of using the nineteenth-century censuses for

research into the lives of individual ancestors need no introduction, their virtually universal coverage and survival and today's
easy accessibility combining to make them already a familiar
source. The actual location of a particular family has a technique
of its own (see Rogers 1989), but one which plays little or no part
in the present exercise (see, however, Part III). 'Community
reconstitution', considered below, involves the amalgamation of
census information with data from other sources in a way which is
scarcely possible before 1841/1851. This is not to say, of course,
that the census is perfect – Benjamin 1954/5, also discussing
modern censuses, talked of there being too few infants recorded,
people giving themselves maximum responsibility when giving
their occupations, and 'women approaching the middle years of
life' understating their ages. Thomson 1980 was concerned with
the accuracy of the elderly in Puddletown, Dorset, finding as
others have done that 20–33 per cent of women lie about their age
by a factor of more than two years. Genealogists are familiar with
the habit of their ancestors telling white lies, especially those
married couples with a significant age difference between them,
but will be alarmed at the conclusion of Razzell (1972) that up to
half the answers to the 'place of birth' question were incorrect,
with parishes showing wide variations in accuracy. (See also
Tillott's chapter in Wrigley 1972 and Levine 1976. In Part III, we
suggest that the research methods could be improved to give a
more optimistic result.) As with earlier listings (for example, see
Appendix 2), there is a tendency to 'heap' answers to certain
points on the age scale, especially to ages divisible by ten.

One of the most significant contributions made by local
historians has been the analysis of the census data to study individual occupations. In the light of the discussion of servants above,
it is interesting to read Penelope Wilcox (1982), who followed the
fortunes of a number of female servants in Victorian Cambridge,
discovering that they had a relatively high age of marriage whatever their individual social background, and that being in service
was not a means of self-advancement for the women and girls
concerned. See also Hinde 1985 for service in two contrasting
districts of Norfolk. Dennis (1977), Kirkman (1986) and
Wojciechowska (1988) have published studies of the migration of
individuals in consecutive censuses.

There have been many studies of communities using the census, with methods described by Wrigley (1966, Ch. 6), Dyos (1968, Ch. by Armstrong on York); Tillott (1968); Wrigley (1972, Chs. by Drake and Tillott). Gwynne & Sill, for example, followed the trail of people born in Wales who migrated to the industry of Middlesbrough. One of the fullest studies is that by Michael Anderson (1971) of Preston in the mid-nineteenth century, the results of which suggest many ideas for both imitation in other locations, and further exploration. Quadagno (1982, esp. Ch. 3) has much to say on the relationship between household patterns and the local economy. It is a very popular choice of project by local history societies, evening classes, and college students. See the list in Mills & Pearce 1989; examples in the references include Smith 1972, 1979, 1980, Hodson & Smith 1981, Redfern 1983 and Gwynne & Sill 1976. Because of the scale of the exercise, large projects may not be possible without a collaborative effort and the use of a computer, and if you are working without such assistance, we would repeat the advice given by many other writers – choose a relatively homogeneous geographical area which includes not many more than 1,000 inhabitants. If you select such an area, you will quickly find that you come to 'know' all the individuals in 'your patch', and even become concerned about their fate, It is a common experience that any area significantly greater will not only develop an unwelcome anonymity, but also become rather unmanageable by traditional, manual means of sorting data.

However, communities did not group themselves neatly into separate parcels, each containing about 1,000 people, and the arbitrary division of larger units to fit this methodological optimum can cause problems. Studies of two-thirds of a large village or township, or an apparently random selection of streets in a town, tend to produce partial and unsatisfying results. If, however, there are topographical, economic or social boundaries which make the selection area viable, then the findings can be presented as fully descriptive. A town will be far too large to tackle, and even its constituent wards will normally have far too many people to handle. Similarly, in rural areas both parish and township may be beyond the individual researcher, particularly in the north of England where the average size of parishes is larger. In both cases, it is necessary not to select an area only by numbers but to relate the area chosen to the questions that will be asked.

If you are working alone on a small geographical area, the advantages of employing a personal computer with the appropriate software are very considerable. (For computerised projects in general, see Edgington 1985.) In processing the data from the census on to the machine, you still enjoy the benefits of a personal knowledge of the area concerned, but you then have at your disposal the means to analyse that data to an extent and at a speed which is not possible manually. Note, however, that the software concerned is not necessarily that with which a genealogist is familiar. Many programs are designed to record and recall family-tree data in a way that brings to the screen material as it is entered in the first place – it is, in short, a convenient way of storing information. What is required now, on the other hand, is the facility to sort the data into new forms which can then, in turn, be used to ask further questions about our ancestors in that area. Computers have been used by historians for this sort of analysis for many years – see chapters by Dyos and Baker in Dyos 1968, a series of articles in *Local Historian* by Beckett and Foulds (1985), and Kirkman 1983, Jackson 1985 and Schurer 1985.

We have found that the best way to record large amounts of information within computer memories that may be limited, compared with the demand you are to make on them, is to convert the data into codes, usually numbers. All columns in the census can be done in this way by giving to each a series of numbers from 0 upwards. Thus, each surname could be given a unique number, though that same number, when applied to the Christian-name column or the occupation column, will represent something quite different for each column. Obviously, you will need to keep a code key handy, preferably manually as well as on the computer itself, and group projects need to maintain the same codes for each part of the exercise – it is no good one researcher allocating a code of '12' for a weaver, and another giving '6' for the same occupation, for that would prevent the ultimate bringing together of a number of different areas for summation or comparison.

The most difficult column to transpose in this way is the one which seems to lend itself most easily – that of age. If only the year could be decimalised! So many of the entries give age to the nearest month – some to the nearest week or even day in the case of very young children – that a means of expressing this quantification is as difficult as it is desirable. You must not, of course, follow the genealogical convention of putting the month as though it were a decimal – for example, '12.6' for twelve years and six months old. When you are to add and average ages of individuals in different categories, any computer will read '12.6' as twelve years and seven months; weeks and days are even more difficult to embrace in a proper system. However, it should also be borne in mind that all ages (not just those in the 1841 census) are rounded down, and a child of '5' might actually be on the eve of a sixth birthday. To be more accurate with large numbers of entries, for the purposes of averaging, six months should be added to whole year ages given in the census.

Arranging place of birth into a three-digit system is not without its difficulties. On the whole, we prefer to codify counties (subcoding places within) rather than calculating distances. The latter idea is not only more time-consuming – it does not provide any directional information which might be required. For a study of migration patterns, see Turner 1983.

For a community reconstitution project, do not limit yourself to the same number of columns as that provided by the census, because the essence of the exercise is record linkage of material from the census with that from other sources in a way which illuminates both, and at the same time creates new insights into our nineteenth-century ancestors.

Originally called 'house repopulation', community reconstitution was demonstrated in the early 1970s by Adrian Henstock, now County Archivist at Nottingham (Henstock 1971, 1973 a, b, 1978), based on work done with an adult evening class in, and concerning Ashbourne in Derbyshire with a population of some 3,500. He showed the great advantages for such a study in collating the data from a census not only with other written sources, as we describe below, but also with maps, so that the spatial distribution and wealth distribution of people in the census can be made apparent. Although estate or enclosure maps can be used for this purpose, a good quality tithe map (i.e. one carrying the Commissioners' seal) is the best, for it is not only likely to be relatively coincidental in time with a mid-nineteenth-century census, but also accurate and complete, giving occupiers as well as owners. For other published examples, see Langdon 1976, Yates 1982 and Mills 1976, 1978 a, b. Kain and Prince (1985) provide a scholarly account of the background to the tithe maps, as well as a chapter on their use in community reconstitution.

Once the geographers get their finger in the pie, because of their interest in the spatial distribution of population over time, historians are usually put to shame in terms of presentation, which produced some entertaining reading in the *Local Historian* some time ago. There is no doubt that cartographic skills can not only enhance the presentation of a research project; they can help to illuminate what would otherwise go unnoticed (see Royle & Pringle 1986).

Earlier, we stressed the advantages of record linkage in order to add significantly to what can be gleaned from any one source on its own. Attempts to collate data from other sources with that from the census can be seen in Williams 1973, using police charge books in Prescot which give, *inter alia*, names, ages, dates and places of birth, address, offence, whether in employment, weekly wages, number of children and (presumably in case of escape or re-offending) physical characteristics. Through community reconstitution, the offenders can be set into their domestic background. Jones (1988) combines census and estate record data. Horn (1982) used the reports of the Parliamentary Commissioners into child employment in her study of eight villages in six counties. Henstock himself (1973a) used local newspapers to discover the location of those with the most influence in the local community. Levine (1977, Ch. 5) compared two Leicestershire villages to study the relationship between family and household structure and the local economy. John Redfern isolated heads of household in Edgbaston whose residences had a rateable value of £20 or more to study the age, sex, and household composition of Victorian suburbia. Mills (1978a) effectively revives the question of the extended family by showing close relatives, especially parents and married daughters, living near each other in Melbourn, Cambridgeshire, though not in the same household. This is a very common experience among genealogists, and we will return to this theme in Part III.

As an illustration of the techniques described above, we returned to Tintwistle in order to illustrate what can be done to extend a census into a community reconstitution, and some of the disadvantages of choosing a project out of interest in the area, rather than knowledge that as full a range of source materials as possible is available. Each household in the 1851 census was first transcribed manually on to cards so that a convenient system of reference was available – each card was given two numbers, one according to the number of the household in the census schedule, and another which located the head of the household in alphabetical order of surname – the cards could then be easily rearranged in either order. There is a well-known danger to avoid – incorrectly transcribing households which cross over to the next page. Notice the household numbers which should be included in the census itself. We could, of course, have made a card for each person, which would have had the advantage of being able to locate lodgers and visitors with specific surnames more quickly, but as this can be done on the computer, it was not felt to be worth the extra trouble. Every element in each census column was given a code number, and half a dozen columns were left blank so that data from other sources could be added later. The 1847 tithe schedule was then transcribed, and the occupiers identified on the map via the schedule numbers.

This immediately gave three results which were not possible without such a record linkage. The first was the identification of the exact route taken by the census enumerator in a rural area where, as one would expect, no addresses in our sense of the word were given, and the description at the start of each enumeration district was rather vague. As a result of this information, we were able to pinpoint the dwellings of many inhabitants who were not listed as occupiers in the tithe schedule, but whose dwellings were now located between those of people who were occupiers. From that information, we were able to return to the tithe schedule, and identify the landlords of all but a few inhabitants, living in houses built between 1847 and 1851.

Those houses which existed in 1847 were then identified on the ground and photographed for future reference. In order to confirm that these were indeed the houses concerned, and not later buildings on the same site, householders were asked for information from their deeds. This request produced a wide spectrum of reaction, from those whose answer could not be printed without making even our publisher blush, through those whose early deeds were lost, to those whose solicitor would make a charge for access, and finally to the interested neighbours who obtained all the data we required. Many were very interested in the project, and in the history of their own houses, some of which had been altered over the centuries in a most curious fashion. Fortunately, many houses in this area were built in terraced rows, and normally you have to find the age of only one in order to know that of the remainder; however, part of the terrace may not have been built at the same time, and you have to take a careful look at the brick or stonework in order to assess the sequence of events – often, a 'join' is hidden behind a downspout, but a break in the mortar line is usually a good guide. (On the dating of houses, see Cunnington 1988.)

It might be thought that a useful source of information about the age of individual dwellings would be local estate agencies. Here, there is bad news and good news. Firstly, they do not cover all the houses for sale, for many are advertised privately. Secondly, once a house is clearly older than the First World War, estate agents tend to lose interest in the date unless it can be clearly labelled as simply 'Georgian' or 'seventeenth-century'. (Indeed, we found that we were eventually able to provide estate agents with data about the houses which neither they nor the owners knew.) Thirdly, the number of agents dealing with only a small place such as ours is surprisingly large, and they do not always display a sign on a property for sale.

What estate agents are very good at, however, as well as seeing all property through rose-coloured spectacles, is in providing an accurate physical description, with measurements, of the inside of the houses. Once you have eliminated those parts which have clearly been built on since, you then have an excellent basis for assessing the relationship between the number and status of the Victorian residents of individual houses, and the area they had to occupy. About 10 per cent of houses, on average, change hands every year in this country, and it is very easy for a long-term project to build up a useful body of information in this way. The figure is much higher in an inner-city area.

We also looked at the religious affiliation of the inhabitants of 1851, which Anderson (1971, p. 103) believed to have had little influence on binding together primary social grouping among the mass of the working class, at least in towns. A rough guide as to numbers involved can be obtained through the 1851 religious census, though this gives only the numbers who attended all churches on a specific date, and who normally attended, in that year. In Tintwistle, there were three places of worship, Anglican (from 1837), Wesleyan (from 1830) and the oldest, an Independent chapel having its origin in the seventeenth century, and to which many inhabitants had gone before the newer denominational buildings had been erected. We assumed that a family (as opposed to a household) worshipped together, so we keyed in religious affiliation according to the head of the family; we were interested in knowing how far religious belief played a part in deciding who to admit as a servant or lodger, and in the motives of those who, over the years, apparently changed from one church or chapel to another. Each place of worship was given a code number on the computer, as were the three possible changes of affiliation; no number meant that the name did not occur in any of the registers or lists of church members concerned.

Political affiliation is where the choice of Tintwistle as a subject let us down, and had we been mainly interested in this aspect, we would have had to choose another location to study. Gibson & Rogers (1990 a, b) provide details of which electoral registers and poll books have survived. The first show who, from 1832, had the right to vote, and a good deal about the property qualification which gave them the franchise – including who occupied the property of absentee owners. However, no poll book showing how people voted before the Ballot Act of 1872 has survived for the constituency of north Cheshire after the election of 1841, and that one is in manuscript form, and therefore less accessible. With determination, however, it will be possible to identify some of the voters who were still there ten years later.

Other sources, easily available in other areas, have not survived for this. There are no rate books, and we have been unable to find references to wages except on a regional or national scale. We could, however, have added genealogical data from parish and non-parochial registers, linking individuals genetically and by marriage, which would have added enormously to the benefits of the exercise.

The computer can now begin to answer questions which are possible to answer manually only by expending an enormous amount of time by linking the data in different columns. Take again just one 'popular' area, illegitimacy, as an example. What were the ages and social status of the mothers of illegitimate babies ? Did they come from two-parent or one-parent homes, or were they already living alone? Was there a relationship between illegitimacy and religious belief ? Was it the product of living in relatively overcrowded conditions ? Who took in the new mother – relatives or a landlord ? Were illegitimate children more likely to be in one part of the parish rather than spread evenly? Were the mothers relatively immobile despite the social shame among their close relatives? On the other hand, the computer throws up information which creates further questions. For example, why did a large proportion of mothers of illegitimate children take them to be baptised by a denomination not normally their own ? Once the English census of 1891 becomes available, we will be able to add others. Where did the self-employed and the employers live? People with which occupations were forced to live in fewer than five rooms?

When this collated information is added to maps described earlier, an extraordinarily detailed picture emerges, as if we were able to look down through the mists which often cloud this part of the Pennines and almost see our ancestors trudging to work, looking after an enormous brood, or escaping into one of the twelve pubs available for the 1,200 inhabitants. 'Community reconstitution' is very aptly named.

Aggregative analysis

We have seen how lists, listings and censuses of inhabitants can be extensively analysed so that what is an apparently bald list of names and associated data can be converted into an understanding about social relationships. With the technique of the grand-sounding 'aggregative analysis', we can begin to make that picture move more continuously, and over a length of time not really feasible by merely adding together 'snapshots' taken perhaps ten years apart. In so doing, we can observe changes, including some of which our ancestors were possibly unaware, and which do not show up at all through the documents studied above so far.

Aggregative analysis involves the identification of social change by adding together a series of apparently unconnected events, and it is because these events are spread over time that the result is a moving, if rather two-dimensional, picture. Our ancestors, whether they knew it or not, form part of that picture – indeed, some of the major events in their lives provide the mechanism which causes the picture to change.

Borrowing ideas from France, but developing and adapting them to suit the records of this country, E. A. Wrigley and colleagues set out in the 1960s what remains the best account of how to study demographic history at a local level using this technique (see Wrigley 1966a, Ch. 3). It involves sorting and counting the vital events (baptisms, marriages and burials) in a normal Anglican parish register into categories which vary according to the main purposes of the study. These may be, for example, 'all baptisms between 1700 and 1750', or 'all marriages involving one party from outside the parish during the seventeenth century'; or 'all burials of children, 1780–1810'. Forms suitable for recording the data are reproduced in Drake 1982, pp. xxxi–xxxiii and Wrigley 1966a, pp. 67–70, 113–15, but they are easily enough devised to suit the researcher's own purposes.

As with all projects of this kind, the researcher must be quite clear as to why the parish has been selected. Basically, there are three main reasons behind such a selection, and it is only in the happiest of circumstances that all three will be fully satisfied. You may be mainly interested in the population of a specific geographical area (whether it be a parish, county or region) and therefore reliant on the quantity and quality of the documents which happen to have survived for that area. This is a popular basis for research, and the main reason why there is such a potential overlap between family and local history. If, however, your concern is for a subject (perhaps measles or marriage during the Industrial Revolution) you would not be confined to one area. Thirdly, you could be attracted by a register which is particularly suited to this form of analysis, the vehicle itself justifying the ride.

Whatever the motivation, there are some useful guidelines for choosing suitable registers which we attempt to summarise below, with acknowledgments to the following, much fuller, accounts – Wrigley 1966a, Ch. 3; Schofield 1970b; Drake 1974, Unit 6, 1982; Wrigley & Schofield 1981, Ch. 1, 2; Willigan & Lynch 1982, Ch. 3; Rogers 1977, Ch. 5. Drake suggests a useful test algorithm to apply to parish registers in order to eliminate those which are unsuitable. The ten main questions are:

1. How complete does the parish register appear to be? Bearing in mind that no register is complete in our modern sense, it is a useful preliminary exercise to make a simple count of the annual and even monthly number of baptisms, marriages and burials in the register during the period which you have selected for study, and to represent those numbers in the form of histograms (see Appendix 5). If desired, violent annual fluctuations can be ironed out by the use of five- or nine-year moving averages – see Schofield 1970b. Several features will immediately become visually apparent in a way difficult to spot from the text itself. Whole years may be missing; there will be fluctuations, especially in the number of burials; small parishes will show greater proportional fluctuations than larger ones; major fluctuations in burials may be an indication of epidemics; a distinct drop in the number of baptisms might indicate the opening of another church, not necessarily Anglican, nearby, an interregnum between incumbents, or a very inefficient incumbent. We should perhaps add that this is a very salutary exercise to undertake for parishes in which you are expecting in vain to find records of ancestors. It is very difficult, without recourse to an index, to notice how many children were baptised twice (pace Wrigley

1973, pp. 76–7, who seems to suggest that this could not happen) and it is evident that burial before baptism was sometimes not entered at all. Drake (1962) estimated that 11 per cent in the Yorkshire parish of Rothwell, 1634–48, were in this category. See also Finlay (1980), who believes that clerks may have used the word 'abort' to indicate any pre-baptismal death. Eversley's rule of thumb (Wrigley 1966a, p. 55) is to take an assumed total population (based on the 1801 census figure, halved for a century earlier) and to proceed only if the total baptisms and burials exceed 50 per 1,000 people probably alive at that time. (Bear in mind that the increase in population was much more rapid towards the end of the eighteenth century.)

More subtly, there may be particular groups of individuals who are underrepresented in the registers. Finlay (1980), for example, found what genealogists have long suspected – the under-registration of families who lived at a considerable distance from the parish church (in this case Hawkshead, Ulverston and Cartmel in the Lake District), though nevertheless within the parish. Wrigley (1977b) discusses some of the reasons for this under-registration; Razzell's study (1972) of forty-five parishes found an average omission rate of about one-third between 1760 and 1834, but with wide variations between parishes. Yasumoto (1985), on the other hand, found 947 out of 1,078 expected baptisms at Methley, Yorkshire, in the same period. (However, see Part III for a more optimistic prospect for these results.) Servants and lodgers are almost 'invisible' in parish registers – for example, only 3 of the 101 servants at Cogenhoe (1618–28) appear. Calculating the male/female ratio among the burials is a useful device for identifying whether there are significant numbers of mobile unmarried people in the area. On underregistration generally, see Wrigley (1977b), who estimates that some 5 per cent of births went unrecorded because of death before baptism. This was especially true in parishes which had a large geographical area. Finlay (1980) has some interesting observations on a method of assessing the amount of neonatal underregistration. (See also Schofield 1970a, also on Hawkshead, and Levine 1976.) Levine concluded that individual children within large families were not baptised, but that this omission was haphazard, conforming to no recognisable pattern. Once again genealogists, take note!

Wrigley and Schofield (1981) give a national assessment of underregistration of baptisms, marriages and burials since the sixteenth century, but of course that can be only a rough guide to the particular parishes which might be catching your eye.

2. Has the register been collated with extant Bishop's Transcripts? For their location, see Gibson (b). There are many years in which such a collation would make little or no difference to the text of the register; there are others, however, in which the BT can be much fuller than the register, providing not only additional entries, but also more information on some. Anyone tackling a project involving an Anglican parish register must, as all genealogists already know, incorporate this extra data when preparing a transcription, or must ensure that any published version has already done so – the introduction to the volume should tell you.

3. Using a published version has many other advantages, and it is always worth asking if such a thing exists. The main reason will become more apparent in our discussion of family reconstitution, but it makes counting easier, and it should ensure that entries which are out of proper chronological order in the register are either highlighted, or, better still, have been transferred to the right place with an appropriate editorial note. With BT collation built in, such a register is in by far the most convenient form for aggregative analysis,

4. provided, that is, the quality of the transcript is good, and that question is one of the most difficult to answer without recourse to the original register. Not all published versions are completely faithful to the original, as they depend so much on the ability of the transcriber to decipher old handwriting, to indicate how many entries are no longer legible, to compile a completely accurate index, to check the printer's proofs against the original to eliminate errors, and so on.

5. Does the parish concerned bear significantly on what you wish to study ? If, for example, your main interest is in the relationship between population and the growth of a local industry, the boundary of the parish might not coincide with the economic boundary which would need to be considered; it would not necessarily cover all the population immediately involved. Remember that you are studying a geographical area

which is normally quite arbitrarily drawn compared with the population changes which occurred over the possibly hundreds of years since its designation; equally, an urban parish created in the early nineteenth century, in addition to all the other problems described below, will probably be drawn within artificially designated street boundaries.

6. Is there an Anglican chapelry or non-parochial (i.e. non-Anglican) church or chapel in the parish ? If so, it must be drawing worshippers away from the parish church, and distorting the figures from which you are about to attempt to draw conclusions. There are two further associated words of warning. Do not judge whether such a church or chapel existed from lists of registers, for the fact that such a register does not exist does not mean that the institution did not exist. Often, the Bishop's Transcripts (and even the registers) of large parishes contain entries from chapelries within its overall boundaries. There are many other sources, such as directories, Anglican visitation articles of enquiry, local history books, the local archive office, for example, which will give you a more accurate answer. Secondly, do not attempt to get round the problem by transcribing the local non-parochial register and merely adding the two sets of figures together. Nonconformist chapels did not normally have catchment areas within fixed geographical boundaries, and even those which did would not normally coincide with the Anglican parish (with the possible exception of Methodists). The non-parochial registers therefore contain entries relating to individuals who lived outside the parish, and who would invalidate any conclusions drawn about the parish as such. Equally, though not in equal numbers, people from 'your' parish might have gone beyond its border to worship in, for example, the Presbyterian, Quaker or Roman Catholic faiths. Unless you are prepared to examine each in turn, extracting only the residents of your parish (even provided such data is given in the register), then it may be that you have chosen the wrong parish to analyse. It is for this reason that so many studies using aggregative analysis are for periods before the Industrial Revolution, which saw a significant growth in nonconformity. Eversley suggests (Wrigley 1966a, p. 51) that it is probably safe to go ahead if Nonconformists appear to provide less 10 ten per cent of all events in the area.

7. Does the register show evidence of local customs which would render conclusions invalid ? Have a look at the marriage patterns in Billinge, near Wigan, in Appendix 5. Something very strange is going on here, which could not be accounted for by the temporary closure of a nearby church, for example; it is clear that, for whatever reason, Billinge was the place to marry between 1779 and 1803 in the Wigan area.

8. While burial is normally within days of death, the same cannot be said for baptism, which can take place when the child is minutes or years old or not at all. It is most unwise, therefore, to base uncritical conclusions about births from registers of baptisms. There have been several studies of this problem – see, for example, Finlay 1980, Drake 1971, Ch. 6, Berry & Schofield 1971, Wrigley 1977b.

9. If you are basing your figures on an annual count, you need to decide when the year begins. Remember the change of date for New Year's Day in 1752, and that before then the year in the register did not comprise the same twelve months as afterwards. (Wrigley 1966a, recommends basing all figures on New Style, using 1 January as the date of the new year even before 1752.) Additionally, there are some studies which are based on the agricultural (or 'harvest') year. You should choose between 1 January, 25 March or 1 August according to the individual needs of your project, be internally consistent, and ensure that, if you are comparing your findings with those of someone else, you are comparing like with like. All other things being equal, 1 January is recommended.

10. Is the parish so small as to render conclusions invalid ? Well, what is small? Different writers offer different advice – for example, Drake (1982, p viii) suggests that a parish having fewer than 100 entries per annum should not be used. Schofield (1972a) advises that no conclusions should be drawn from parishes with a population less than 1,000 (inferring about 30–40 baptisms per annum); Eversley (in Wrigley 1966a, p. 57) advises against using a parish which has less than an average of 15–20 events per annum, There is no simple formula; only that the smaller the parish, the less likely it is that conclusions drawn from it would apply to other parishes nearby. If the locality is of central importance to you, therefore, you should consider the possibility of adding

together figures from a number of small, adjoining parishes in order to reduce the danger of being distorted by a single maverick register.

By now, you will have realised that aggregative analysis is quite impossible, because you will not find a register which fits all the requirements implicit in the above list of questions. Don't worry – that is everyone's reaction at first. Indeed, Chambers (1972, pp. 59–61) seems to suggest that using a single parish is never advisable, though some of his reasons equally apply when several parishes are aggregated for analysis. At the opposite extreme is the view that, providing you are keeping the results to yourself, none of the above matters – it is the interest of doing the exercise which controls the end product, and so what if 'your' parish had only ten baptisms a year – that is the only parish you wish to study.

Between these two extremes, an application of a modicum of common sense enables some considerable progress to be made in the public domain, for unless others can see your results and benefit from them, we are wasting a valuable opportunity to contribute to the sum of human knowledge. The important things are to bear in mind the major problems incurred if the strictures above are disregarded, and to make sure that whatever conclusions you reach are qualified by statements relating to interpretations in the light of the quality of the raw material – in other words, do not deceive yourself, for you may be sure that you will not deceive others. Sometimes, it is just as useful to provide the reasons why your findings may not be entirely credible as it is to provide the findings themselves.

See Eversley (in Wrigley 1966a, pp. 87–8) for a preliminary summary of results which can be obtained from aggregative analysis, (though in the intervening years, many discoveries have been added to them).

Marriage

Marriage is the point at which the great majority of families start, and the simplest analyses of marriage registers can throw a great deal of light on to the history of the family at both national and local levels. As was clear in Part I, researchers have noted the strong relationship between marriage and socioeconomic circumstances at the time. Occasionally, even our epidemiological history has an influence on age and rates of marriage. Defects in first the Anglican baptismal, later the burial registers, especially following the Industrial Revolution, do not apply to the registers of marriage, because of Hardwicke's Marriage Act of 1753, in force effectively until 1837. By this Act, only weddings in the Anglican, Quaker or Jewish faiths were recognised as legally valid, so nonconformists, even if they went through a form of marriage outside, also repaired to the parish church in order to legitimise the union in the eyes of the state.

For national estimates of marriage numbers and rates (as of so many other events which are the subject of this book) see Wrigley & Schofield 1981, where the best available assessment, based on their study of the registers of 404 parishes, is given with which to compare any local results of research, though do not be surprised if individual parishes show marked variations from the norms. It is also excellent for discussing the methods used in such projects. For local rates, population totals should be known, so unless the results are for 1801 or since, only crude rates can be arrived at, from (e.g.) estimates based on the Hearth Tax. The least suspect of the pre-1754 marriage registers would seem to be those during the period of the Marriage Duty Acts of 1695–1706 which tried to tax even common-law marriages, (Schurer & Arkell 1991.)

Beyond the mere counting of events are several aspects of marriage which can be studied to varying degrees according to the amount of information yielded by the register concerned. Only a defective register, for example, would not provide the date of the marriage, which means that the question of seasonality and its significance can be raised. Leslie Bradley's articles in *Local Population Studies* (reprinted in Drake 1982) examined seasonality in detail, finding the 'prohibited' period from February to Easter easily demonstrable until the early nineteenth century, though the others had fallen into disuse earlier. Summer months were also unpopular for timing weddings; see also Wrigley & Schofield 1981, Ch. 8, Edwards 1977, 1987 and Hunter 1985, relating seasonality to occupation. Duration of individual marriages cannot be gleaned through aggregative analysis, though access to the hundreds of pedigree charts lying otherwise idle in Family

History Society vaults might be very revealing on this subject. Remarriage of widow or (post-1754) widower, however, can be picked up fairly easily from parish registers or marriage allegations which often provide marital status; when they are compared with the complete marriage register, they can show over long periods of time the different proportions of men and women in this category. How far, for example, was marriage used as a defence against being left a widowed parent, or as a defence against old age, and how did such strategies differ for men and women?

Few registers provide age at marriage, however, before 1837, so if you wish to study this aspect you must either find a register which does, at least for the dates you require, or you get the information by family reconstitution (see below). Another useful source of age at marriage is the allegation given by those applying to be married by licence instead of by banns, but this has the significant methodological defect of not being a representative sample of the population.

Marriages arranged by licence were more expensive than banns, though W. E. Tate (1951, p. 64) believed that all 'save the humblest' had recourse to them. The incidence of marriage by licence was also markedly different between parishes, perhaps in relation to the physical difficulty of obtaining one. In the remote parish of Urswick in Furness, the proportion increased from one-third to two-thirds as soon as the incumbent, Henry Holme, was allowed to issue licences (as well as marry the couples concerned) in 1722. Chambers (1972, p. 43) quotes the much more extreme example at Fledborough in Nottinghamshire where in 1730 the incumbent increased the number of couples he married from less than one a year to over twenty by virtue of being able to grant licences.

Outhwaite (1973) uses this source, finding that about 15 per cent of all marriages were by licence, that the practice was popular in the North, North Midlands, Wales and Monmouthshire, especially when the bride and groom were of disparate ages, or when parties were 'cursed with unfortunate names'. We also believe that a licence was more common than usual when the parties were from two different parishes – perhaps the cost was less than having to pay for a double set of banns. Drake (1962) provides some interesting figures for age at marriage in the West

Riding of Yorkshire in the late seventeenth and early eighteenth centuries, again using marriage allegations. For their location, see Gibson (b).

Few researchers seem to have used banns as their principal source of information, though they are recorded regularly from 1754 onwards. Banns are therefore, as it were, virgin territory, and we believe worth exploring not only for marriage across parishes, but also for the smoothness (or otherwise) of the psychological processes leading up to the wedding itself. Reference to Appendix 5 indicates something quite extraordinary going on in Billinge where, it seems, the clergyman still faithfully recorded the banns of marriages which did not take place either in his church or perhaps even anywhere else. Unfortunately, not all clergymen were prepared to waste valuable space in the register in this way, recording only those banns of marriages which were to be performed in their own church.

An excursion into mobility

A 'marriage horizon' is the geographical distance between the homes of the bride and groom as stated at the wedding, and has been the subject of a number of research projects. Finlay (1980) was able to identify townships; Coleman (1984) and Küchemann (in Drake 1971) were interested in the genetic implications of different horizons, and in the spread of disease; Maltby (1971) and Eversley (in Wrigley 1966a) and Küchemann examine the effects of physical obstacles (rivers and hills, for example) on the likelihood of marriage. Spufford (1973–74) noted that migration seems to have been easier by water than by land, and Stanier (1987) suggests that 'communal solidarity', especially among immigrant communities, was a less physical, though no less real, obstacle to freedom of marriage partner. Coleman worked out what most genealogists had suspected for a long time – that the graph of marriage horizons is like the gamma decay of radioactive elements, the frequency falling very rapidly with distance, but with a long, thin tail.

This generalisation hides local and regional skews, with the gravitational attraction of large urban centres, especially London, being felt at great distances. In the seventeenth century, London is estimated to have received about one in every six adults in England, in-migration being believed to be the mechanism for population growth when burials far exceeded baptisms (see Spufford 1973–74, Part II and Wrigley & Schofield 1981). Migration to London was also over much greater distances than the normal 10–20 miles, and amounted to a net gain for the capital of some 8,000 a year in the seventeenth century. Possibly a third of London's population were servants, apprentices and lodgers, all highly mobile groups (for London's earlier demographic patterns, see Finlay 1981).

Not enough studies have been made of provincial towns in order to see whether they exhibit similar, though of course much smaller, features. Dyer (1973) explains a system of relating parish register data with other sources of information about the size of Worcester in order to arrive at an estimate of in-migration which would account for half of the city's doubling in size between 1540 and 1640. Levine (1987) suggests that urban centres (most of which consisted of only a few thousand people before the Industrial Revolution, incidentally), were responsible for absorbing large numbers of 'excess women' from the countryside. Spufford (1973–74, Part II) assembles evidence that mobility into provincial towns was little different from that within the countryside; a commoner pattern was movement *between* towns by labourers who had already lost their roots. Anderson (1971, p. 38) found the same phenomenon in nineteenth-century Preston. All this evidence, however, begs the question of how and when those landless labourers had appeared in the smaller towns in the first place.

Since 1985, there has been a project on the history of small towns from 1600 to 1850 based at the Centre for Urban History at the University of Leicester which may discover the answer – family history societies should consider contributing to this project (see Clark *et al.* 1989, who provide estimates for 644 towns and 218 other communities).

While such features are relatively easy to discover using aggregative analysis, you should try to bear in mind that what is being measured in the first place is what people said at the time of marriage. Not everyone has had the incentive to tell the truth, however, and genealogical experience often shows ancestors paying for one set of banns when two would have been more appropriate to their circumstances, especially in urban areas where the clergyman was unlikely to know all his parishioners. Furthermore, the clergy were not equally assiduous in recording the parish of both parties, especially before 1754, and after 1780 a suspiciously high number of couples in some areas said they were both 'of this parish', which can skew any conclusions about mobility based on this source. On the other hand, the substantial numbers of youngsters going out of their own parish to become servants, and marrying from their adopted parish, disguise much mobility if the marriage entries alone are taken as sources of information; but the marriage allegations of 1823 had to be accompanied by a baptismal certificate, and these could form a much more useful basis for estimating mobility.

Pain and Smith (1984) and Millard (1982) identify considerable problems in accepting marriage horizons as a basis for measuring mobility. Unless due recognition is paid to the geographical (and indeed the population) size of a parish, large towns will paradoxically appear to be the most isolated, simply because people had plenty of marriage partners to choose from. Pain and Smith's research into Stanhope, Co. Durham, forced them to conclude 'that the direct interpretation of marriage horizons as migration is simply no longer credible'.

Fortunately, there are many other sources which can provide data on pre-census mobility. Settlement certificates and examinations are too well known to require any introduction. Constables' accounts, which include the distribution of alms to (or the punishment of) vagrants, gypsies, soldiers, foreigners, and poor travellers) were used by J. R. Kent (1981) in her study of immigrant Irish and Scots in the Midlands during the early seventeenth century; settlement certificates, explained alongside other sources for studying migration by Drake (1974, Unit 8) were used by Parton (1987) for a study of migration into and out of Birmingham (see also Laslett 1983). For an earlier period, depositions of witnesses are available in some parts of the country – see Cornwall 1967 and Dils 1987. They formed the basis of studies by Hanley (1975), Siraut (1981) and Souden (in Clark 1984) into urban migration in the sixteenth century, one estimate being as high as 7 per cent of the population having made such depositions. A surprisingly high proportion, up to one-fifth, had moved over forty miles during their lifetime, mobility being especially high among tradesmen.

A useful 'marker' attached to the mobile individual or family is the surname and Souden and Lasker (1978) illustrate a method of calculating mobility through surname distribution. Over a long period, much can be discerned about the movement of people generally once the origin of the surname is known – see, for example, articles by Buckatsczh (1951), Escott (1988), and Prideaux (1986), the last of whom is a genealogist who has tried to apply some of the family history techniques in this book to all known instances of his own surname. It is an interesting example of the possible interfaces between genealogy and demography, though extrapolations from national figures to one surname are probably too extreme.

We advise that the estimating of mobility by surname distributions is not straightforward, and should really be attempted only with rare surnames, or those which have single points of origin. With rarer names, the IGI can be of significant advantage, though only infrequently (e.g. Willan 1983) does it appear to have been used by non-genealogists. Grace Wyatt (1989) has used this source in association with marriage horizons and a family reconstitution exercise.

In the north of England, following an order by Archbishop Markham in 1778, there are a number of parish registers which can significantly increase our knowledge of mobility, because they include grandparents, as well as parents, at the time of baptism, and parents (even of adults) at burial. There are a few such registers found before 1778. See Sheils (1979) and Long and Maltby (1980) who analysed intergenerational occupational mobility and change (not surprisingly finding that farming was the most 'hereditary' occupation); they also suggested that changes in social status, intermarriage within occupations and occupational change in relation to distance travelled could be investigated. (In contrast to Spufford's suggestion, they found that Skipton was more attractive than more rural areas, but do not give figures for how many of the migrants came from other towns.) Wrigley (1977a) analysed the Colyton register from 1765 to 1777 when this information is given for the bride's parents' at marriage. Once again, however, we would urge caution, because a grandparent's place of residence at the time of baptism does not mean place of birth; full exploitation would be safer by family reconstitution (see below, p. 132).

Levine (1977, Ch. 4) analysed mobility into and out of two places in Leicestershire (Shepshed and Bottesford), concluding that mobility was particularly high in the smaller villages and was differentially affected by employment prospects in places with widely different economic backgrounds, including the willingness (or otherwise) of the Lord of the Manor to encourage industrial development. Laslett (1977) offers a rough analysis of the causes of mobility, suggesting that two-thirds was in consequence of birth and death, about 7 per cent the result of marriage, 20 per cent was migration for the purpose of seeking work (especially servants, only half of whom stayed longer than one year in the same household), and the remainder random. His studies of Clayworth and Cogenhoe suggest that at least a third of the population changed parish every ten years before the industrial revolution, a rate which has probably doubled since. Chambers (1957) concluded that half the population did not die in their parish of birth, and that the two main causes were service, in which occupation mobility was often annual, and apprenticeship. Often, it was the landless who never returned, though Wrightson and Levine (1979, p. 81) report that it was the highest of their four social classes in Terling which was the most mobile. Hey (1987, pp. 76–82) summarises the differences between 'betterment' mobility, in search of improved wages, and 'subsistence' mobility, trying to avoid the worst effects of local demographic crises. By the nineteenth century, service as a cause had been replaced by factory work in the industrial areas, but the age of leaving home remained about the same.

Birth and baptism

Until 1837, we are dependent upon baptismal records for a knowledge of family groups, family sizes across different times and places, and birth rates; although other sources, such as wills or listings can give an indication of family size, parish registers with all their imperfections are the most complete available source for analysing many aspects of family history.

Estimating birth rates depends on a knowledge of the size of the parish or area concerned. Such a knowledge is rarely obtained direct before 1801. In the absence of a listing, a multiplier could be used (see above) if a list is conveniently close in time. Alternatively, an estimate of population size can be based on the average number of baptisms in a parish which does not contain a significant number of non-Anglicans; but if the purpose of arriving at a population size is to establish birth rates, this becomes a self-fulfilling prophecy, and should not be used. Most pre-industrial parishes had crude birth rates of between 28 and 40 per 1,000 persons alive, according to Wrigley & Schofield (1981).

However, simply counting the number of baptisms (adding those available from nonconformist registers if residence is given) will provide a rough indication of the growth of parishes over decades, if not centuries, which can be compared to the estimated national growth described by Wrigley & Schofield (1981, Ch. 3).

It is normal for annual totals to fluctuate, though not as much as those of burials, and it is sometimes difficult to see trends even on a histogram. You may find the idea of a 'moving average' based on an odd number of years useful in such circumstances – a five-year average is recommended for most purposes, with the mid-point moving forward in time. This irons out many of the individual irregularities without hiding short-term trends as nine-year moving averages tend to do. (Odd years in which the number of baptisms seems unbelievably low, or missing altogether, should be given a notional figure taken from a wider average, however.)

At a slightly more detailed level, many studies have been made in those parishes whose registers give both date of birth and date of baptism in order to see what can be gleaned about families of different social status (Berry & Schofield 1971; Drake 1982), and different distances from the church (Finlay 1980). The interval has varied with both time and location, the period lengthening during the eighteenth century, but generalisations hide some strange variations from parish to parish, and even from one day of the week to another.

A histogram showing monthly, rather than annual totals opens out the questions of seasonality which have been explored at length by Bradley (1970–71, reprinted in Drake 1982) and Dyer

(1981). The latter has weekly figures based on an assumption about human gestation being thirty-nine weeks, and suggests that harvests and holiday celebrations had an observable effect on our ancestors' reproductive patterns. In the period 1580 to 1620, conceptions were found to peak in April–June and in December, and trough in September/October in towns, September–December in rural areas. There are major problems of interpretation in the seasonality of baptisms, however, which do not apply to marriages nor burials, not the least of which is the normally unknown date of birth, and therefore of conception. Dennis Mills (1973) discovered a local custom of July baptisms in Melbourn, Cambridgeshire, which in the last decade of the eighteenth century resulted in almost half the annual total occurring in that month; Melbourn was not alone in having such customs.

Much has been written about illegitimacy, described by Wrightson and Levine as 'an offence of the poor and the obscure' (1979, p. 128). Ratios (the number of illegitimate births compared with the total number of births) can be easily gleaned through aggregative analysis (see Laslett 1977, Ch. 3; Laslett et al. 1980, and Laslett 1983, Ch. 7). Illegitimacy rates however depend once again on knowing something of the total population – but this time, the numbers of women of child-bearing age. For this, we need recourse to family reconstitution. However, a study of ratios can be revealing, and as in so many other areas of family history, there are many more studies needed on a local basis in order to confirm or modify what has been learned in other areas. It has been shown, indeed, that numbers and ratios change over space as well as over time, the North-West, especially Prestbury of all places, being notoriously high (Laslett et al. 1980, pp. 29–31). Demographers have established a close relationship between illegitimacy, pre-nuptial pregnancy, and age at marriage – oddly, the first two rise together as the last falls, and vice-versa; see Laslett 1983 (Ch. 7). As a consequence, it has been suggested that illegitimacy should be considered as part of the history of courtship and marriage rather than a question isolated with other births, or a question of morality.

We should perhaps add here that illegitimacy within marriage is a highly contentious area, and one on which very few have written (see Laslett 1977, 1980 (p. 8) and Swart 1989). Needless to say, we believe that aggregative analysis has at best a secondary role to play in a discussion of this topic.

Death and burial

Again, national trends in totals and rates over three centuries can be obtained from Wrigley and Schofield (1981, Ch. 3), and once again there is immense scope for local studies to augment and refine the national picture which has been obtained only by aggregating burials from individual registers. London, however, has had a particularly important role, as the number of deaths there has been so high that only immigration on a massive scale has maintained its growth; there is continuing controversy as to the age groups concerned in the high death rates, but that is an issue we must leave for consideration by family reconstitution.

There are several aspects of death, as shown through the burial records, which can be tackled using aggregative analysis. The most obvious is seasonality (see Bradley's articles, republished in Drake (1982). The differential effects of the seasons on death numbers and rates is well known, and can be easily traced, with children and adults distinguished as a result of the common practice (before 1813) of including parents at the time of burial of children (actual ages afterwards, though often without the names of the parents). What was a 'child' in this context was never defined, but the general feeling is that they included unmarried under-20s living at home, with some above that age being balanced by others under it not so presented (Eversley in Wrigley 1966a, p. 71). Less well researched are differences which can be associated with economic activity other than farming.

Cause of death is measurable in those registers which, largely from the last quarter of the eighteenth century, supply the information. There are, however, immense difficulties of interpreting the data supplied, and it was to be another century before one could be reasonably sure that a medical practitioner gave a proper diagnosis. How can we achieve a meaningful estimate of cause of death when registers referred to 'gradual decay', 'old age', 'teething', 'bad legs', 'inflammation of the midriff', 'shaking', and so on; half the people in the Heaton Norris burial register in 1808 had died of 'decline'. 'Visitation of god' and other euphemisms survived long into the age of civil registration.

Finlay (1980) writes of 'endogenous' and 'exogenous' deaths (i.e. from causes which are from the internal circumstances of an individual birth, or external to it), from which he draws evidence of under-registration of burial. He was also able to measure the recording of abortions (uncommonly found in parish registers) in relation to geographical distance from the parish church. Death in childbirth is likewise more difficult to measure without recourse to family reconstitution, but here is another area in which an analysis of the thousands of available pedigree charts would be of considerable interest. Aggregative analysis can also be used to assess the incidence of infanticide, though of course the registers include only those cases which come to light, not the unknown number whose bodies have never been found. Unbaptised infants are often included with the names of the parent(s) only or omitted altogether, many clergy believing they should not acknowledge the names by which parents wished them to have been known (thus, even today, increasing the trauma of a neonatal death); but where the parents are not given, we must assume a high proportion to have died through want of attention at birth, if not actual bodily harm. For an interesting and surprising assessment of the extent to which mothers died in childbirth, see Schofield in Bonfield et al. 1986, Ch. 9.

Relatively few registers supply age at death before the last quarter of the eighteenth century, though Johnston (1971a) was able to use those for Trentham for 1727–30 in his analysis of the effects of crisis mortality in the West Midlands, based on data from seventy-one parishes.

Of all the activities under the broad heading of aggregative analysis, however, none has produced more interest than that of 'crisis mortality', accepting Schofield's definition (in 1972b) of a year in which more than twice the average number of people died (whatever the geographical area). The normal histogram of annual total of burials over a long period of time will very quickly indicate the years in which this happened even at the level of the parish or below, and often these visitations were taken for granted so much that the clerks did not bother to give the cause. Some years are well known to have affected the whole country, or considerable sections thereof – 1597, 1623 and 1727–30, for example. (See Wrigley & Schofield 1981, Ch. 8, 9, Appendix 10; there is a chronological table on p. 333; see also Drake 1974, Unit 7, 1962; Schofield 1972b; Local Population Studies 1977; Barker 1981; Bradley 1971; Rogers 1974; Willan 1983; Levine 1977 Ch. 6, appendix; Long & Pickles 1986; Appleby 1973, 1978; Johnston 1971a; Gooder 1972 and so on.) Much of this research has now been assimilated and carried forward by Walter and Schofield (1989), who pay particular attention to Laslett's original question of whether the peasantry in pre-industrial England had good cause to fear starvation as an endemic problem. (See Laslett 1965, Ch. 5, 1983, Ch. 6) There should always be a suspicion that the crisis was basically one of subsistence, even though disease can be shown to have been present, and recourse should be had to contemporary prices of food, especially if these are available at a local level. Indeed, Wrigley and Schofield recommend that researchers have available running indices of wages, prices, temperature and rainfall when undertaking this sort of exercise; see, for example, Mitchell & Deane 1962 and Mitchell & Jones 1971.

Once individual years have been identified (and there were many at a local level which do not appear on the national lists), the next step is to represent the histogram on a monthly rather than an annual basis, so that the seasonal incidence can be seen. An historical 'disease identification chart' can be found in Rogers 1974, and an improved version in Local Population Studies 1977. The histogram technique can also be used in order to distinguish males from females, and adults from children (see above for provisos), though actual ages would have to await family reconstitution. Alan Dyer (1984) illustrates how a detailed analysis of burials during the seventeenth century could identify outbreaks of measles. The outcomes are interesting enough in themselves; but when they are used in conjunction with other data, they can throw considerable light on the way our ancestors reacted to the misunderstood forces acting on their lives. For example, the deaths of a large number of girls would have the effect of reducing the population, whereas the deaths of numbers of elderly people have the medium-term effect of increasing it – housing (often a scarce commodity) was made available, thus reducing the average age at marriage, and thus increasing the number of children per marriage (see Howson 1961).

Family and total reconstitution

So far, we have tried to show how historical source material can be used in ways which are far from obvious at first glance. Several directions for doing so have been suggested – the analysis of all the data, taking into account the sequence in which they were originally written; comparing data for more than one geographical area, and more than one time slot; and the linking of data from more than one source about the same individuals. These suggestions prove useful whatever the period studied, but the resulting pictures are static, or at best intermittent, and we had to use aggregative analysis of parish registers to get an idea of gradual change over time. (Civil registration records from 1837 would be better, but are not yet available for historical analysis to any but the richest with immense amounts of free time, However, see Pearce 1973 and Wilcox 1982 for examples of demographic research using this source.) Aggregative analysis can considerably advance our knowledge of change, but it is rather poor at offering explanations as to why changes occurred. For one example of the extent and limitations of linking aggregative analysis with economic history, see Pickles 1976.

Family reconstitution, on the other hand, has the capability of bringing together a number of different strands of research described in this book, and it is not surprising that it has become central to the most significant findings of family history research. It uses as background and corroborative information the results of all the methodologies described so far; it employs the skills of the genealogist for genuinely historical purposes; it is ideally suited to group or society projects; and it produces results concerning the family history of a parish which relate much more directly to its social and economic history. At the same time, for reasons which will become apparent, relatively few of these studies have been undertaken and results published (and moreover they are unevenly distributed – see Appendix 6), leaving the field open for those whose imaginations can be caught by the rewards which such a subject can bring. Those rewards have been vividly described by R. B. Outhwaite (1973, p. 55) as enabling CAMPOP to go 'between the sheets of history'. N. L. Tranter, in a general introduction to family history research sources and their limitations, adds to Wrigley's list (1966a, p. 149) of the output from family reconstitution as

age at, and duration of, marriage; the frequency of adult celibacy, both among males and females; the average interval between the date of marriage and the birth of the first child, and between successive births; the average duration of the child-bearing period; the number of multiple births; the proportion of children born illegitimate; the average number of births per marriage or by age group of a woman within marriage; the sex-ratio of births; mortality rates by age-group and sex; life expectancy at various ages. (Tranter 1973, p. 16)

If life expectancy is estimated, it can be compared with the earliest of the estimates published by the Registrar General (Appendix to 9th Annual Report PP1849 xxi) or the tables provided by Richard Price (1803). To these could be added many other possible outcomes, particularly relating to occupation and social class. Nevertheless, it has its limitations, and as Stone (1977) and others are eager to point out, it still cannot deal properly with human relationships. We are still seeing the past through a dark and uncertain filter – for example, Wrigley's calculations of the average age of marriage in Colyton was based on only 30 per cent of all the brides between 1538 and 1837.

The rules of the game follow, and are easily understood in the context of the basis of the methodology concerned – put simply, whereas genealogists trace their own family tree, historians undertaking family reconstitution trace all the trees in a parish or area, and the conclusions drawn are therefore about a particular geographical area over time, not merely the collection of data about a few specific individuals from whom, by chance, we happen to be probably descended. Because of the requirements of family reconstitution, the data from aggregative analysis will also be incorporated (using New Style for preference) as what E. A. Wrigley called the 'preliminary analysis of the register'; the results of any studies of lists or listings can also be used, as can the many sources of personal relationships, notably probate records, with which genealogists are so familiar, exploited for exactly the same reasons – the clarification of relationships. The forms used are very similar to some pedigree charts used by genealogists, but with significant additions – for example, length of marriage and length of widowhood.

The fullest account of family reconstitution and its methods is probably still Wrigley 1966a, pp. 111–53, though he himself described it in 1973 as too rigorous; there are other accounts – e.g. Barker 1985. All data from within the period determined for study by the researcher are transferred on to slips, one for each baptism and burial, two for each marriage. Surnames with variants are collected together into sets arranged chronologically, and the data then transferred on to Family Reconstitution Forms (see Wrigley 1966a, pp. 126–7 for illustrations), first marriages, then baptisms and finally burials, each linking to the marriages. Schofield (1972a) and Levine (1976) discuss the important issue of how to ensure that conclusions drawn from the exercise can be regarded as representative, both believing that it is unlikely that those omitted are significantly different from those families which can be reconstituted. Through the Cambridge Group for the History of Population and Social Structure (CAMPOP), there is the possibility of aggregating the findings from several family reconstitution projects (Appendix 6) – see, for example, the study of mobility by David Souden (1984) from sixteen widely separated parishes.

The linking of records about individuals is that part of the method which enables family reconstitution to be distinguished from, and produce results much more advanced than aggregative analysis. It talks exactly the same language as genealogists because it is genealogy, but for all the families in the parish. Thus, ironically, those who have traced their own family tree through the period concerned are among the best qualified for these studies, which require patience, skill, and attention to the significance of detail. It is said to take a notional one hundred times as long to undertake as does aggregative analysis for the same area and time period, but since that estimate, access to personal computers with the relevant software can cut both times considerably. Willigan and Lynch (1982, Ch. 8) describe the additional advantages of computerising a family reconstitution exercise.

There are other snags which should be recognised at the outset. As with aggregative analysis, parishes should have a population of at least 1,000, giving about thirty baptisms per annum, on average, before the Industrial Revolution; register entries from smaller but adjoining parishes can be merged to produce meaningful results. One thousand souls is certainly larger than the average village in which most pre-industrial Britons lived, numbering but a few hundred (Laslett 1983, pp. 53–4). As long a period as possible should be tackled, a good run of 200 years yielding more results than two single centuries from separate parishes. Unlike aggregative analysis, family reconstitution cannot compensate for irregularities in the form of omissions any more than genealogy can. It is probably safe to start the exercise only half a century after the date of commencement of the register itself – otherwise too little can be known about those who were already adults when the project commences. Comparatively few parishes have been fully reconstituted – a list was issued by Laslett in 1983 (p. 288) and those available at CAMPOP are listed in Appendix 6.

Genealogists are already only too familiar with the problems of identifying individuals with certainty – on this subject, see Wrigley 1973. This, added to the familiar problems caused by geographical mobility, means that not all families in the parish will contribute data to all the results obtained, and the caution advised when choosing a parish for aggregative analysis (pp. 114–19) still applies. Additionally, beware of choosing a parish where apparent mobility can be great, especially those in urban areas, and those in which the church is situated close to the parish boundary. Souden (1984) suggests, however, that this very deficiency could be turned to advantage by using it as the basis for a study of mobility, though the registers are very poor at giving any idea of direction to the mobility concerned. Once again, an application of the IGI would help considerably in certain counties where the proportion of entries is high.

Either Nonconformity must be accommodated by linking data from the non-parochial registers (ensuring by your choice of parish that they are extant and accessible) or that parish avoided altogether. The former sounds attractive, but it must be remembered that Nonconformists normally ignored Anglican parish boundaries, thus distorting results which are ostensibly about those parishes. It should also be remembered that it was not uncommon for individual Roman Catholic couples to marry in both Catholic and Anglican churches between 1754 and 1837. As a result, family reconstitution has been undertaken for periods significantly before the start of the nineteenth century, and for relatively few parishes in view of the difficulties involved.

Any failure to find families which did reside in the parish (because those families did not have baptisms, marriages, or burials recorded therein) produces a further problem which must be recognised – they can add up to a quarter or even a third of the total population. If conclusions are to be drawn from the majority, but not from the totality, it should always be questionable whether those results are meaningful for the whole parish – and ultimately, therefore, whether the whole exercise would be better left undone if its conclusions are erroneous or misleading. If omissions are random, there is no problem; but if they are systematic through local custom, high mobility or non-conformity, for example, the results may be skewed. Schofield (1984) also has some interesting if cautionary words about the burial of non-parishioners.

A useful description of the operations of a group undertaking family reconstitution is that by Johnston (1970), though of course there are many others which emphasise more the results of the exercise (e.g. Dyer 1973; Levine 1977; Loschky & Krier 1969). Johnston's group studied Powick in Worcestershire, on the main road from the Midlands to South Wales and the South-West. There were about 500 inhabitants in 1676, and 1,172 in 1801. The period from 1663 to 1801 was tackled by ten researchers, collating the data from 2,783 baptisms, 815 marriages, and 2,711 burials. Some families were discarded from consideration – surnames with fewer than five instances in the registers (some 17.2 per cent, genealogists will note with horror), and a further 668 entries which could not be fitted into family groups (perhaps a consequence of the parish being on a main thoroughfare). The percentage of the entries eventually used was 72.8, and the total research hours were 'beyond computation' – probably over 1,000. (Macfarlane (1977) estimates that some 1,500 working hours are needed to complete the family reconstitution of a parish of 1,000 inhabitants over a 300 year period.) Many swore they would never do it again, but that was during the collection stage, and several later went on to similar studies. (We suspect that the group were not genealogists, so did not have that peculiar bent for historical jigsaw puzzles!) 'Total dedication, inexhaustible patience, and infinite leisure' were required in those pre-computer days.

Johnston's group were able to investigate family size, premarital pregnancy, duration of marriage, the demographic significance of the widespread mortality crisis in the late 1720s, the association of local families and wealth through marriage patterns, and other features of major significance to the history of the family – but there were also spin-offs which were more unexpected – dating of documents of hitherto unknown origin; establishing the context for other documents (e.g. settlement certificates) which were difficult to explain in isolation; and providing a permanent record of the family history of the parish, indexed and cross-referenced, for use by other researchers.

As already suggested, most family reconstitution exercises investigate certain family history features which change over time – age at marriage, duration of marriage, fertility, and so on. These investigations can be carried a stage further by relating kinship to social class, a classic study being undertaken by Keith Wrightson (see Wrightson & Levine 1979, R. M. Smith 1984, Ch. 9 and Levine 1977, Ch. 8). Over half the householders in the 1671 Hearth Tax return for Terling in Essex were found to be unrelated to other householders, and most of the remainder had only one such link, throwing into question any belief in the inbred pre-industrial community with extensive blood ties. Half the households were judged to be in the lowest of four social classes (gentry and large farmer; yeomen, substantial husbandmen and craftsmen; husbandmen and most craftsmen; and labourers, cottagers and widows), and they showed little evidence of marriage with other classes; yet most kinship links among classes I, II and III were vertical, rather than horizontal within each class. They married above or below their class, unlike the lowest, over two-thirds of whom married each other. Class II women were found to marry below their station, but this did not necessarily result in upward mobility for their husbands. You should beware, however, of trying to study social class over long periods of time, and the significance of certain terms, notably 'husbandman' changed (and in that case actually disappeared, of course, during the first quarter of the nineteenth century). On the difficulties of assigning social classes before the Industrial Revolution, see Laslett (in Wrigley 1966a, pp. 192–8), and Wrightson and Levine (1979, p. 22–3) who discuss the problem of men having multiple occupations.

Loschky and Krier (1969) also examined the relationship between family history and social class, this time dividing the population in three north Lancashire parishes into eight groups. They found a direct relationship between social class and completed family size, the lowest having the most children, but their class II (tradesmen) having the fewest, evidently practising some form of birth control. (On family limitation see Wrigley 1966b.)

The linking of Wrightson's study to the 1671 Hearth Tax return, and the termination of Johnston's work on Powick in 1801 illustrate yet again the advantages of linking parish register data with other sources, for both are illuminated in and by the process. Brown (1971) linked a family reconstitution project with the 1803 enclosure map of Aldenham, Herts., overseers' accounts, militia rolls, and of course probate records, the last of which are particularly useful in confirming and supplementing family history. Ingram (1985, Ch. 4) discusses the possibility that there was a deliberate effort on the part of the local gentry, against the canons of the Church of England, to prevent the poorest from marrying at all, in order to reduce the poor rate which would have been needed to support their growing families. Wrightson & Levine (1979, pp. 69–72) reported the Poor Law officials driving labourers surplus to local needs out of the community; two centuries later, they were to be driven out to the colonies.

The overall relationship between the fluctuations in the local economy and such indices as the age of marriage, family size, family limitation and expectation of life is described by Levine (1977, Ch. 6) in his family reconstitution of Shepshed in Leicestershire, which he rather unusually brought forward as late as 1851. In Chapter 7, in contrast, he relates a period of restricted fertility in Colyton, Devonshire, to that village's de-industrialisation, as production of woollen goods declined. Similar conclusions were drawn by Minoro Yasumoto (1981) about Methley in the West Riding of Yorkshire. See Roger Schofield's chapter in Walter & Schofield 1989, which assembles some main conclusions.

Among the many fascinating problems thrown up by aggregative analysis which family reconstitution can answer, some concern the remarriage of widows and widowers (especially at a time when marital status is not evident in the parish register entry itself), the proposition that illegitimacy runs in families, bridal pregnancy, and the mystery of 'missing' baptisms. (See chapter by Smith in Bonfield et al. 1986, and Dyer 1981 who found that only 11.6 per cent of fertile couples had a child within fourteen months of marriage, some 63.3 per cent having their first child between eighteen and twenty-six months after the ceremony.) According to Grace Wyatt (1981), about eight per cent of all marriages were involuntarily infertile.

A facet of marriage which can be related to others is occupation. How far did the occupation of the groom (far more than the bride, of course) influence the age and date of marriage? Family reconstitution can also relate age of marriage to migration; for example, a high age of marriage for men might be the result of out-migration of women and/or occupational insecurity for men. Newall 1987 notes that the average marriage age of tradesmen's wives was lower than those of farmer's wives, but not those of agricultural labourers. She also found a significant difference in the ages of women according to whether they were marrying parishioners or non-parishioners. Did certain occupations offer a better chance of a stable or long-lasting marriage? What was the relationship between occupation and the distance apart of the parishes of bride and groom, the so-called 'marriage horizon'? (See above.) These and a number of other questions are addressed in a fascinating chapter by V. B. Elliott in Outhwaite 1981 and in Bonfield 1986, which examines the impact on marriage of, for example, being a craftsman, an apprentice, a carpenter, a servant, as well as of being a migrant or being fatherless. She discovered that, in London at least, widowers had a tendency to marry their own servants. Levine (1987) discovered that those he chooses to term 'peasants' preferred to marry older brides, as they had fewer children and were 'better units of production',

Illegitimacy, which has been the subject of research using aggregative analysis, can be taken to much greater depths by family reconstitution because the questions are asked about identifiable, individual mothers, children, and sometimes even the fathers. This means that questions can be asked about the age of the mothers concerned, about the age at baptism, whether illegitimacy runs in families, and the connection between illegitimacy and social class. Once again, reference to the IGI would be a very useful technique for acquiring data towards some of the answers. Questions about the number, ratios and rates of illegitimacy have thrown up some interesting answers, the proportion apparently increasing as the number of births increases, and Levine (1977) also notes that illegitimacy rose and fell with the price of grain during the eighteenth century – a simple example of linkage of records across apparently unrelated data which opens out a whole new area for investigation, and raises once again the connection between changes in the economy and family history.

A major study of illegitimacy is in Laslett 1977, especially Ch. 3, where the tricky question of the relationship between the truly illegitimate, the children of clandestine marriages or of spousal relationships, and the children conceived but not born before wedlock is discussed. Levine (1977, Ch. 9) concluded that illegitimacy was largely the result of 'marriage frustrated' among those who could not accurately predict the demand for their labour rather than the mark of a more or less promiscuous society. Essentially, when there were seen to be few impediments to marriage, pre-marital sex was a normal course of events; when barriers to marriage were more effective, couples abstained rather than turned to promiscuous behaviour. Incidentally, Levine reported (p. 129) some difficulty in locating the mothers of illegitimate children in the reconstitutable families of Terling, 1538–1625, believing that many must have been servants. Mothers of illegitimate children *were* often servants, but not necessarily in the parish concerned (see Part 1, p. 56). It was certainly common practice in a later period, however (the late eighteenth and early nineteenth centuries, if not longer) that illegitimate children were not baptised in the mother's own parish (or, in the case of Nonconformists, in the mother's own chapel – she might have taken the child to the Anglican church). It would be worth investigating whether researched figures for illegitimacy require re-examination in the light of this phenomenon, which could possibly skew the results for any one parish (or indeed for any one incumbent). See above, p. 112.

Bridal pregnancy can be tackled only by piecing together the genetic relationship between those involved in different events in the parish register, and has been researched by Hair (1966, 1970), Ingram (1985) and both Smith and Brodsky (in Bonfield *et al.* 1986). Church presentments can throw additional light on individual cases, and on the attitude of the authorities to presenting, or otherwise, the offending couple. Laslett *et al.* (1980, p. 4) also has an interesting if uncharacteristic note on the wide variety of circumstances in which bastards appear to be brought up in works of literature.

Paul Hair's study of seventy-seven parishes in twenty-four counties accepted a definition of pre-nuptial pregnancy as baptism within 8.5 months of a wedding, and once again, use of the IGI would nowadays improve his record of tracing the families of only half of those married in the subsequent baptismal register. About a third of brides traced were pregnant at the time of the wedding, but the proportion varied widely (between one-sixth and one-half) according to the parishes concerned and the time period, the highest rates being in the North and West, and after 1700. There are other interesting variations within the main pattern, including the not unexpected decrease in the likelihood of pre-nuptial pregnancy with the increasing age of the bride (Bonfield 1986, pp. 88–9).

Another subject for investigation has been the incidence of mothers dying in childbirth. After a probable rise, there is a remarkably steady decrease being noted in each fifty-year interval from the second half of the seventeenth century (at twenty-one in every 1,000 births) to 4.6, the Registrar-General's figure for the mid-nineteenth century. First births are shown to be particularly dangerous for the mother (Schofield, in Bonfield 1986, Ch. 9). However, we are now at one of the limits of what family reconstitution can reveal; as Roger Schofield points out, the technique cannot identify the mothers who died during pregnancy, though it is known that the last three months of pregnancy are particularly prone to disease.

For the potential researcher sitting aghast at the amount of time which is required to undertake family reconstitution, there are several silver linings. The first is that they are much easier to undertake as a group, and although this requires a group organiser, it can also involve everyone participating in the planning and publication stage, not simply feeling like a research 'dogsbody'. Secondly, access to a computer can take a lot of the drudgery out of processing the data, once transcribed, though there are problems about identifying individuals whose names are spelled radically differently in different documents (see Sharpe 1990). Both of these mitigations can be applied by family history societies which have the skills, the volunteers, and often the computing power and know-how required.

It should also be stressed that family reconstitution in its full glory might not be required if the purpose of the research is more limited. Rosalin Barker (1981) demonstrated how a study of an outbreak of plague in Great Oakley, Essex, could be enhanced by identifying family relationships of the victims through the parish register. In 1973–74, one of the present authors conducted an investigation into a significant increase in the number of burials in Lancashire in 1623 (Rogers 1974). Aggregative analysis of some eighty parishes indicated the geographical spread and statistical extent of this 'population crisis'. Counting events was able to provide monthly totals (indicating that it was a problem of winter and early spring), and the number of children as opposed to adults, females as opposed to males, and so on. However, aggregative analysis could not tell us the ages of the victims concerned, or provide specific rates, such as infant mortality (the death rate of children under the age of one year); nor could it indicate the social class of the victims – all questions which required a greater level of detail than that provided by the registers on the surface.

The first of these could be obtained by even a limited application of family reconstitution. The age of children (admittedly post-baptismal) could be found by merely linking the deaths to the earlier baptismal entries, just as genealogists are used to doing in their own family tree. When related to all baptisms, this gave a rough measure of infant mortality. By reconstituting all the families alive at the date concerned, we could learn whether this increased mortality affected large families rather than small, and gain an estimate of how many families were affected by the crisis. Similarly, changes in the age of marriage could be studied independently of other variables, without the need to have a full-blown family reconstitution of the whole parish. By 1965 (Laslett), the myth of common child marriages had been exploded; but the average age of marriage, particularly of women, has turned out to be of critical importance to the understanding of the steady but nevertheless dramatic increase in population from the mid-eighteenth century, and needs much more investigation on a local level. Dyer (1973), for example, discovered that the average age of marriage for women in towns was two years younger than in the countryside around sixteenth-century Worcester. Professor Chambers (1957 and 1972, pp. 63–4) noted a higher fertility rate among the partly industrialised parishes of Nottinghamshire compared with their agricultural counterparts; this, he suggested (p. 117), rather than mobility from the countryside, explains the huge increase in urban growth during the eighteenth century. We return to this major subject in Part III.

We have already indicated that the basic family reconstitution exercise using parish registers can usefully be augmented by record linkage with other sources. V. Newman Brown (1971), for example, used overseers' and constables' assessments and accounts, wills, a local marriage index, militia rolls and estate records as well as the Enclosure map referred to above. This extension into collation with other records is taken to its natural conclusion by Alan Macfarlane's suggestion for 'total reconstitution' which, it has been estimated, takes about twenty times longer, (See Macfarlane 1977 and Sharpe 1990, whose work took eighteen months after the basic family reconstitution had already been done – and this was in Colyton where no early wills survive!) This can best be tackled by a large group, perhaps only one which has relatively easy access to London repositories. It would last a number of years, and involve adding to the family reconstitution results the data from all surviving records of the parish concerned. Macfarlane indicates how the sixteenth century saw an 'explosion' of records created in the Tudor state, though their survival rate varies considerably across districts until the nineteenth century. He provides an inventory of the major sources of information on individuals which makes them 'visible' to historians, and examines the problem of data collection and storage, once again eased by computers (see, e.g., Beckett & Foulds 1987). One conclusion of considerable interest to genealogists as well as to family historians is his estimate that very few individuals can have escaped through the web of record systems so as to appear in none of them. Total reconstitution allowed Paula Sharpe to identify sex-related migration patterns among unmarried persons in Colyton, the very people who are normally invisible in the parish register, and therefore in normal family reconstitution. On the other hand, Wrightson and Levine (1979), despite having used wills, manorial and estate records, parish accounts, taxation returns, Quarter Sessions and Assize papers and records of ecclesiastical courts to supplement their family reconstitution of Terling, balked at total reconstitution. They concluded that the work necessary to find all the references to its inhabitants in a wide variety of other documents was far greater than the results would merit.

Many local features – the physical background of the parish or settlement being tackled, the patterns of weather, housing, furniture, and modes of heating; the economic background of the parish – its modes of production, capital investment, occupations, the market in land, the distribution of wealth; its demographic history, with data from community and family reconstitutions being linked; and the social framework, including patterns of crime, literacy, education, religion and (its inevitable concomitant) sin, could be linked through total reconstitution, which can best be organised on a scale which only a family history or local history society can provide.

Part III

A family history
research agenda

Organisation

We have tried to challenge local historians and, perhaps more directly, genealogists with the proposition that neither group has paid sufficient attention to the history of the family as a major area for research. We summarised in Part I the ways in which demographers and economic and social historians have changed perceptions of the history of the family from the sixteenth to the twentieth centuries; in Part II, we explored many of the techniques by which the source material can be analysed in order to shed light on shifts and changes, whether local or national. We now turn to how those techniques may be used in order to enhance that knowledge and understanding which both groups can bring to bear on the subject of their own passions, and to make that research more relevant for other historians. In so doing, we shall include a few specific suggestions, but as examples only – to cover a wide range of possible topics would not only be tediously long; it might also discourage the very ingenuity which we hope will emerge from looking at any source material in unaccustomed ways. Several others, of course, emerge naturally out of the examples in Parts I and II.

As Alan Rogers's guide to project development (1977) shows, projects can have considerably different aims, requirements and outcomes. They can be national or local, thematic or chronological, and be undertaken by an individual or a group. In every case, however, we are involved with learning by doing, so that if any reader, however interested in what we have written, merely passes on to the next book on the shelves, we will have failed in one of our major objectives. We are looking for action, but action with a purpose that is meaningful and significant to others.

Such action may be on three broad levels. You may feel, as many people do, that you want complete control over your project, that you decide what to research and how to do it, taking full responsibility for its outcome. We have no quarrel with this strategy so long as its scope is properly limited to a subject or area within the competence of the researcher to undertake. Motivation tends to be very high, and you do not have to suffer the psychological pressures of working with other people.

Secondly, you can volunteer to work in a group project whose parameters are already set, either by your own Society, by a national organisation such as CAMPOP, or by the Church of Latter-Day Saints (for example, the effort to index the 1881 census of England and Wales). We hope you will choose one with an historical rather than one with only an antiquarian or genealogical relevance, and you will have the satisfaction of playing a part in a large project which would be impossible to achieve without substantial numbers of volunteers.

We would like to stress the third possibility, however, which covers an enormous range of investigations too large for the individual to tackle, but too local or idiosyncratic to be of interest as national projects. There are ways by which individuals can generate, or become involved in local projects requiring a collective effort when the idea seems worthy but beyond the capability of one person to undertake.

There are certain people who could be approached with the idea first of all. The relevant local history or family history society should have a secretary or (in the case of the larger societies) a projects co-ordinator who can advise on whether the idea would find support from the organisation. Although such individuals are normally volunteers themselves, and therefore very busy with routine administration, we hope they can give thought to the form of support available, and also raise with their societies the possibility of a more active council role, rather than waiting to react to ideas which might happen to come from members or outsiders. Societies should be like good publishing houses, not only dealing sympathetically with scripts which happen to come their way, but actively involved in seeing a need, and commissioning such research in the first place, putting some of their support facilities at the disposal of volunteers who take up the ideas.

Alternatively, especially for those who are not members of a society, go to your local university extra-mural department, local history librarian, or WEA secretary to see whether and how a project could form the basis of a day or evening research class, and whether anyone has already undertaken it. This knowledge comes from a wide variety of sources, though for family history the 'Work in Progress' column in *Local Population Studies* is excellent – it is also a useful source of ideas and contacts. The local librarian or archivist will normally know what serious research is currently being undertaken using documents in their custody. Several of the articles in the Resource Reading List which follows were the outcome of such classes.

Of all the national institutions capable of offering advice, the Cambridge Group for the History of Population and Social Structure at 27 Trumpington Street, Cambridge CB2 1QA, popularly known as CAMPOP, deserves a special mention, and family historians should be aware that the organisation faces something of a dilemma. On the one hand, they are the first to acknowledge that much of the research on which their aggregative analysis and family reconstitution results have been based was undertaken by amateur volunteers, many of them genealogists and local historians. On the other hand, the level of funding available to the Group is such that they have a limited capacity in resource terms to offer all the help which they would wish to give.

It is possible, with prior appointment, for the public to use the excellent library which contains not only books and serials but also a large collection of articles, pamphlets and conference papers. There are aggregative analyses of about 600 parishes, fifty family reconstitutions (see Appendix 6) and photocopies of a large number of listings. Blank forms for aggregative analysis and family reconstitution are available for those who wish to pursue a project manually.

Other forms of assistance may be available through an approach to the Director. We believe that, although CAMPOP is not resourced to provide advice on possible projects to every individual who requests it, they would be willing to help societies who want to organise some substantial research, and probably individuals with an initial track record who wish to investigate something more advanced. This rough distinction certainly applies to computing, which would have to be relatively sophisticated before they could offer time and advice. Societies would also find CAMPOP willing to give advice about possible lecturers for family history or demographic subjects even if they themselves could not provide lecturers for specific occasions.

Try not to be too suspicious of academics, by the way, The days are long gone when volunteers were seen as research fodder for tutors eager to publish in their own name without acknowledgment, and adult classes are much too sophisticated to allow that to happen. Equally, do not assume that they already know all the answers – most tutors are in the game from a thirst for knowledge rather than from a passion to teach others what they already know. The novice often needs advice about the amount of work which would be required for successful completion of a project, and whether the source material exists for the necessary research. Regard with suspicion, however, arguments about academic respectability (especially from male lecturers) and do not be put off merely because your interest does not fall within the mainstream of historical research.

Organisations will provide not only advice but also the means by which a group can be brought together. If you do not wish to lead or co-ordinate the group yourself, they can also provide someone who will perform that role, liaising with any groups undertaking similar research elsewhere, exploiting the skills which are normally found within a group though not normally within a single individual member, liaising on the group's behalf with the custodians of the source material relevant to the research, and encouraging the development of the project in ways not at first anticipated. It may be possible, for example, to link a group studying families in a census to another studying the history of housing in the same area.

The group leader has two other important functions. One is to keep in mind the main objectives of the research. As we noted in the Introduction, it is all too easy to get sidetracked into unexplored byways, even cul-de-sacs, which have little relevance to family history, and this is particularly true when the project is based on a locality. We described local history as a black hole because it is very easy to slip into and virtually impossible to escape once in its beguiling clutches. Those studying mining families, for example, all too often end up studying the history of the local coalfield as an end in itself rather than as a background to the local family history project.

Secondly, the project leader must decide, or must help the group to decide, when to call a halt to the data collection stage of research, when to start the process of arriving at conclusions (and indeed which conclusions to aim for – this can be something of a continuous process), and how to organise its writing-up. A few projects are self-contained – it is obvious what data must be collected, and you know when you have done it. Even in the case of a single parish family reconstitution, however, there is a strong temptation to go outside the parish to glean, for example, dates of marriage, and in more open-ended projects the collection of data could go on indefinitely. Deciding when to stop is vital, and should be based on an assessment of the point at which the law of diminishing returns begins to apply, more data simply not being worth the extra effort needed to collect it. Local historians are prone to what Bernard Jennings called 'antiquarian's palsy', when the sheer amount of material collected becomes a psychological barrier to drawing the threads together and reaching conclusions.

What to investigate

There are many questions relating to the vital events at the core of family history – birth, marriage and death – which fascinate both demographers and genealogists alike, but which have scarcely been tapped by local historians. Yet the answers have to relate to, or be based on local studies, without which the raw data would not be accessible. Whereas, on the whole, demographers have tried to find national patterns by adding together, or generalising from information relating to locations often geographically wide apart, we believe that the family historian should be more interested in the locality, and in the differences between localities. While remembering the caveats about choice of subject given in Part II, the presence of one's ancestors in a parish of study can only heighten interest, and provide deeper understanding and knowledge of their lives.

Of course, in tracing their own genetic roots, genealogists may find that their ancestors were concentrated in one place, often a set of neighbouring parishes, while others find that they have to move hundreds of miles from one record office to another. Most have a mixture, especially when they try to trace all their ancestors. Whatever the pattern, they will have an opportunity to try to discover the family history context which determined the shape of family structures, in those places at those times, and so understand far better the nature of the track by which their genes have descended.

The general suggestion has been made that the age of marriage was crucial for population change, and was closely related to economic development and its social consequences. It seems unlikely that the fall in the age of marriage took place overnight, though clearly there was a quickening in the mid-eighteenth century. What appears more likely is that those groups less dependent on property or its expectations may always have married earlier, and that the eighteenth century simply saw a growth in the number of those orders of society who saw no great economic advantage in waiting so long. Perhaps this has to do with the spread of wage-earning, or with the smaller amounts of capital needed for many forms of domestic industry which were growing before the Industrial Revolution as we commonly understand it. Whatever the reason, it is perhaps useful to think of two regimes of family formation running side by side from the sixteenth to the twentieth centuries. One, the old, was based on property; the other, the new, arose from the expectations of wages or the earnings of manufacture, commerce or the professions. The old preserved later marriage, the new married earlier and tended to have more children.

This tentative hypothesis can be tested out by family historians, with settled or highly mobile ancestors. For those with both, there is the possibility of comparing those who stayed with those who left. Without attempting to be prescriptive or to limit the initiative of any who have their own questions in mind, we include in the following pages a number of basic questions, some answerable only once census-type material is available, which might help to trigger the incomparable curiosity, stamina and perseverance which genealogists display in their basic research.

Our common inheritance of the pattern of these vital events makes their investigation of primary importance, and suggests that the questions should come first before an examination of whether source materials exist to make the answers possible. All too often historians, especially amateur ones, come across a source which sits up and begs to be analysed, or at least written about, even though the results may or may not make any significant contribution to our knowledge of how the world was as it was and why, and therefore how it now is and why.

Questions come first, then, before the discovery of whether we can find the answers. What do we want to know about our ancestors and the way they lived? Once again, the authors' instincts turn to the demographic and the economic, but the point we are trying to stress is that other authors might perfectly legitimately arrive at a quite different set of questions. Ours relate largely to patterns of birth, marriage, mobility and death, and the relationship of all these to local economic circumstances. Others might be far more interested in human relationships, for the study of which much of the source material examined in Part II might be at best peripheral, or requiring a different sort of treatment. Fresh evidence might be required for such questions.

For example, one major source which we have scarcely touched upon is the will and testament so familiar to genealogists. Demographers use wills on occasion as supporting evidence in family and total reconstitution, but local historians have often overlooked them, though the accompanying inventories have proved a rich seam. (See Riden 1985 for some local projects based on probate records.) Unlike inventories, wills do not easily lend themselves to statistical analysis and, compared with parish registers, they exist for only a minority of the people of any parish or township. Nevertheless, we believe that they can shed light on many aspects of family life, and we welcome projects such as that of the Bolton and District Family History Society and the Historic Stockport Research Group in transcribing and publishing wills, inventories and other probate records with minimal abbreviation, allowing all to be studied in conjunction (see Bolton & District FHS 1987; Phillips & Smith 1985). Gibson (d) indicates the present whereabouts of probate records.

Wills are the only documents available in large numbers which were intended to give expression to the true intent of our ancestors regarding attitudes towards their family (as well as towards other people and institutions, of course). Though they can appear stylised and formal they are, in fact, highly individual in content. Some 400 years ago perhaps two-thirds were written less than a fortnight before the testator died (Coppel 1988), but those made earlier were equally concerned with the final disposition of the maker's work and achievements. The will and testament remains the last word not only on the testator's intentions with regard to his or her personal (and occasionally real) estate but on the religious views he or she accepted, however tacitly, on inclinations towards charity, and above all on the attitudes that underlay provision for the family left behind. However, whereas most genealogists consult only those few wills which their own ancestors happen to have left, the local family historian will be interested in learning how they fit into the general pattern of wills left by others at that time and in that locality, and where and why they differ.

What are the main areas of interest, once wills are available for analysis in large enough numbers? Notice, first, the position of the future widow in the eyes of the testator, and what attitudes are implied towards her. Is she entrusted with the care of the children, the business, and/or the property without supervisory help, and, if she is to be helped, by whom? Do the provisions of testators of different occupations or social classes differ significantly? (See Vivien Brodsky's interesting research in Bonfield *et al.* 1986, pp. 144–52.) Was the widow to be sole executrix (as commonly as Nesta Evans suggests in Riden 1985, p. 66), a sure indication of the trust he placed in her? As a legatee, the widow was entitled (at least in the Province of York), to one-third of the worldly goods which God had seen fit to bestow on him – did he leave her more than this minimum, and did the legacy betray that desire felt by so many men to control their wives even after death by making it conditional on certain kinds of behaviour? (On entitlement generally, in relation to different forms of property ownership, see Macfarlane 1978, Ch. 4.) Care of young children, sometimes requiring a tuition bond, was also of common concern. Who was entrusted with their upbringing, for how long, and with what stated outcomes? Do wills of different periods reveal changes in attitudes towards minors? Were girls to be treated the same as boys? Indeed, what do wills inform us of these differences generally, whether minors or adults?

Children too were entitled to one-third of their father's personal estate, though the division of that third between them was not necessarily equal. Some children were clearly struck out for disobedience; others had already received their portions and were left only token bequests, but it is not uncommon to find the daughter who has looked after the father rewarded with the lion's share of his personal estate. Bearing in mind that real estate was often transferred by other devices, property transmission by the will is a strong indication of relationships within the family (see Wrightson & Levine 1979, pp. 94–9). It would be interesting to explore the consequences of inheritance and, even more, non-inheritance for children, an aspect of their own family history that many genealogists must have happily or ruefully considered.

Were there legatees other than widows and children? Were they in the immediate household (servants, for example), more distant relatives, or friends and citizens of substance? Who gave to the poor, to the church, and to other institutions which relied on donations? (On the last, see, e.g., Jordan 1959.) In the case of those dying without close kin or obvious heirs, did the community seem closer to them than their more distant relatives – could water be thicker than blood, and if so, to whom? It would be interesting to compare the wills of bachelors with those of spinsters in their approach to distinguishing between kin and friends. Would other research support Wrightson and Levine's finding (1979, p. 93) that women and men showed no difference in the way they viewed their nearest relatives? In general, the disposition of one-third of the residual estate, after the widow and children had been allocated their portion, should be worthy of analysis. Which relatives were regarded as close enough to merit mention, whether or not they were beneficiaries? Does this analysis throw any light on the extended family controversy, to which we return below?

Wills can also indicate mobility or contacts remote from the testator's own area. Legatees, who may be close kin, may be distant from home and thus described; the testator's choice of burying place can sometimes indicate where he or she came from or indicate which place that family regarded as its ancestral parish. Lists of debtors and creditors similarly show the geographical orbit of testators, those who were moneylenders not less than those in trade, though moneylenders might have felt more secure lending over short geographical distances.

Wills are sometimes believed to be crucial to the understanding of the way in which the inheritance of property relates to family history, structure, expectations, and to some extent even the mobility of daughters and younger sons. However, conclusions about particular areas should only be reached in the light of a knowledge of laws governing the rather complicated forms of landholding. Even more complicated are the customs of individual manors, which often predetermined the limits within which a testator might have freedom of action. Additionally, Lloyd Bonfield (1986, Ch. 6), in a study of Preston in the sixteenth and seventeenth centuries, showed that wills and manorial custom were not the only basis for the transmission of property, and genealogists will not be surprised (though they will be saddened) to learn of the extent of simple gift during life, despite its attendant dangers for the donor.

We believe that wills may therefore be as poor guides to the real estates of testators as inventories are useful accounts of their personal estates. Freehold lands and property are sometimes left in wills, but not always; arrangements and agreements could be made long before the testator made his will, and there was no necessity to repeat them in the will itself. Copyhold estates were held under the customs and traditions of the manor in which they were situated, and those customs were very varied. It was the custom of the manor that determined the inheritance of copyholds, sometimes contrary to common law as in forms of 'borough English' where such lands descended to the youngest son, daughter, or brother. There was similar variation in the widow's right to her husband's copyhold, or her share in it, and in the terms on which it was held. In all copyhold estates, however, it was the court baron of the manor that determined the descent of the estate or judged and decided the intentions of the tenant. It is therefore necessary to understand the customs of any specific manor before trying to reach conclusions. Like freeholds, copyholds are not necessarily mentioned in wills, but the mention of the heriot, payable to the lord on the tenant's death, often provides the clue to this form of landholding. Leases of land or property, not under copyhold, are usually listed as personal estate in inventories and, if not mentioned separately in the will, pass as part of the personal estate.

Finally, wills can offer indications of the place of the testator's family in the local community, judged by the quality of the legatees, and those outside the family who were appointed executors. To these should be added the appraisers who drew up inventories.

Inventories, numbering nationally over two million according to Philip Riden's estimate, have been published in relatively larger numbers than wills, and can be used to gauge not only the relative wealth of individuals but changes in the material quality of life over long periods, two centuries in some parts of the country. There have been many studies of the relative wealth of members of different occupations, but of equal interest would be the revelation, in different areas, of the ownership of particular objects. The ownership of books, for example, has been studied by historians of education and literacy, but there are many other personal possessions revealed in inventories which would lay open the day-to-day accessibility of creature comforts to different individuals.

An extension of this principle within the same families is the linkage of the probate records of husbands and their widows. How far did estates prosper or deteriorate in the hands of widows? How far were they prepared to ignore the wishes of their late husbands in order to defend the interests of themselves or their family? Could they maintain control of the family's source of wealth (farm, shop, or workplace), or had they relinquished it to their children in old age? What were the real, as opposed to the well-known fictional, property consequences of acquiring a stepfather, a feature of family life far more common before the twentieth century than within it?

Until fairly recent times, the history of marriage and remarriage has been inextricably bound up with the history of birth, so that you cannot study one without impacting on the other. We have seen, for example, how a fall in the average marriage age during the eighteenth century is believed to be the key to the rise in population during the first fifty years of the industrial revolution. Still largely unexplored, however, are the many thousands of parish registers which provide the raw data for discovering how and when individual parishes were affected by this change in different parts of the country, and how far the cause proposed by Levine – an increasing dependence on marketable skills rather than the ownership of land or a means of production – can be detected in marriage age in the same area across different occupational groups.

As Gregory King's analysis of the ranking of English society in 1688 shows, there was already a substantial proportion of the population, perhaps between a third and a half, with virtually no hope of inheriting property. Their decisions concerning when to marry could not have been governed by hopes of portions, dowry or inheritance; they were similar to the early factory workers rather than to the propertied orders around them. Did more of them marry, and marry earlier, and therefore have more children? Did more of their children die in infancy? Was their general life expectancy so much lower than that of the propertied classes that their marriage decisions had only a restricted effect on population growth?

It may well be, of course, that many members of the groups that King dismissed as lessening the wealth of the country, servants, soldiers and sailors, for example, were not devoid of property expectations; they could also be sons or daughters of farmers and smallholders who would in due course inherit portions or property that would shift them into higher groups. It may be also that it was from these propertyless orders that the emigrants to the New World were drawn.

As we have suggested, it seems probable that different social orders had different strategies for family formation from the sixteenth to the twentieth centuries with a major shift to earlier marriage in the eighteenth century. Changes in the age at marriage, in so far as they were related to economic developments, must have taken place at different periods in different parts of England. Each region had its own natural resources and its own ways of exploiting them, and within regions there were differences between their constituent parishes and townships. Thus the great national shifts in economic life break down into a kaleidoscope of thousands of contributing changes when individual parishes are examined in detail. Thus, believing that a national picture of a change is already 'known' should not prevent you from testing out that change in the locality which may be of interest to you, whether it be in agriculture or in industry. What was the age of first marriage for the man and woman? When they married, were they resident at the parental home, or elsewhere? At what time of year did they marry? What were their occupations? What capital or assets were they likely to have accumulated to start their married life?

In agriculture, the great shift was that from subsistence farming, with production for local markets, to production determined by regional, then national markets. London had consumed the produce of many parts of England from the sixteenth century or before, but turnpike roads and canals, and the urban growth of the late eighteenth century, began to make England one market. This process did not proceed uniformly; enclosure, expansion into the waste, drainage and land improvement, changes in animals, crops or husbandry methods, the replacement of resident farm service by day labour, all vary in their timing from place to place.

Industrial change could be more dramatic. The finding or exhaustion of minerals could transform communities. In manufacturing, the development of new products from the sixteenth century or the search for cheaper production changed the distribution of trades, often at the expense of the corporate towns. New products or fashions also introduced new skills and damaged old ones; feltmakers replaced capknitters, turners of treen dishes gave way to potters, carpenters and thatchers had to bow to brickmakers and bricklayers, stonemasons and slaters.

The introduction of cotton was the greatest of all these innovations. From the late sixteenth century, it produced a stream of new cloths and, in the eighteenth century, inventions. It redistributed the textile industry in a continuous series of shifts that proceeded at different speeds even within the 'cotton' counties. The industries that grew out of it had equally uneven consequences for particular places.

The experiences of families have to be understood against the background of their specific time and place, as Levine's family reconstitution studies of Leicestershire villages, referred to in Part II, amply demonstrate. Parish registers form the archival bread and butter for the researcher into local family history, and enough has been said in Part II covering methodologies which can be applied to them to the effect that they are not simply about baptism, marriage and burial, but conceal between those entries an enormously detailed story of the individual development of each parish.

The assumed corollary of an earlier age of marriage is an increase, however small when taken at the level of the individual family, in the numbers of children per marriage. Genealogists will be very familiar with the pattern of pedigrees indicating very large families in Victorian times compared with their direct ancestors a couple of hundred years earlier, far greater than a drop of a couple of years in the average age of marriage could produce. See Martin 1977 for a study of the small household in the 1760s. (One of many possible contributory factors may have been a reduction in the age of weaning, for which there is some slight evidence in the eighteenth century, which would have the effect of reducing the time interval between births to the same mother; see Fildes 1986.) An easy measurement of the scale of this phenomenon might be through the numerous pedigree charts which are, at the moment, lying too idle in the libraries of family history societies. Would a study of those charts which show siblings relate it to time, place and occupation? Is there any evidence, for example, for a sequence of marriages being in age order of siblings, and if so, is that pattern long-lasting? (see Laslett 1983, p. 100). What about the youngest daughters? Have they always been blessed and cursed with the pressure of having to stay at home to look after elderly parents, with consequent reduction of their chances of marriage?

Currently, these charts are deposited with societies, we suspect, largely to give other members an opportunity to locate others searching for the same family, and even to save someone else's efforts if they can show that they are related genetically to a family which has already been researched. It will now come as no surprise that we believe that the potential use of the charts is far wider and more historically important than that, and we believe that societies should have a radical rethink of the pro forma of pedigree charts in order to facilitate research into family history. Methods should also be devised for their regular updating, rather than the 'once-and-for-all' deposit, which is often at the point of initial membership. This brings us back yet again to the message at the core of this book – that individual genealogists, but particularly their societies (which can be far more that the sum of their parts) should consider a strategy for historical rather than antiquarian research, a strategy which should embrace not only their present activities but also a more purposeful steer which would affect decisions about publishing, library purchase, lecture programmes, and other aspects of their usual activities, including the design of pedigree charts and a more positive drive to collect and use them.

Even without such changes, charts *en masse* can provide the raw data for several other studies relating to vital events – age of marriage, for example; time intervals between the death of a spouse and remarriage; the relationship between both of these and occupation or social class; or the time interval between wedding and baptism of first child. Local historians would not find these charts easy to use, because they are not grouped together on a local or even a regional basis. People join particular societies not only because their ancestors lived in that area, but because *they* happen to live there nowadays; when geographical mobility is also taken into account, it will be clear that the charts are best used for subject or chronological, rather than area studies.

However, massing people together is distasteful, or at best irrelevant, to many genealogists, largely because they see their ancestors as individuals and have no great interest in population change in its own right. We like to believe in free will, and the thought that our forebears were somehow at the mercy of economic forces which they could neither control nor resist is abhorrent. Symptomatic of this impersonal approach is David Levine's suggestion that in the period immediately before the Industrial Revolution, 'the decision to marry was being determined by conditions beyond a betrothed couple's control and understanding' (1977, p. 12). Such studies seem to depersonalise our ancestors, whereas the very essence of genealogy is to pick out the wheat from the chaff, to identify particular individuals and thereby to ignore others.

We suggest, however, that ignoring the others is very short-sighted, for only by placing individuals into a wider human and physical context can we discover just how individual they were, and the investigation of the maverick has been just as significant in other subjects, such as biology or psychology, as it may be in family history. Only by knowing the normal spread of events can we identify those outside it. Why, for example, choose to marry someone of a widely different age or social status? Could it be that, despite all the pressures to conform to a pattern, to obey parents, the church, the landlord, the poor law authorities, love played a major part in their action? To the individualist, what question is more important, and what question more of an archival challenge, than 'Did your ancestors love each other?' Did they all follow Keith Wrightson's suggested maxim that 'one should love prudently' (1982, p. 83)? Does a narrow age gap imply greater choice of partner, making it more likely that affection has played a role? Or does a great disparity of ages imply that a greater love has had to overcome the social barriers against such a union? Just how do we decide whom to marry, and is there any evidence that the answer might have changed over several generations?

As we have seen, one aspect of maverick behaviour which has been widely studied, and is so widespread as to be of interest to all genealogists, is illegitimacy. This, however, is merely the core of a penumbra of related questions which are of relevance to the entire spectrum of historical interest, psychological, genealogical, sociological, demographic, legal, and even socio-economic. Until the last thirty years, sex outside marriage was an expression of nonconformity, and shows up in a number of different ways. Children can be born out of wedlock; is this the same phenomenon as bridal pregnancy, and if not what are the causes of difference? Is there any significant difference between illegitimacy, or bridal pregnancy, in spinsters and in widows? How, in this morass, are we to regard common-law marriage, beloved of the legal historian and surprisingly difficult to study in the absence of evidence that no wedding had taken place?

Common-law marriage is an archival, and therefore an historical problem; it is also a genealogical nightmare, as large amounts of time can be spent looking for a wedding when you don't know whether the record has survived, whether you simply cannot find it, or whether the wedding never took place. Even a wedding following the birth of children is no proof that there had been a common-law marriage beforehand. Discovering the extent of such arrangements is a major challenge to family historians, and the answer will be of considerable interest to many other historians. Were the children of such marriages treated as illegitimate before 1753 as they were afterwards? (See Macfarlane in Laslett 1980, pp. 73–5) Is there any evidence of common-law marriage in probate or poor law records? Is the use of 'alias' a clue, in the absence of any other obvious explanation? Can we know anything about the extent and social characteristics of the phenomenon? It is one of the many areas in which the genealogist's familiarity with the IGI could be used in order to challenge, or at least modify, some of the findings of demographers who have not used it, particularly those studies which rely on identifying individual baptisms or marriages within the parish under review. See, for example, Razzell (1972) or Levine (1976), who tried, seemingly without going outside the parish concerned, to assess the efficiency of parish registers in recording vital events. Gibson (e) lists the current holdings of the IGI around the country.

Who had illegitimate children? Did illegitimacy really run in families, as many writers have suggested, collectively forming a 'bastardy prone sub-community'? (See Laslett 1980, Ch. 8, and pp. 240–6, where R. M. Smith discusses a means of analysing the necessary data from the parish registers.) Did it run in individuals, the same women giving birth to more than one in any statistically significant way? Why was there a regional skew to illegitimacy? Was there any occupational difference between the mothers of illegitimate children and other women of the same age (a question which probably cannot be answered before the nineteenth century)? How far was illegitimacy associated with the removal of parental oversight through the death of one or both of the parents of the mothers concerned? How did religious persuasion, economic or occupational circumstances, or the implementation of the poor laws, affect individual mothers? Has anyone studied the fathers of illegitimate children in your area, the 'supposed's' and 'believed to be's' of the baptismal registers? Such references are relatively few in number in any single parish, and once again the IGI, pedigree charts and church court records contain the most accessible clues to the information. Ingram (1985, p. 154) observes that the fathers were named in up to 80 per cent of bastardy presentments in the Archdeaconry of Wiltshire in the early seventeenth century.

The study of the time interval between wedding and first baptism has raised a number of interesting questions about natural abortion, infant mortality, and fertility in relation to the age and occupation of the mother, and child-rearing practices. Unresolved, however, is the alternative model answer to the problem of why, apparently, a large number of couples failed to have babies in the first two years of marriage. Did women giving birth for the first time return to their own mother's home to have the child in relative comfort and familiar surroundings, and then have the child baptised in the mother's parish rather than her own, establishing that as its place of settlement, and removing it (statistically speaking), from her own parish? Here is what three writers say on the subject:

It is important to remember that it was customary for the first child of a marriage to be born and baptized at the native parish of the mother and this often applied to subsequent children as well. (Steel 1968 p. 147)

We are certain that it was not general for brides living away from their pre-marital parish to return for their first birth, and we have found no positive evidence that brides commonly returned to their mother's house. (Hair 1970 fn 10)

It was . . . very common for a mother to deliver a child (particularly the first) in her father's parish . . . The child would be baptised and then go back with the mother to the husband's parish (Snell, 1984, p. 30)

Here is one of the many opportunities for genealogists to come into their own, using not only parish registers to reconstitute that aspect of the vital history of individual couples, but also sources so far scarcely touched by historians – most obviously the IGI, and pedigree charts, though there is also the possibility of exploiting the sequence of names of children in wills, testing the existence and survival of children whose baptism might pre-date the earliest child in the local register. Establishing whether it is the baptism which is missing, or whether it is the child who was never conceived, or at least did not survive, is very important to arguments about population growth, about the relationship between mothers and daughters, and for the genealogist concerning the likelihood of having to go outside the obvious parish for the baptism of the eldest child.

Peter Laslett, and all researchers since, reached the conclusion that the extended family in historical times is a myth as the evidence, from early listings through to the censuses, indicates that the normal English household consisted of the nuclear family of parents and children, augmented normally only following bereavement or perhaps illegitimacy. Two married couples, for example, have not normally lived with each other, and the loss of mutual support, which is a supposed consequence of the welfare state in the twentieth century, may have been grossly exaggerated because of a false folk memory of how people used to live. The apparent disparity between this memory, and the research findings of Laslett and others discussed in Part II, prompted Michael Anderson's investigation of family life in mid-nineteenth-century Preston. He found a considerable reliance of kinship self-help even among that highly mobile society (Anderson 1971, especially Ch. 5), but did not undertake the genealogical research necessary to make an accurate picture of where relatives lived. We do not know how far his findings were true outside Lancashire towns, and most importantly of all, how far this strong kinship is demonstrable before the nineteenth century. One of the great challenges to the local family historian is to discover whether the neighbourhood family existed before the nineteenth century. Laslett (1972, pp. 157–8) acknowledges that the evidence is either not there, or requires considerable analytical effort to reveal; Anderson suggested that it probably did not exist, because the nuclear family's own domestic and economic problems were too great to afford spare capacity for charity, even when begun at home. This assertion appears to be supported by Wrightson and Levine's discovery that 93 per cent of householders were related to fewer than two other householders in seventeenth-century Terling (1979, pp. 85–7). We believe, however, that the reason for this apparent distancing of close relations might have a simpler explanation – that the number of children surviving to adulthood in the seventeenth-century family was so small that it was much less likely that siblings would be neighbours.

We think that local family historians should therefore reopen this debate, not so much because we believe that the conclusion is false, but because the evidence on which it is based may not yet be detailed enough. The effectiveness of the extended family does not require it to be living under the same roof; on the other hand, geographical distance could not be easily overcome before the age of the train. We believe that in the shifting kaleidoscope of rural and urban life in the sixteenth, seventeenth and early eighteenth centuries some families maintained family networks (what sociologists call 'propinquity of kin') in which relatives were close enough to respond to each other's needs or to celebrate happy events at a respectful yet supportive distance, each person close enough to be gravitationally affected by each other's needs, especially during times of personal crisis. This might have become more important during the eighteenth and nineteenth centuries if, as is believed, couples were marrying on the basis of expectation of wages rather than on the certainty of acquired wealth.

This meaningful distance will vary with time and place, and the type of needs concerned. When children went away from home into domestic service, was it to relatives, and was it at such a distance that home visits were out of the question? Did that apply equally to boys as well as to girls? (See Sharpe 1990.) Did young couples reside in such a place that grandmother could easily look after the young children, allowing mothers to go out to work as soon as possible, and to offer advice and support in times of crisis? If so, was the gravitational pull stronger through the male line which normally controlled property, or the female – was the extended family based more on economics, or more on psychological relationships?

The source material for answering these questions is equally available to all historians, but only an application of genealogical techniques will create the linkages necessary to show who was related to whom so that, for example, we can see if members of the same family are found scattered at random across a Victorian city or in a seventeenth-century Poll Tax return, or whether they are clustered in a significant way in order to facilitate, or be a consequence of, an effective extended family network. They might live close to each other in *order* to provide mutual support, or in consequence of that support being necessary in order to acquire a place to dwell with the same landlord, or a place to work with the same employer. Anderson (1971, pp. 38–9) suggests that migration to other towns may have been when relatives could no longer assist in finding jobs, but also (p. 141) lists the apparent disadvantages of mutual intergenerational aid.

Many questions relating to women in paid or salaried employment remain unresolved because of the unsatisfactory nature of the data recorded by census enumerators, which bedevils not only discovering the extent to which it occurred, but also therefore hides the true extent of regional, social and religious variations. What are we to make of the occupation 'grocer's wife', for example? Did childless women remain at home, perhaps because they had less economic need to work, or because their income was not from a recognisable occupation; or did they go to work because two cannot live as cheaply as one (how old is that aphorism, by the way?), or perhaps to keep the work habit from before marriage? As usual, we have to find out *what* happened before it is worth speculating on *why* it happened,

When genealogists are looking at their ancestors, or local historians at a specific area, they should ask themselves certain questions and set the answers into the context of what was happening to the community around them. What was the nature of the wife's occupation? Was it on the farm or in the trade or domestic workshop? If she worked outside the home, was it in a trade related to, or different from her husband's occupation? Did she continue to work after she had children? If not, did she return to work after they had reached a given age? What effect did her parent's widowhood have on her working pattern?

As we saw in Part II, mobility is another area of major concern to both historian and genealogist alike, and there are many questions worthy of investigation. The census has long been used as a source for this purpose, but the IGI is largely untapped; so are the baptismal certificates attached to 1823 marriage allegations, and the 'Markham' registers in the north of England. Perhaps the best of these is that of Witton, Cheshire, which continues from 1778 past the point where others stop in 1812, through to 1852, and largely untapped by thorough investigation into family history. There is also movement related to the development and decline of occupations. What did happen to the hand-loom weavers, for example? Did they rely on the Poor Law Guardians, or did they diversify into new forms of labour; was this the weavers themselves, or their children? Again, there is the possibility for a major contribution by genealogists, whose normal research cannot be geographically confined by a family reconstitution based on a limited geographical area such as a single parish. Of particular relevance would be for an individual or society to link up with the Small Towns Project based at Leicester University. The patterns of movement into urban centres are of considerable interest to genealogists, often in a period long before the census becomes available, and the keys to the research are marriage and occupation, both the product of genealogical research.

Finally, the study of old age and death should throw up questions and conclusions which are peculiar to family historians. One starting-point is the immediate effects of widowhood, not only in occupational terms as a source of income, but change of residence for a source of support. We have seen how much more difficult it was for a single woman to survive than it was for a single man. How did the widow, not merry enough to remarry, support herself? Did widows and widowers find towns equally attractive in their old age? Were widows and widowers equally likely to move in with married, or unmarried children? If so, was it with sons or daughters? Or, did grown-up children go to live with a widowed parent – if so, was this more likely to be with the mother rather than with the father? Could two women really share the same kitchen – if so, whose kitchen was it likely to be? Did the attitudes of those who had risen in the social scale differ from those who had not? Whatever pattern emerges, can you explain its cause, hopefully in a way which can be tested against other data for corroboration or otherwise? In short, what strategies for survival were employed by the newly widowed, as an alternative to parish or Poor Law Guardians' support before the Old-Age Pension Act of 1908, and were the strategies adopted by women different from those of men? See Anderson 1971, Ch. 10 for a detailed picture of Preston in the mid-nineteenth century; he suggests that, however much reliance was placed on kinship self-help before the twentieth century, it was that Act which enabled families to be able to afford to maintain an extended family in the folk-memory sense.

Surviving Poor Law records are so vast, and largely unindexed, that they are an almost untapped source for family history, and are in our opinion far more worthy of volunteer indexing programmes than some which are currently being undertaken. So far, studies of the poor have been largely statistical, the paupers being anonymised in a mass of returns from which only genealogical research can rescue them as individuals. In the case of a fortunate few areas, registers of the names and addresses of the friends and relatives have survived; for the majority, it will require painstaking reconstitution in order to discover the relatives of those incarcerated in workhouses and hospitals (see Gibson & Rogers 1991/2). Two major groups throughout the nineteenth century were mothers with illegitimate children, and the elderly and infirm who were incapable of looking after themselves. Did both groups have close relatives outside who might have supported them? Why did the 'extended neighbourhood family' let them down? What can institutionalisation tell us about contemporary attitudes to the supposed obligations of parents to grown-up children, and of grown-up children towards their elderly parents? (See Quadagno 1982, Chs. 4, 5.) Are conclusions about such attitudes capable of generalisation, and do they have any relationship to social class, religious belief, occupation, or to location?

Death itself has been the subject of considerable investigation since the actuarial and medical concerns of the eighteenth century, and has been investigated more thoroughly by historians than either birth or marriage. Nevertheless, much which should be investigated is still submerged through the former inaccessibility of parish registers and post-1837 death entries on a large scale. In the case of the latter, we are still (at the time of writing) entirely dependent on what the Registrar-General determines shall be investigated including, in the present day, projects outside the NHS which require the prior support of the British Medical Association. However, it may be possible to discover the home and family circumstances of infant deaths, or of centenarians, for example, by picking up references to age at death from the national indexes from 1866. For the location of the indexes, see Gibson (e).

Until legislation opens the way for free public access to death entries, most investigations will centre on much earlier periods, particularly in those areas where burial in the local Anglican churchyard was by far the most likely fate for a corpse, though even after the gradual introduction of cause of death into many pre-1813 registers, we would not recommend acceptance of the stated cause of death as anything more than a layman's guess and therefore a poor basis for analysis. The London Bills of Mortality appear to be the only source for causes of death over a very long period, but of course they are only statistical, and skewed to metropolitan conditions.

Patterns of death are yet another good example of the way in which local conditions can play a significant role in the outcome across different localities, and national averages can hide considerable variations relating to physical conditions, child-rearing practices, and so on. As indicated in Part I, Jews in late nineteenth-century Manchester had a far lower rate of infant mortality than their Gentile neighbours, despite the similarity of their economic circumstances. Their adherence to breast-feeding saved their babies from the perils of poor and infected diets, and it was medical investigation, seeking the causes of low infant mortality in their district, which revealed the importance of this cultural factor. There may be many similar local influences that affected family health, and through it the society around it.

Each parish should therefore be treated as potentially unique in its pattern of death, likely to be different from its immediate neighbours, and to change over time. Again, the role of the urban areas should be of particular interest in the extent to which smaller towns showed the same features as London in balancing an excess of burials by in-migration; who formed the majority of these urban burials remains to be investigated. The role of societies here may be crucial, in the sense of having the potential to research this field. The immense contribution of the Church of Latter-Day Saints in gathering and making available data contained in the IGI does not extend to death or burial records on any substantial scale, and we are therefore dependent on laborious research either in fragile original documents or in eye-straining microfilm in the great majority of English parishes whose registers are not available in published, or even in transcript form.

In this regard, therefore, a society has a role to play which may have to precede projects which investigate death, a role which facilitates the accessibility of the registers themselves. In an area as fortunate as the North-West, this is already showing itself in volunteer help in the work of the Cheshire Parish Register computerisation project, and the Lancashire Parish Register Society, and is potentially able to revive the parish register section of the Cumberland and Westmorland Archaeological and Antiquarian Society. In Bedfordshire, indeed, perhaps half of the pre-1813 registers are now in print, making research into the family history of that county one of the most thorough in the country. With modern printing methods and their substantial volunteer force, there is every reason for Societies to found self-financing parish register publication projects in their area, not only relieving the immense pressure currently on the original registers and Bishop's Transcripts, but also making them available verbatim to all classes of historian.

Making it public

This returns us to the plea we made in the Introduction: that properly conducted historical research might be of interest, and therefore should be available to others whether they are family historians or otherwise. Whereas genealogical research, being essentially for the benefit of researcher or client, normally stays private, historical research should be made public, and be seen as a contribution towards society's understanding of its own past. As we have tried to show, acquiring genealogical techniques by tracing one's own family is an excellent training for research which can be of relevance to others. This then begs the question of how the fruits of research reach the public domain.

Publishing – or making public – can take many forms, and your selection of the most appropriate is not always a straightforward matter. We assume, of course, that your results (if not the mass of your working papers) will be made available by being deposited in the local library and/or record office. Additionally, at one end of the publishing spectrum, there is a talk to be given to a group (be it WI, extra-mural class, or society) interested in the subject concerned. To be significant, a talk must be well researched and illustrated, but is normally a by-product of a larger outcome rather than an end in itself; it can also be unsatisfactorily ephemeral. The presentation of a paper for publication in the journal of a society, however, can be more demanding because it will be available to a much wider audience, and will become a permanent record of your results for others to copy as well as to criticise.

You might be aware already that these journals fall into two main categories. The decision to publish always lies with an editor, who is appointed to satisfy the membership's thirst for knowledge. Often, pressure of papers for publication is not overwhelming, quite the reverse, so that unless an article is defamatory, irrelevant or badly written, it will probably be published, enjoyed by thousands of readers, and cross-referenced by librarians or by the FFHS so that it is known to potential readers who are not members of the society concerned. A glance at the excellent summary of articles, arranged by subject and by geographical area, in the digest section of the six-monthly FFHS *News and Digest* gives an idea of the enormous range of material published by family history societies alone.

The more ambitious, however, should be aware that other publications which have pretensions to a consistently higher level of academic respectability are known as 'refereed' journals. In these cases, editors can probably choose from several papers competing for space, and will probably take the advice of an independent expert in the field of study on the way in which the article has been researched, conclusions drawn, and related studies by previous writers considered. This does not necessarily mean that you should be put off submitting an article for consideration – only that, until you become experienced in the art, it is best to seek the early advice of those tutors or fellow members who have overcome the humiliation of being initially rebuffed, lived to write another day, and learned from the experience. We know of no source which will tell you in advance whether a journal is refereed or not: the editor should be approached for advice.

That sort of advice should also be available for suggesting different outlets for your research, whether refereed or not, and it is normally worth considering a final target publication at a relatively early stage in your writing up. *Local Population Studies*, for example, is unlikely to accept an article which of necessity includes a substantial content of local, as distinct from population history, whereas such an emphasis might be more acceptable to *The Local Historian*. Length, house style, and emphasis are useful to bear in mind at as early a stage as possible. In the context of the subject of this book, the editor of *Local Population Studies*, at 27 Trumpington Street, Cambridge CB2 1QA, will be happy to give advice to prospective authors of articles.

Having encouraged the maverick, or tangential research project, however, we should not risk strangulation at birth by mentioning only those publications which can be in the straitjacket of traditional academic life. If you want the world to hear you, private publication of pamphlet or even book is a real possibility. The financial outlay is not great, even using old-fashioned methods of typesetting, and sponsors may be found through the judicious lure of a share in profits; desktop publishing makes the process even cheaper. So great is the market for any material based on local or family history (and you will probably be offering both) that you should comfortably recover those costs and finish up in the black. There are, we are told, easier ways of making money, but few can give the satisfaction of seeing your own research read, enjoyed, and used by other people.

Appendix 1 *see pp. 87–92*

Hearth Tax return for Tintwistle, Cheshire, 1664
(Public Record Office E179/86/145, Crown
copyright)

Macclesfield
Hund'

Chargeable		Not Chargeable	
John Bostocke	iij	Samuell Knott	i
Robert Sike	ij	Widdow Knott	i
Allin Hollingworth	ij	John Knott	i
Thomas Newton	i	Mary Deauson	i
John Doxon	i	James Mosse	i
Widdow Heaward	i	Roberrt Mosse	i
Nicolas Deason	i	William Beelie	i
John Watson	i	Alice Roade	i
Widdow Heaward	i	Alice Taylor	i
Raphe Hollingworth	i	Hugh Lawton	i
Raphe Heaward	i	Josuah Knott	i
Henery Heaward	i	James Buckley	i
Thomas Hadfield	i	Widdow Dyson	i
John Hall	i	Jane Heaward	i
John Sikes	i	Francis Knismith	i
William Heaward	i	Edward Boare	i
Nicolas Marshall	i		
Thomas Earneshawe	i		
Henery Whitehead	i		
Thomas Brownill	i		
John Hayward	i		
James Heaward	i		
James Buckley	i		
William Woolley	i		
Robert Heaward	i		
Robert Buckley	i		

16 —

Tintwistle

Henery Mellon	i
John Ouldham	i
James Broadbent	i
Raphe Heaward	i
George Hollingworth	i
Robert Heape	i
Hugh Garsid	i
Thomas Deansnay	i
Edward Hulme	i
John Hollingworth gent	iii)
George Disburie	i
George Booth	i
Richard Wood	i
John Turner	i
John Deausnay	i
Thomas Marshall	i
Adam Wilde	i
Reginould Hollingworth	ij)
John Wolley	i
Widdow Booth	i
Thomas Heaward	i
John Woolley	i
Robert Bradleeke	i
John Woolley	i
George Ward	i
William Field	i
John Shawe	i
Richard Harrey	i
Robert Knowles	i

N 63

A knowledge of local names suggests that this list was written later by a clerk copying the collector's handwriting, with 'Dewsnap' and 'Harrop' being misread.

Appendix 2 *see pp. 95, 100*

Population pyramid constructed from the list of inhabitants of Ealing, Essex, 1599

Normally, population pyramids distinguish only males (on the left) and females. With a little ingenuity, however, you can make visible many aspects of family and household structure by such a diagram. Individuals can be placed into a group context; groups can be distinguished within the entire community; and the age structure can indicate the direction of career change – above, for example, wives phase in as female domestic service phases out.

This exercise is also good at revealing probable errors in the source document – in this case, a 2-year-old 'husbandman', a 2-year-old 'maid', and Adam Mathew, a 16-year-old maidservant.

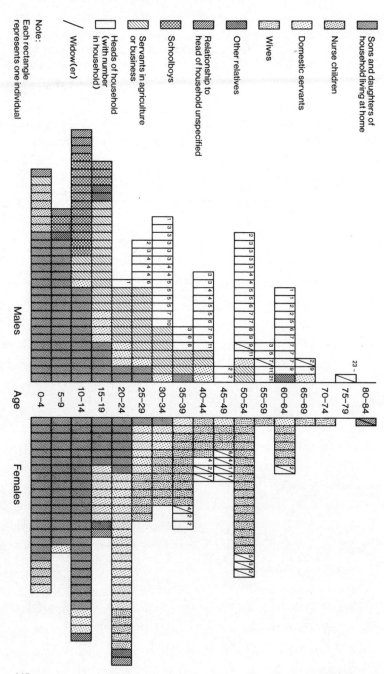

Appendix 3 see p. 96

A listing of inhabitants of Ringmore, Devon, 1698 (British Library Harleian MSS 6832 f146)

Transcript of a listing, believed to be in the hand of Gregory King. Households are numbered, and wives distinguished (incorrectly in families 19 and 20) by the letter W; with that exception, relationships are a matter for surmise, as in the 1841 census, without genealogical investigation. King's calculations derived from the data in each column show his interest in the number of under-16-year-olds (perhaps with the poll tax in mind?), the 16s–59s, and those aged 60 or more. An apostrophe is used instead of a decimal point. The number of persons is then multiplied by the average age in each column, giving the total in years, and numbers in age group cohorts are added.

Those who delight in spotting errors of the great and famous should enjoy checking this document.

Devon Ringmore   A List of all men, women & Children in ye parish
                      taken Sept 14th 1698

		121 146
1. Tho: Lee	52	7. John Cotly	56	14) Eliza: Maunder	70
Eliza: Lee W	34	Thomasin Cotly W	60	Eliza: Hingston	24
Sampson Lee	50	Marg't Cotly	28		
Mary Frowd	17	Marg't Row	55	15) Tho: Cocker	54
Barbara Steer	60	Phill'p Cotly	27	Marg't Cocker W	51
Mary Steer	22	Charles Cotly	17	John Penhay	
a boy	13	Sarah Hatch	26	Marg't Cocker	
2. Rob't Gilbert	66	........Cotly	6	16) Agnes Fox	70
John Gilbert	34			Agnes Fox	24
Prisc: Gilbert W	30	8. John Frowd	61	17) John Cocker	54
Mary Frowd	23	Bridget Frowd W	60	Deborah Cocker W	51
John Edgecomb	19			Mary Cocker	17
Susanna Frowd	11			James Bear	17
3. Marg. Frowd	64	9. Phillip Palmer	69		
Benj. Frowd	28	Clara Palmer W	74		
........Frowd	27	Mary Palmer	39	18) Jeptha Edgecombe	50
Agnes Frowd	34	Mary Palmer	8	Agnes Edgcombe	60
4. Dan'll Kennard	40	Eliza: Edgecomb	17	19) Rob't Lee W	45
Mary Kennard W	35	W'm Bound	27	Mary Lee	41
Dan'l Kennard	13	John Blackler	14	Mary Lee	5
Barb. Kennard	6	10. Ann Torkington	60	20) Nich: Head W	70
John Kennard	5	Mary Torkington	59	Grace Head	72
5. Francis Yeabsly	75	Eliza: Torkington	31		
Agnes Pearse	40	Tho: Torkington	26	21) Phill: Elliot	69
Thomasin Pearse	30	Francis Torkington	19	Alice Maunder	43
6. John Skinner	42			John Maunder	10
Joan Skinner W	34	11. Eliza: Ford	68		
John Skinner	8	Hannah Ford	38	22) John Ford	40
Joan Skinner	6	12. Hugh Flashman	60	Marg't Ford W	35
Eliza: Skinner	5	Mary Flashman W	66	Hon'r Ford	7
Ric'd Skinner	1	Hon'r Ward	77	Hon'r Nichols	70
John Berry	69	13. Mary Gilbert	52	23) John Rickham	40
Tho: Roach	13	Mary Gilbert	26	Wilmot Rickham	60
Rebec: Roach	14	Cath: Gilbert	11	24) Rebecca Cotly	44
		W'm Gilbert	10	Rebecca Steer	23
		James Gilbert	9		

          persons agr   4+17+9=30+43'4=1304
11+18+5 = 34 × 30 = 1020y
 5+18+9 = 32 × 39 = 1250y
 4+17+9 = 30 × 43'4=1304
20·53·23   96×37 = 35

25)	Rebecca Genney	38	35)	Rich'd Derry	54	42) Timothy Hatch	33
	George Genney	5		Eliza: Derry W	52	Mary Hatch W	35
	Rich: Genney	5		John Derry	18		
	Tho: Genney	2		Rich'd Derry	10	43) John Hatch	30
26)	Ann Hill	67		Eliza: Derry	7	Elinor Hatch W	26
	Grace Hill	29				Mary Frowd	48
27)	James Hoopell	76	36)	W'm Anthony	54	44) Walt'r Crosman	70
	Grace Hoopell W	60		Eliza: Anthony W	30	Eliza: Crosman W	40
	W'm Hill	21		Joan Anthony	69	Eliza: Crosman	2
	John Stidston	18		Tho: Wakeham	13		
	Hon'r Fox	30		Hannah Woodmaston	22	45) Peter Prideaux	60
28)	Nich: Hoopell	24	37)	Mary Skinner	75	Ann Prideaux W	26
	Alice Hoopell W	23		Abigail Skinner	16	Ann Prideaux	3
	John Hoopell	3		Joan Skinner	49	Mary Prideaux	1
	Alice Hoopell	2				a maid servant	18
	John Frowd	21	38)	Franc: Fox	34	46) Joan Lidston	49
	And. Frowd	11		Frances Fox W	40	Abigail Lidston	18
29)	Nich: Hoopell	60		Fran: Fox	9		
	Hester Hoopell W	56		Tho: Fox	8	47) W'm Roach	40
	Ric'd Steer	21		Rich'd Fox	5	Hannah Roach W	36
30)	Rich'd Fox	61		Charity Fox	2	Elias Roach	10
	Grace Fox W	26	39)	George Terry	38	Mary Roach	3
	John Wakeham	25		Eliza: Terry W	40	48) Tho: Heskett	27
	Mary Hele	15		Nich: Terry	5	Henry Tippett	49
	Sam'l Lidstone	21		Phill: Hatch	58	Willmet'a Tippett W	42
31)	Andrew Treby	40		Eliza: Hatch	32	John Tippett	14
	Mary Treby W	36		Dorothy Hingston	62	Rich'd Tippett	3
32)	Rob't Farley	48	40)	James Hoopell	26	Marg't Tippett	10
	Eliza: Farley W	40		Mary Hoopell W	25		
33)	Mary Bear	52		Mary Hoopell	1		
	Mary Bear	21	41)	John Stidston	61		
34)	W'm Badcock	34		Mary Stidston W	50		
	Joan Badcock W	27		Mary Stidston	22		
	Ruth Badcock	6		Joan Stidston	13		
				Eliza: Stidston	7		

Fam   persons

$8+15+2 = 25 \times 28 = 693$ years

$11+18+4 = 33 \times 36 = 1007$

$\underline{7+21+5 = 33 \times 35 = 1019}$

$24 - 26+59+11 = 91 \times 29'9 = 2719$

$\underline{24 - 20+53+23 = 96 \times 37'2 = 3574}$

$48 - 46+107+34 = 187 \times 33'65 = 6293$

$7+21+5 = 33 \times 35 = .099$

$11+18+4 = 33 \times 36 = 1007y$

Incl. 5 – 17. at 2 –   34
Incl. 15 – 29. at 9 –   261
Incl. 25 – 25 at 19 –   475
Incl. 40 – 35 at 32 – 1296
Incl. 60 – 40 at 48 – 1920
Incl. 70 – 24 at 64 – 1534
Incl. 76 – 10 at 73 –   730
                                6170

Appendix 4 see p. 103

1801 census 'return' for Croston, Lancashire
(Lancashire Record Office PR2644 Croston 1801)

	Above 60		From 15 to 60		From 10 to 15		From 5 to 10		Under 5 yrs old			
	M	F	M	F	M	F	M	F	M	F	M	F
Hillock												
Marg Hardiker												
Catherine Hardiker		1										
Richd Pemberton				2								1
Edwd Nutter			1^w	11								
John Field			1	1								4
Rob Baron			1	1								5
Ann Norris		1		1			1	1				
John Smith			3	1	1							4
Jenney Bromley		1		1								
Jennet Rigby		1		1								
D Geo Molyneaux }			2a	2					2			
Henry Hargraves			3	2					1	1		
Richd Smith	1a											
Rob Park	1											
Baxtonden Lodger			x^w		1							2
William Miller	1	1	2	1	1		1			1		
	3	6	14	26	3		2	1	3	4		16

Houses inhabited 14
Families 15
Houses uninhabited —
Males 25
Females 28
Total 53
4: R:C.

Street	Above 60		From 15 to 60		From 10 to 15		From 5 to 10		Under 5 yrs old		
	M	F	M	F	M	F	M	F	M	F	
Mrs Collins	1		2		1		1	x	3	x	2
Henry Varley			1	1							2
Aaron Langton		1	1	1							4
Ja. Waring			1								
William Taylor		1		3							
Miss Withingtons											
Richd Watkinson			1	1			1		1	1	
Henry Nelson $\}$			1^w	1^w	1^w			2	1	1	
Spiby				1							
Law^e Farrington		1	1				1				
Richd Nelson Junr			1								
Eliz^t Hesketh			1								
Thomas Allerton			1								
Richd Baxtonden		2	2	1	2						
Miss Taylor											
John Park			2	2	1	2	2	2	2	1	6
Jane Coxhead			1	1						1	6
William Cookeson		1	1	2		2	2			1	3
John Jones											
Rob Norris											
Jenny Rigby											
Mr Dickinson											
Ann Waring		4	19	19	3	2	7	2	8	4	23

41 M
37 F   6 R:C
78 total

	Above 60		From 15 to 60		From 10 to 15		From 5 to 10		Under 5 yrs old		
	M	F	M	F	M	F	M	F	M	F	
Margaret Varley		1									
Thomas Faviar		1	1								
Margrey Miller		1	1	x							
Thomas Aspinwall			x	1							
James Thornton			2	1							
x John Pemberton			1	1							
Marg Critchley			1	1							
Andrew Worthington Pinfold	1w	1a	1ow	1	1						
Hugh Almond			1	2		1					
John Spiby			1	1							7
3 dogs kept											
Andrew Worthington Butcher }			3	2	2			1		1	
Ann Norris	1	1		1	1	1		1	1		
Richd Nelson Senr											
Helen Banister (stuck through)				3	1	1					
Aggy Banister			2w		1						
Rob Banks (Dog kept)			1	1	1						
Eliz^th Tomlinson with d^o			1								
ja^s Worthington			1								
John Worthington with d^o			3	2		2		2		3	12
Robt Holding Dog kept			3	2						2	4
John Catteral			1	1						1	
William Eastham			1	1							
Geo Eastham with d^o	1	1	1	3			1	1	1		4
Jane Eastham with d^o											1
Henry Rutter	3	8	23	24	6	5	1	5	1	9	34

In the workhouse

	Above 60		From 15 to 60		From 10 to 15		From 5 to 10		Under 5 yrs old	
	M	F	M	F	M	F	M	F	M	F
Thomas Baxtondens family			2	1				2	2	1
Alice Bank		1		1						
Henry Spiby Blind	x			1		1	1		1	1
Thomas Howard			1	2	1	1	1		1	
Charles Taylor			1	1						
Eliz' Silcock				1		1		1		
Eliz' Banks				1						
Ann Hough				1						
Marg' Saziker		1								
Jennet Welsh (later insertion)				1						
Agness Nelson (struck through)				x						
Helen Spiby				1						
Eliz' Hodson Blind				1						
Helen Hesketh				1						
Mary Howarth										
Mary Nelson		1	1	1						11
Governor & Family	1		1	1		1	1	1	1	
James Wilding	1	4	5	13	1	3	5	3	4	4

4 R:C

Kennelleach

	Above 60		From 15 to 60		From 10 to 15		From 5 to 10		Under 5 yrs old		
	M	F	M	F	M	F	M	F	M	F	
Thurstain Hunter Dog kept			2	2					1	2	5
Peter Buck			1^w	1					2	1	3
Ellen Staziker		1					1	1			8
Mary Trafford				2	1^w		1	1			6
Ann Holding		x		1							3
Marg^t Thornley		1									
Richd Hunter			1^w	1		1	1	1			5
John Clarkson Dog kept			2^w	1					2	1	5
John Staziker Dog kept			1	1					1	1	3
Ja^s Catarall											
Richd Abbot	1		1	1					2	1	5
Willm Holding				1							3
Mary Holding		1		1					1		5
John Rutter	1		2^w	2							8
Thos Hunter	1	1			1				1	1	8
Henry Duckworth Dog kept			1	2		1	1	1		1	8
Alice Molineux				1					2		4
Thos Rigby Dog kept		1	1	1	1		1	1		1	5
Cath^e Catarall			x	1	x	1	1	1	2	1	4
Richd Whitle			1^w	2					1		8
Richd Watkinson			1	2					1		8
Wm Watkinson			3^w								4
Richd Watkinson Dog kept		1	1	3^w	2	1	1	1	1	2	
Betty Fisher				2					1	1	7
Wm Holding											8
3 R:C	3	7	21	25	2	5	8	7	15	9	80

(Marg^t Thornley and Richd Hunter are bracketed together with the note "(later insertion) Alms House")

Name	Above 60		From 15 to 60		From 10 to 15		From 5 to 10		Under 5 yrs old		
	M	F	M	F	M	F	M	F	M	F	
Nanny Cattarall		1		2							3
Thoˢ Hodson Dog kept			2ᵒʷ	3ʷ					1	1	7
Betty Holding		1		1		1					3
Mary Rigby			1	3				1			5
Mary Holding		1	1	2ʷ		1³			1	1	5
Willᵐ Monk			1	1			1	1	1		3
Wᵐ Steel			1	1					1	1	3
Richᵈ Blackston			1	1				1	1		4
Sarah Watkinson			2	2	1	1	1	2	1	1	8
Richᵈ Watkinson			2	1							3
Willᵐ Hodson's Widow	1			2ʷ					1	1	4
Ellen Moon		1		1							
John Norris			3ʷ	1	2		2	2	2		4
Henry Farrington Dog kept	1		1	1	1	1	1	1			5
Jaˢ Higham		1	1	1							5
Thoˢ Cattarall			3	2							4
Alice Wignall			1	2ʷ		1			1		4
John Whitle			1	2		1				1	5
Thoˢ Holding			2	3		2	1	1	1	1	12
Thoˢ Holding			4	1	1				1	2	5
Samˡ Rigby			1	1				3			3
Richᵈ Worthington Dog kept											
John Hough	2	4	28	35	5	7	6	10	10	6	86

	Above 60		From 15 to 60		From 10 to 15		From 5 to 10		Under 5 yrs old		
	M	F	M	F	M	F	M	F	M	F	
Hanging Bridge											
Richd Alty Junr			1	5					3		6
Betty Alty Senr			3	2			1	1	2		
Thos Almond			3	3						1	
Highfield Lane											5
Willm Wrennall			2	2			1	1	3	2	
John Sumner			3	1	2						
Mary Worthington			1	2		2^w	2	2			6
Groap Lane											
James Mayor Dog kept			2^a	3^w					1	1	
Mrs Master (later insertion)		1	1	4							
Mr Price			1	1		1			1		
Peggy Smith			2	1							
Thos Smith			1	1					1	2	
John Spybie			1	1					1		
Willm Smith			2	2							
Mrs E: Master (later insertion)			1	1							
Thos Rigby Dog kept	1	1		1		1^w					
Richd Staziker			1	1^a					2	3	2
Thos Holding				1							7
Thos Taylor				1					1	1	6
Thos Croston (scored through)											
John Russel	1		1						1	2	
Alice Nelson									1	1	
John Pemberton	1	1^a	1	1		1	1		2	3	2
James Wright with D°		1		1^w						1	3
Maria Smith		1		2							1
2 R:C	3	8	26	36	3	6	8	5	12	9	33

Name	Above 60 M	Above 60 F	From 15 to 60 M	From 15 to 60 F	From 10 to 15 M	From 10 to 15 F	From 5 to 10 M	From 5 to 10 F	Under 5 yrs old M	Under 5 yrs old F	Total
John Gill			1	1							2
Jane Beardsworth		1		1			1	2			4
Peggy Norris		1									1
Mary Unsworth		1		1				1		1	5
Jane Dewhurst			1	1							
Ellen Trafford	1		1	2	1				1		1
Henry Nelson		1							1	4	6
Mary Trafford Dog kept			x	x							
James Taylor			2[w]	1[w]	1	1	2[w]		1	2	2
Rich[d] Mawdesley			1	1							4
Rich[d] Hardiker			x	1						x	4
Tho[s] Ditchfield			1[t]	1[w]		1				1	2
Betty Bolton with D[o]			1	1[w]				1		4	4
Hannah Ditchfield Dog kept		1[ow]	2[a]	1			1[w]	1	1	1	4
Rich[d] Ditchfield			1[w]	3[w]				2	1	1	6
Marg[t] Sumner Dog kept			1[w]	1[w]							8
John Watkinson			2[ow]	2[w]						2	7
John Walmsley			1[w]	1[ow]		1				3	5
Tho[s] Iddon	1		1[w]	1[ow]						1	4
Roger Dawson			2[w]	1[ow]						2	8
Roger Dawson Jun[r] with D[o]	1		1[w]			1[a]	1[w]	2		1	
Will[m] Norris			1[ow]	1[w]				1		3	6
Mr Wagstaff			2[a]							1	6
Will[m] Ilsley Dog kept			1[a]	1[ow]		1		1		7	7
Will[m] Trafford Dog kept											
W[m] Trafford (later insertion, struck through)											
Ann Whalley Dog kept			4	2	1	1		1	1	2	6
Tho[s] Baxtonden Dog kept				3							7
Rich[d] Staziker	1	1	2	2	1			1		1	7
39 72 33 R:C	3	6	29	32	5	4	7	12	5	17	97

	Above 60		From 15 to 60		From 10 to 15		From 5 to 10		Under 5 yrs old		
	M	F	M	F	M	F	M	F	M	F	
Willm Staziker			1^w	1^ow							
Richd Heys 2 Dogs kept			3^a	3	1		1	1	2	1	
Ja^s Grayson Dog kept			2^a	2^a				1	1		
John Norris Dog kept			2^ow	1^a		x	1	1	1	x	
James Molyneux Dog kept			2^w	1^w			2		1	2	
Mr Trafford			4	1	1		2	1	1	2	3
Rev^d S Master				7							
5 R:C			14	16			4		4	3	3

	Above 60		From 15 to 60		From 10 to 15		From 5 to 10		Under 5 yrs old			
	M	F	M	F	M	F	M	F	M	F		
Drinkhouse Lane												
Tho⁵ Farrington			2ᵃ	3ʷ								7
Wⁿ Dalton			1	3								1
Bety Hunter	1		1	1	2	2						6
James Spybie					1	1						7
James Hardiker			3ʷ	2ʷ								
John Critchley			1ʷ	2ᵃ								
John Worthington			3	1		1						
Roger Waddington			1ᵃ	2	2			1		1		
John Holding			1	1				1		1		
Willᵐ Ashhurst			1	2ʷ	4ʷ		2	1	1	2		8
John Silcock	1ʷ		1ᵃ	4						2		4
Willᵐ Holding			1	1						1		1
Alice Haugh		x										4
John Critchley	1	1	1	1			1	1	1	1		4
Ann Critchley		1	2	2	2	2						
James Iddon			1	1								2
Roger Farrington			2	2			2	2				3
Rob⁵ Norris	1		2	3	1	1	1		1			7
Wᵐ Moss	1	1	1	3ʷ	2	1	1			1		2
Tho⁵ Yates Dog kept			1	1							9	4
Henry Bretherton Dog kept												
Mary Worthington			1	1				1				
Betty Fazakerley		1	2									
Peter Forrest				1								
Willᵐ Farrington			1	3								7
Will Critchley			4	2		1						2
Edwᵈ Monk			1					1		1		3
8 R:C	5	4	30	43	11	10	8	8	5	12		4
												61

Tho⁵ Dobson Dog kept
John Iddon Dog kept
Richd Cottham Dog kept
School House

	Above 60		From 15 to 60		From 10 to 15		From 5 to 10		Under 5 yrs old		
	M	F	M	F	M	F	M	F	M	F	
			2	2	2	1			2	1	16
			3	2	1	1			2	1	23
			2	3							34
			1	1							80
	1		8	8	3	2	1	1			86
		1									33
											97
											3
											61
											433

A load of meal =

£
240
4
960
2
1920
480
2400

Houses inhabited	Families	Houses uninhabited	Males	Females	Total	Agriculture	Trade	Other work
1/ 14	15	—	25	28	53			
2/ 21	23	—	41	37	78			
3/ 20	24	—	34	51	85			
4/ 1	17	—	16	27	43			
5/ 22	23	—	49	53	102			
6/ 21	22	—	51	62	113			
7/ 22	23	—	52	61	117			
8/ 25	27	—	49	71	121			
9/ 7	7	—	59	77	136			
10/27	27	—	23	20	43			
11/ 4	4	—	13	13	24			
			412	503	915	412	278	
			409	506	910	503	123	
184	212	—	403	507	915	915	511	511
			408	503	910		912	
	4		5	4				
	6		2	1				
	4		410	504				
	3			410		123		
	2			914				
	33							Total
	5							
	8							
	65 Rom: Catholics							

Account taken of the population of Croston March 10th 1801

Houses inhabited	Family	Houses uninhabited	Males	Females	Total	Employed in agriculture	Employed in trade	Employed in other work	Total	Roman Catholics
184	212	—	412	503	915	125	274	516	915	65
119	119	1	313	346	Mawdesley 659	100	115	444	659	166
27	34	—	95	77	Bispham 172	32	17	123	172	51
99	104	—	286	281	Bretherton 567	162	189	216	567	none
87	91	—	229	224	Ulneswalton 453	65	193	195	453	34
71	—	—	174	179	Hesketh with Becconsal 353	—	—	—	—	6
235	—	—	542	574	Tarleton, Sollom & Holmes 1116	—	—	—	1116	none
822										322

Note that the letters in the age columns are placed above the digits in the original, and that x signifies that a digit has been crossed out. Any digit crossed out and replaced has not been transcribed.

Appendix 5 see pp. 114, 118, 122

Aggregative histogram of parish register entries
for Billinge, Lancashire, 1772–1812

A parish register histogram, visually demonstrating changes in the volume of events in a way that reading the register itself cannot do. Baptisms and burials in this chapelry on the outskirts of urban Wigan are much as one might expect, but the marriage registers show erratic and hitherto unexplained variations in the number of events, including the reading of banns which did not lead to weddings here. In many cases, the ceremony involved minors, and was stopped by an irate parent.

The solution to this mystery awaits family history research.

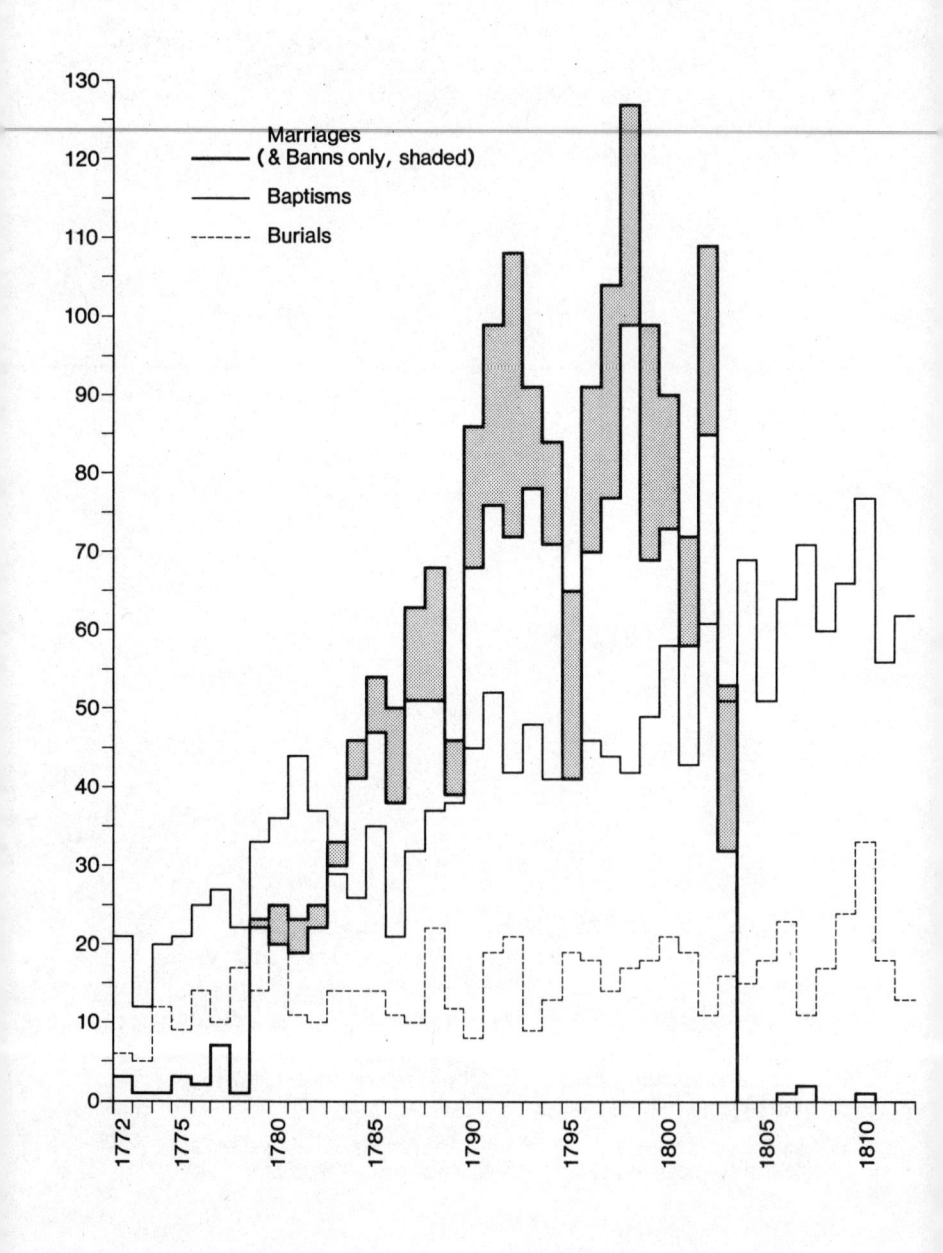

Appendix 6 see pp. 134, 148

List of family reconstitutions held by the
Cambridge Group for the History of Population
and Social Structure

This is the list of family reconstitutions which are currently available for
consultation at the Cambridge Group for the History of Population and
Social Structure. There are also a few from abroad, and a study of combined Quaker data from a number of different communities.

'N' indicates that names are included in the data, 'I' that there are only
initials, and 'O' that there are neither – only statistics.

County	Place	Dates	
Bedfordshire	Southill & Campton with Shefford	1538–1841	N
Cambridgeshire	March	1558–1751	N
	Willingham	1561–1812	I
Devonshire	Bridford	1538–1749	N
	Colyton	1540–1837	N
	Dawlish	1654–1837	N
	Hartland	1559–1837	N
	Ippleden	1675–1836	O
	Kenton	1645–1837	N
	Morchard Bishop	1660–1851	N
	Moreton Hampstead	1603–1837	N
	Sedgeley	1558–1837	N
	Tavistock	1741–1871	N
Durham	Wickham	1579–1779	N
Essex	Great Oakley	1559–1838	N
	Terling	1538–1849	I
Hampshire	Odiham	1539–1849	N
Hertfordshire	Aldenham	1559–1839	N/I
Kent	Ash	1654–1840	N
Lancashire	Hawkshead	1582–1841	N
Leicestershire	Bottesford	1581–1849	N
	Shepshed	1538–1849	N
Lincolnshire	Gainsborough	1564–1812	I
London	St James Clerkenwell	1551–1752	N
	Quaker community	1660–1850	N
Northumberland	Earsdon	1656–1841	I
Nottinghamshire	Gedling	1565–1841	I

County	Place	Dates	
Oxfordshire	Banbury	1564-1837	N
	Bletchingdon	1559-1840	N
	Chesterton	1539-1837	N
	Hampngay	1657-1836	N
	Hamptnpyl	1545-1840	N
	Islip	1591-1841	N
	Kirtlington	1558-1751	N
	Liddington	1572-1840	N
	Lower Heyford	1540-1840	N
	Middleton Stoney	1599-1839	N
	Rousham	1543-1840	N
	Shipton	1654-1836	N
	Tackley	1575-1840	N
	Weston	1599-1840	N
Staffordshire	Eccleshall	1575-1783	N
Suffolk	Lowestoft	1561-1730	N
	Thurleston	1650-1950	N
Surrey	Reigate	1560-1769	N
Warwickshire	Alcester	1562-1841	N
	Austrey	1559-1836	N
Yorkshire	Birkstall	1595-1800	N
	Great Ayton	1672-1837	N
	Methley	1560-1812	O

Resource reading list

Please note that the following list of books and articles is presented to give some idea of the range of publications which are available to help to clarify many aspects of family history, to indicate the location of any background reading, to provide a convenient reference list for the main text, and, perhaps most important, to provide a resource for the study of particular aspects of family history on which you may be concentrating for projects you may be undertaking. The titles of books, but not articles, are given in italics, their place of publication being London unless otherwise stated.

Abbreviations

A	*Archives*
AH	*Amateur Historian*
BHRS	*Bedfordshire Historical Records Society*
BIHR	*Bulletin of the Institute of Historical Research*
BLHEM	*Bulletin of Local History (East Midlands)*
CS	*Chetham Society*
D	*Daedalus*
EcHR	*Economic History Review*
EEH	*Explorations in Economic History*
EHR	*English Historical Review*
FH	*Family History*
GJ	*Geographical Journal*
GM	*Genealogists' Magazine*
HSLC	*Transactions of the Historic Society of Lancashire and Cheshire*
JEH	*Journal of Economic History*
JFH	*Journal of Family History*
JHG	*Journal of Historical Geography*
JRLS	*Journal of Regional and Local Studies*
LH	*Local Historian*
LPRS	*Lancashire Parish Register Society*
LPS	*Local Population Studies*
MH	*Midland History*
ns	*new series*
PP	*Past and Present*
PS	*Population Studies*
RES	*Review of Economics and Statistics*
RSEH	*Records of Social and Economic History*
RSLC	*Record Society of Lancashire and Cheshire*
TCS	*Transactions of the Cymmrodorian Society*
TLCAS	*Transactions of the Antiquarian Society of Lancashire and Cheshire*

TPIBG   Transactions and Papers of the Institute of British Geographers
TRHS   Transactions of the Royal Historical Society
TSAS   Transactions of the Shropshire Archaeological Society
TSRS   Thoroton Society Record Series

Abrams, P. & Wrigley, E. A. (1978) Ch. 9 in Towns in societies, Cambridge
Aiken, J. [1795] (1968) A description of the country from thirty to forty miles round Manchester
Aldridge, N. (1986) 'The mechanics of decline: immigration and economy in early
     modern Chester' in M. Reed (ed.), English towns in decline, Leicester
Allison, K. J. (1963) An Elizabethan 'census' (BIHR XXXVI)
Anderson, M. (1971) Family structure in nineteenth-century Lancashire, Cambridge
Anderson, M. (1980) Approaches to the history of the western family, 1500–1914
Anderson, M. (1984) The social position of spinsters in mid-Victorian England (JFH
     9.4)
Appleby, A. B. (1973) Disease or famine? Mortality in Cumberland and
     Westmorland 1580–1640 (EcHR XXVI.3)
Appleby, A. B. (1978) Famine in Tudor and Stuart England, Stanford, CA
Ariès, P. (1965) Centuries of childhood
Arkell, T. (1982) Multiplying factors for estimating population totals from the
     Hearth Tax (LPS 28)
Aubrey, J. (1962) Brief lives, ed. O. L. Dick, Harmondsworth
Bagley, J. J. (1971) Historical interpretation 2: sources of English history 1540 to the present day,
     Newton Abbot
Bagley, J. J. (1975) Lancashire diarists: three centuries of Lancashire lives, Chichester
Baker, D. (1973) The inhabitants of Cardington in 1782 (BHRS 52)
Barker, R. (1981) The local study of plague (LH 14.6)
Barker, R. (1985) Reconstituting the family (GM 21.9)
Barker, T. C. & Harris, J. R. (1959) A Merseyside town in the industrial revolution: St. Helens,
     1750–1900, Liverpool
Baugh, W. E. (1985) Introduction to the social services
Beckett, J. V. & Foulds, T. (1985) Beyond the micro: Laxton, the computer, and
     social change over time (LH 16.8)
Beckett, J. V. & Foulds, T. (1987) 'Reconstructing an English village in the
     eighteenth and nineteenth centuries using FAMULUS 77: Laxton, Notting-
     hamshire' in P. Denley & D. Hopkin (eds.), History and computing, Manchester
Benjamin, B. (1954/5) Quality of response in census taking (PS 8)
Berry, B. M. & Schofield R. S. (1971) Age at baptism in pre-industrial England (PS 25)
Blundell, M. (1952) Blundell's diary and letter book 1702–1728, Liverpool
Bolton & District Family History Society (1987) Bolton wills and inventories 1545 to 1600
     (Vol 1, surnames A to M), Bolton
Bonfield, L. et al. (1986) The world we have gained: histories of population and social structure,
     Oxford
Bradley, L. (1970–1) An enquiry into seasonality in baptisms, marriages and burials
     (LPS 4–6)
Bramwell, B. S. (1939) The frequency of cousin marriages (GM 8.6)
Brown, M. (1970) Hathersage 1851–1861, Sheffield
Brown, V. Newman (1971) Wider reconstitution (LPS 7)
Browning D. (1984) The registers of the chapel of Billinge (LPRS 123)

Buckatsczh, E. J. (1951). The constancy of local populations and migration in England before 1800 (PS V.1)

Burn, J. S. (1829, 1862, 1976) *The history of parish registers in England*

Bythell, D. (1969) *The handloom weavers*, Cambridge

Chambers, J. D. (1957) The Vale of Trent 1670–1800 EcHR Supplement No. 3

Chambers, J. D. (1972) *Population, economy and society in pre-industrial England*

Champion, W. A. (1988) The frankpledge population of Shrewsbury, 1500–1720 (LPS 41)

Chorley, K. (1950) *Manchester made them*, 3 vols. Cambridge

Clapham, J. H. (1926–38) *An economic history of modern Britain*

Clark, A. (1919, 1968) *The working life of women in the 17th century*

Clark, P. (ed.) (1984) *The transformation of English provincial towns, 1600–1800*, chapter by D. Souden

Clark, P., Gaskin, K. & Wilson, A. (1989) *Population estimates of English small towns*

Clay, C. G. A. (1984) *Economic expansion and social change: England 1500–1700*, Vol. 1, Ch. 1

Clegg, J. (1978–81) *The diary of James Clegg of Chapel-en-le-Frith, 1708–55*, ed. V Doe, 3 vols., Derbyshire Record Society

Cobbold, R. (1977) *The biography of a Victorian village*, ed. R. Fletcher

Cockroft, W. R. (1974) 'The Liverpool police force 1836–1902' in S. P. Bell, *Victorian Lancashire*, Newton Abbot

Coleman, D. A. (1984) 'Marital choice and geographical mobility' in A. J. Boyce (ed.) *Migration and mobility*

Collier, F. (1965) *The family economy of the working class*, Manchester

Coppel, S. (1988) Willmaking on the deathbed (LPS 40)

Cornwall, J. (1967) Evidence of population mobility in the seventeenth century (BIHR xl)

Creighton, C. [1891] (1965) *A history of epidemics in Britain*, 2 vols.

Cruickshank, M. (1981) *Children and industry*, Manchester

Cunnington, P. (1988) *How old is your house?*, Sherborne

Dennis, R. J. (1977) Inter censal mobility in a Victorian city (TPIBG II.3)

Dils, J. (1987) Deposition books and the local historian (LH 17.5)

Disraeli, B. (1845) *Sybil*

Dowell, S. (1884) *A history of taxation and taxes in England* (4 vols.)

Drake, M. (1962) An elementary exercise in parish register demography (EcHR 2nd series XIV)

Drake, M. (1971) *Applied historical studies*

Drake, M. (1974) Course handbooks for D 301 Historical Demography, Open University, Milton Keynes

Drake, M. (1982) *Population studies from parish registers* (Introduction by Drake and reprints of various LPS articles), Matlock

Dyer, A. (1973) *The city of Worcester in the sixteenth century*, Leicester

Dyer, A. (1981) Seasonality of baptisms: an urban approach (LPS 27)

Dyer, A. (1984) Epidemics of measles in a seventeenth-century English town (LPS 34)

Dyos, H. J. (1968) *The study of urban history*

Edgington, S. (1985) *Micro-history: local history and computing*

Edwards, W. J. (1977) Marriage seasonality 1761–81: an assessment of patterns in seventeen Shropshire parishes (LPS 19)

Edwards, W. J. (1987) The definition of prohibited areas (LPS 38)

Elliot, V. (1973) Marriage licences and the local historian (LH 10.6)

Engels, F. [1845] (1969) *The condition of the working class in England*

Escott, M. M. (1988) Residential mobility in a late eighteenth-century parish – Binfield, Berkshire, 1779–1801 (LPS 40)

Faraday, M. A. (1971–72) The Ludlow Poll Tax return of 1667 (TSAS lix)

Fieldhouse, R. (1971) The 1811 census of Thirsk (LPS 7)

Fildes, V. A. (1986) *Breasts, bottles and babies – a history of infant feeding*, Edinburgh

Fildes, V. A. (1988) *Wet nursing*, Oxford

Fildes, V. A. (1990) *Women as mothers in pre-industrial England*

Finlay, R. (1980) Distance to church and registration experience (LPS 24)

Finlay, R. (1981) *Population and metropolis: the demography of London 1580–1650*, Cambridge

Fletcher, A. J. (1971) *The Hope Valley in 1851*, Sheffield

Fletcher, R. (1977) *The biography of a Victorian village*

Flinn, M. W. (1982) The population history of England 1541–1871 (EcHR XXXV. 3. This is a lengthy review of Wrigley & Schofield 1981; see also L. Bradley's Review in LPS 27 (1981)

Fox, V. C. & Quitt, M. H. (1980) *Loving, parenting and dying*, New York

Gibson, J. S. W. (a) (1990) *Census returns 1841–1881 on microfilm: a directory to local holdings* (also contains references to publish census returns, 1801–31), Birmingham

Gibson, J. S. W. (b) (1991) *Bishop's transcripts and marriage licences, bonds & allegations*, Birmingham

Gibson, J. S. W. (c) (1990) *The Hearth Tax, other later Stuart tax lists, and the Association Oath rolls*, Birmingham

Gibson, J. S. W. (d) (1989) *A simplified guide to probate jurisdictions: where to look for wills*, Birmingham

Gibson, J. S. W. (e) (1987) *General Register Office and International Genealogical Indexes: where to find them*, Birmingham

Gibson, J. S. W. & Dell, A. (1991) *Tudor & Stuart muster rolls*, Birmingham

Gibson, J. S. W. & Medlycott, M. (1990) *Militia lists and musters 1757–1876*, Birmingham

Gibson, J. S. W. & Medlycott, M. (forthcoming) *Guide to listings provisional title*, Birmingham

Gibson, J. S. W. & Mills, D. (1987) *Land tax assessments c1690 – c1950*, Birmingham

Gibson, J. S. W. & Rogers, C. D. (1990) *Poll books c.1696–1872: a directory to local holdings in Great Britain*, Birmingham

Gibson, J. S. W. & Rogers, C. D. (1990) *Electoral registers since 1832; and burgess rolls*, Birmingham

Gibson, J. S. W. & Rogers, C. D. (1991/2) *Poor Law Union records* (provisional title), Birmingham

Gibbs, G. G. (1988) Child marriages in the Diocese of Chester 1561–1565 (JRLS 8.2)

Gillis, J. R. (1985) *For better, for worse, British marriages 1600 to the present*, New York

Glass, D. V. (1973) *Numbering the people*, Farnborough

Glass, D. V. & Eversley, D. E. C. (1965) *Population in history*, Chicago

Gooder, A. (1972) The population crisis of 1727–30 in Warwickshire (MH 1)

Gough, R. [1834] (1981) *The history of Myddle*, ed. D. Hey, Harmondsworth

Gwynne, T. & Sill, M. (1976) Census enumerators' books: a study of mid-nineteenth-century immigration (LH 12.2)

Hair, P. E. H. (1966) Bridal pregnancy in rural England in earlier centuries (PS XX)

Hair, P. E. H. (1970) Bridal pregnancy in earlier rural England further re-examined (PS XXIV)

Hanley, H. (1975) Population mobility in Buckinghamshire 1578–1583 (LPS 15)

Henstock, A. J. M. (1971) House repopulation in the mid-nineteenth century (*BLHEM VI*, reprinted with minor changes as the next entry)

Henstock, A. J. M. (1973a) House repopulation from the census returns of 1841 and 1851 (LPS 10)

Henstock, A. J. M. (1973b) Group projects in local history: house repopulation in the mid-nineteenth century (LPS 10)

Henstock, A. J. M. (1978) *Early Victorian county town: a portrait of Ashbourne in the mid-nineteenth century*, Ashbourne

HMSO (1949) *Royal Commission on Population*

HMSO (1971) *Trends in population*

Hewitt, M. (1958, 1975) *Wives and mothers in Victorian industry*

Hey, D. (1986) *Yorkshire from AD 1000*

Hey, D. (1987) *Family history and local history in England*

Higgs, E. (1989) *Making sense of the census*

Higson, J. (1859) *Historical and descriptive notices of Droylsden*, Manchester

Hinde, P. R. A. (1985) Household structure, marriage, and the institution of service in nineteenth-century England (LPS 35)

Hindson, J. (1983) The Marriage Duty Acts and the social topography of the early modern town: Shrewsbury, 1695–8 (LPS 31)

Hodson, J. H. & Smith, J. H. (1981) *Three Sundays in Wilmslow*, Wilmslow

Hollingsworth, T. H. (1968) The importance of the quality of the data in historical demography (D 97)

Hollingsworth, T. H. (1969) *Historical demography*

Holmes, R. S. (1973) Ownership and migration from a study of rate books (*Area* 5.4)

Horn, P. (1980) *The rural world 1780–1850*

Horn, P. (1982) Victorian villages from census returns (LH 15.1)

Houlbrooke, R. A. (1984) *The English family 1450–1700*

Howlett, N. M. (1983) Family and household in a nineteenth-century Devon village (LPS 30)

Howson, W. G. (1961) Plague, poverty and population in parts of north-west England (HSLC 112)

Hunter, A. (1985) Marriage horizons and seasonality: a comparison (LPS 35)

Hutchins, B. L. & Harrison, A. (1911) *A History of factory legislation*

Ingram, M. (1985) 'The reform of popular culture? Sex and marriage in early modern England' in B. Reay, *Popular culture in seventeenth-century England*

Ingram, M. (1987) *Church courts, sex and marriage in England 1570–1640*, Cambridge

Jackson, S. (1985) Using micro-databases in local history: Bromborough Pool 1861 (LH 16.5)

Jackson, S. (1986) Death and disease in Bradford-on-Avon 1711–1734 (JRLS 6.2)

Jenks, E. (1928) *A short history of English law*

Johnston, J. A. (1970) Family reconstitution and the local historian (LH 9.1)

Johnston, J. A. (1971a) The impact of the epidemics of 1727–30 in south-west Worcestershire (*Medical History* XV)

Johnston, J. A. (1971b) Group research methods in local history (LPS 6)

Jones, M. (1988) Combining estate records with census enumeration books to study nineteenth-century communities: the case of the Tankersley ironstone miners c. 1850 (LPS 41)

Jordan, W. K. (1959) *Philanthropy in England 1480–1660*

Jordan, W. K. (1962) *The Social Institutions of Lancashire* (CS 3rd series XI)

Kain, R. J. P. & Prince, H. C. (1985) *The tithe surveys of England and Wales*, Cambridge

Kennedy, M. (1988) Changing perspectives on the Victorian family (GM 22.11)

Kenny, S. A. (1975) 'The evolution of the Lancashire cotton industry 1750–1900', unpublished MA thesis, University of Manchester

Kent, J. R. (1981) Population mobility and alms: poor migrants in the Midlands during the early seventeenth century (LPS 27)

Kilvert, F. (1974) *Kilvert's diary 1870–1879*, ed. W. Plomer

Kirkman, K. (1983) Computerising the census enumerators' returns (LH 15.8)

Kirkman, K. (1986) Mid-nineteenth-century rural change: the case of Pinner (LH 17.4)

Knodel, J. (1979) An exercise on household composition for use in courses in historical demography (LPS 23)

Krause, J. T. (1967) 'Some aspects of population change 1690–1970' in E. L. Jones & G. E. Mingay (eds.) *Land, labour and population in the Industrial Revolution*

Küchemann, C. F. *et al.* (1976) A demographic and genetic study of a group of Oxfordshire villages (*Human Biology* 39)

Langdon, G. (1976) *The year of the map: portrait of a Wiltshire town in 1841*, Tisbury

Langton, J. & Laxton, P. (1978) Parish registers and urban structure: the example of late eighteenth-century Liverpool (*Urban History Yearbook*)

Laslett, P. (1965/71) *The world we have lost*

Laslett, P. (1972) *Household and family in past time*, Cambridge

Laslett, P. (1977) *Family life and illicit love in earlier generations*, Cambridge

Laslett, P. et. al (1980) *Bastardy and its comparative history*

Laslett, P. (1983) *The world we have lost further explored* (3rd edn of *The world we have lost*)

Law, C. M. (1969) Local censuses in the eighteenth century (PS 23.1)

Lawton, G. O. (1979) *Northwich Hundred Poll Tax, 1660, and Hearth Tax, 1664* (RSLC 119)

Lawton, R. (ed.) (1978) *Census and social structure: an interpretative guide to the nineteenth-century censuses for England and Wales*

Laxton, P. (1981) Liverpool in 1801: a manuscript return for the first national census of population (HSLC 130)

Leech, E. Bosdin (1990) The registers of Langho, 1725–1837 (LPRS 130)

Levine, D. (1976) The reliability of parochial registration and the representativeness of family reconstitution (PS XXX; forms of an appendix to the next entry)

Levine, D. (1977) *Family formation in an age of nascent capitalism*, New York

Levine, D. (1987) *Reproducing families: political economy of English population history*, Cambridge

Lewis, J. (1984) *Women in England 1870–1950: sexual divisions and social change*

Lindert, P. & Williamson, J. G. (1982) Reviving England's social tables 1688–1812 (EEH 19)

Local Population Studies (1977) *The plague reconsidered: a new look at its origins and effects in 16th and 17th century England* (LPS supplement)

Long, M. & Maltby, B. (1980) Personal mobility in three West Riding parishes 1777–1812 (LPS 24)

Long, M. & Pickles, M. (1986) An enquiry into mortality in some mid-Wharfedale parishes in 1623 (LPS 37)

Loschky, D. J. (1967) The usefulness of England's parish registers (RES 49)

Loschky, D. J. & Krier, D. F. (1969) Income and family size in three eighteenth-century Lancashire parishes: a reconstitution study (JEH XXIX. 3)

Lowe, R. (1938) *The diary of Roger Lowe*, ed. W. L. Sachse

Lown, J. (1990) *Women and industrialization*, Cambridge

Macfarlane, A. (1977) *Reconstructing historical communities*, Cambridge

Macfarlane, A. (1978) *The origins of English individualism: family, property, and social transition*, Oxford

Macfarlane, A. (1986) *Marriage and love in England: modes of reproduction, 1300–1800*, Oxford

McIntosh, M. K. (1984) Servants and the household unit in an Elizabethan English community (JFH 9.1)

McLaren, A. (1978) *Birth control in nineteenth-century England*

Maltby, B. (1969) Easingwold marriage horizons (LPS 2)

Maltby, B. (1971) Parish registers and the problem of mobility (LPS 6)

Malthus, T. R. [1798] (1973) *An essay on population*

Marsh, D. C. (1958) *The changing social structure of England and Wales 1871–1951*

Martin, J. M. (1977) An investigation into the small size of the household, as exemplified by Stratford-on-Avon (LPS 19)

Matthews, W. (1950) *British diaries*, Berkeley, CA

Matthews, W. (1955) *British autobiographies*, Berkeley, CA

Meacham, S. (1977) *A life apart*

Medlycott, M. (1990) Local census listings (GM 23.8)

Mendelson, S. H. (1987) *The mental world of Stuart women – three social biographies*, Hemel Hempstead

Menefee, S. P. (1981) *Wives for sale*, Oxford

Millard, J. (1982) A new approach to the study of marriage horizons (LPS 28)

Mills, D. & J. (1988) Rural mobility in the Victorian census: experience with a micro-computer program (LH 18.2)

Mills, D. & Pearce, C. (1989) *People and places in the Victorian census*

Mills, D. R. (1973) The christening custom at Melbourn, Cambs. (LPS 11)

Mills, D. R. (1976) A social and demographic study of Melbourn, Cambridgeshire, c. 1840 (A 12)

Mills, D. R. (1978a) The residential propinquity of kin in a Cambridgeshire village (JHG 4)

Mills, D. R. (1978b) The technique of house repopulation: experience from a Cambridgeshire village, 1841 (LH 13.2)

Mingay, G. E. (1968) *Enclosure and the small farmer in the age of the Industrial Revolution*

Mitchell, B. R. & Deane, P. (1962) *Abstract of British Historical Statistics*

Mitchell, B. R. & Jones, J. G. (1971) *Second abstract of British Historical Statistics*

Mowat, C. L. (1964) *Britain between the wars 1918–1940*

Musgrove, F. (1964) *Youth and the social order*

Musk, D. J. (1983) Courtship distances (Suffolk Roots, 9.2)

Newall, F. A. C. (1987) 'Who married whom?' some comments on 18th-century marriage patterns (GM 22.8)

Newman, G. (1906) Infant mortality

Nixon, F. (1969) The industrial archaeology of Derbyshire, Newton Abbot

Outhwaite, R. B. (1973) Age at marriage in England from the late seventeenth century to the late nineteenth century (TRHS 5th series 23)

Outhwaite, R. B. (1981) Marriage and society: studies in the social history of marriage

Owen, D. (forthcoming) The register of the chapel of Rivington (LPRS)

Pain, A. J. & Smith, M. T. (1984) Do marriage horizons accurately measure migration? (LPS 33)

Palliser, D. M. (1984) What to read on population history (LH 16.4)

Parton, A. (1987) Poor law settlement certificates and migration to and from Birmingham (LPS 38)

Patten, J. (1971) The hearth taxes 1662–1689 (LPS 7)

Pearce, C. G. (1973) Expanding families (LPS 10)

Pearson, S. (1985) Rural houses of the Lancashire Pennines 1560–1760

Pepys, S. (1970–83) The Diary of Samuel Pepys, ed. R. Lathom and W. Matthews, 11 vols.

Percival, T., & Heberden, W. [1789] (1973) Population and disease in early modern England, Farnborough.

Perkin, H. (1969) The origins of modern English society 1780–1880

Phillips, C. & Smith, J. H. (1985) Stockport probate records 1578–1619 (RSLC 124)

Pickles, M. F. (1976) Mid-Wharfedale 1721–1812: economic and demographic change in a Pennine Dale (LPS 16)

Pinchbeck, I. (1981) Women workers and the industrial revolution 1750–1850

Pollock, Sir F. & Maitland, F. W. (1898) The history of English law before the time of Edward I, 2 vols.

Pollock, L. A. (1983) Forgotten children: parent/child relations from 1500 to 1800, Cambridge

Price, R. (1803) Observations on reversionary payments 2 vols.; 6th edn

Prideaux, R. (1986) Descending lines and the search for connections in an expanding population (LPS 36; cf. Paul Hair in LH 12.1)

Pryce, W. T. R. (1971) Parish registers and visitation returns as primary sources for the population geography of the eighteenth century (TCS 11)

Quadagno, J. (1982) Aging in early industrial society, New York

Quaife, G. R. (1979) Wanton wenches and wayward wives

Razzell, P. E. (1972) The evaluation of baptism as a form of birth registration through cross-matching census and parish register data (PS 26)

Redfern, J. B. (1983) An early Victorian suburban elite: heads of household at home (LPS 30)

Richardson, R. C. (1972) Puritanism in north-west England, Manchester

Riden, P. (1985) Probate records and the local community, Gloucester

Rogers, A. (1977) Group projects in local history, Folkestone

Rogers, C. D. (1974) The Lancashire population crisis of 1623, Manchester (see also LPS 36, 37)

Rogers, C. D. (1975) 'The development of a teaching profession in England 1547–1700' unpublished PhD thesis, University of Manchester

Rogers, C. D. (1986) Tracing missing persons, Manchester

Rogers, C. D. (1989) The family tree detective, Manchester

Rose, L. (1986) Massacre of the innocents: infanticide in Britain 1800–1939

Roy, I. & Porter, S. (1982) The population of Worcester in 1646 (LPS 28)

Royle, S. A. & Pringle, M. E. (1986) Map making for local historians (LH 17.3)

Rushton, P. (1986) Property, power, and family networks: the problem of disputed marriage in early modern England (JFH 11.3)

Schofield, R. S. (1970a) Perinatal mortality in Hawkshead, Lancashire, 1581–1710 (LPS 4)

Schofield, R. S. (1970b) Some notes on aggregative analysis in a single parish (LPS 5)

Schofield, R. S. (1970c) Age-specific mobility in an eighteenth-century rural English parish (Annales de Démographie Historique)

Schofield, R. S. (1971) Historical demography: some possibilities and some limitations (TRHS 5th series 21)

Schofield, R. S. (1972a) The representativeness of family reconstitution (LPS 8)

Schofield, R. S. (1972b) 'Crisis' mortality (LPS 9)

Schofield, R. S. (1984) Traffic in corpses: some evidence from Barming, Kent (1788–1812) (LPS 33)

Schofield, R. S. (1985) English marriage patterns revisited (JFH 10.1)

Schurer, K. (1985) Census enumerators' returns and the computer (LH 16.6)

Schurer, K. & Arkell, T. (1991?) Surveying the people

Scott, J., Smith, J. H. & Winterbottom, D. (1973) Glossop dale, manor and borough, Glossop

Shahar, S. (1983) The fourth estate. A history of women in the middle ages

Sharlin, A. (1978) Methods for estimating population total, age distribution and vital rates in family reconstitution studies (PS 32.3)

Sharpe, P. (1990) The total reconstitution method: a tool for class-specific study? (LPS 44)

Shaw, T. (c.1906) Unpublished reminiscences (in the possession of J. H. Smith)

Sheils, W. J. (1979) Mobility and registration in the north in the late eighteenth century (LPS 23)

Shorter, E. (1975) The making of the modern family

Silverthorne, E. (1986) Hayes parish census 1790 (North West Kent Family History 4.4)

Siraut, M. (1981) Physical mobility in Elizabethan Cambridge (LPS 27)

Skinner, J. (1984) The jouurnal of a Somerset rector 1803–1834, ed. H. & P. Coombs, Oxford

Smith, J. H. (1972) Hayfield in 1851, Manchester

Smith, J. H. (1979) Glossop in 1851, Glossop

Smith, J. H. (1980) Ten acres of Deansgate in 1851 (TLCAS 80)

Smith, J. H. & Symonds, J. (1975) A short history of New Mills, Manchester

Smith, R. M. (1984) Land, kinship and life-cycle, Cambridge

Smith, V. (1969) The analysis of census-type documents (LPS 2)

Snell, K. D. M. (1984) Parish registration and the study of labour mobility (LPS 33)

Souden, D. (1984) Movers and stayers in family reconstitution populations (LPS 33)

Souden, D. & Lasker, G. (1978) Biological inter-relationships between parishes in East Kent: an analysis of the Marriage Duty returns for 1705 (LPS 21)

Spufford, M. (1974) Contrasting communities: English villagers in the sixteenth and seventeenth centuries

Spufford, P. (1973–74) Population mobility in pre-industrial England (GM 17.8, 17.9, 17.10)

Stanier, A. M. (1987) Communal solidarity in a migrant community (GM 22.6)

Stapleton, B. (1984) Sources for the demographic study of a local community from the sixteenth to the mid-nineteenth century (JRLS 4.2)

Steel, D. J. (1968) *General sources of births, marriages and deaths before 1837*, Vol. 1 of the *National index of parish registers*

Stone, L. (1977) *The family, sex and marriage in England 1500–1800*

Stone, L. (1990) *The road to divorce*, Oxford

Strachey, R. (1928) *The cause*

Swart, E. R. (1989) A computer simulation of the ineradicable uncertainty in genealogical research (FH 14.118)

Talbot & Shrewsbury papers (1966, 1971) *Calendar*

Tate, W. E. (1967) *The English village community and the enclosure movements*

Tate, W. E. (1951, 1983) *The parish chest*, Chichester

Teitelbaum, M. S. (1974) Birth underregistration in the constituent counties of England and Wales, 1841–1910 (PS 28.2)

Thompson, F. (1945, 1948) *Lark rise to Candleford*

Thomson, D. (1980) Age reporting by the elderly and the nineteenth-century census (LPS 25)

Tillot, P. M. (1968) The analysis of census returns (LH 8.1)

Tilly, L. A. (1987) Women's history and family history – fruitful collaboration or missed connection? (JFH 1–3)

Tranter, N. L. (1973) *Population and industrialization*

Tranter, N. L. (1985) *Population and society, 1750–1940*

Turner, T. (1979) *The diary of Thomas Turner 1754–1765*, ed. G. H. Jennings, Oxford

Turner, W. (1983) Patterns of migration of textile works into Accrington in the early nineteenth century (LPS 30)

Tusser, T. [1580] (1984) *Five hundred points of good husbandry*, Oxford

Wadsworth, A. P. & Mann, J. deL. (1931) *The cotton trade and industrial Lancashire 1600–1780*

Wall, R. (1982) The inhabitants of Summertown, Oxford in the year 1832 (LPS 28)

Wall, R. (ed.) (1983) *Family forms in historic Europe*, Cambridge

Walter, J. & Schofield, R. S. (1989) *Famine, disease, and the social order in early modern society*, Cambridge

Watts, J. (1866) *The facts of the cotton famine*

Webster, W. F. (1980) *Protestation returns 1641/2 – Notts. Derbys.*, Nottingham

Webster, W. F. (1988) Nottinghamshire hearth tax 1664:1674 (TSRS 37)

Whiteman, A. (1986) The Compton Census of 1676 (RSEH ns X)

Wilcox, P. (1982) Marriage, mobility and domestic service in Victorian Cambridge (LPS 29)

Willan, T. S. (1983) Plague in perspective: the case of Manchester in 1605 (HSLC 132)

Williams, E. C. (1959) *Bess of Hardwicke*

Williams, J. A. (1973) A local population study at a college of education (LPS 11)

Willigan, J. D. & Lynch, K. A. (1982) *Sources and methods of historical demography*, New York

Wojciechowska, B. (1988) Brenchley: a study of migratory movements in mid-nineteenth-century rural parish (LPS 41)

Wolfram, S. (1987) In-laws and outlaws: kinship and marriage in England

Wood, G. H. (1910) The history of wages in the cotton trade

Woodforde, J. (1978) The diary of a country parson, 1758–1802, ed. J. Beresford, Oxford

Woods, R. I & Hinde, P. R. A. (1985) Nuptiality and age at marriage in nineteenth-century England (JFH 10.5)

Workman, R. (1981) Analysing a tithe map in depth (LH 14.5)

Wright, S. J. (1989) A guide to Easter books and related parish listings (LPS 42, 43)

Wrightson, K. (1975) Infanticide in earlier seventeenth-century England (LPS 15)

Wrightson, K. (1982) English society 1580–1680

Wrightson, K. & Levine, D. (1979) Poverty and piety in an English village: Terling, 1525–1700

Wrigley, E. A. (1966a) An introduction to English historical demography

Wrigley, E. A. (1966b) Family limitation in pre-industrial England (EHR 2nd series xix)

Wrigley, E. A. (1972) Nineteenth-century society: essays in the use of quantitative methods for the study of social data, Cambridge

Wrigley, E. A. (1982) Age at marriage in early modern England (FH 12.91/2)

Wrigley, E. A. (1973) Identifying people in the past

Wrigley, E. A. (1976) The significance of appropriate source material to the progress of historical population studies (A XII, 55)

Wrigley, E. A. (1977a) A note on the life-time mobility of married women in a parish population in the later eighteenth century (LPS 18)

Wrigley, E. A. (1977b) Births and baptisms: the use of Anglican baptism registers as a source of information about the number of births in England before the beginning of civil registration (PS 31.2)

Wrigley, E. A. & Schofield, R. S. (1981) The population history of England 1541–1971: a reconstruction

Wrigley, E. A. & Schofield, R. S. (1983) English population history from family reconstitution: summary results 1600–1799 (PS 37.2)

Wyatt, G. (1981) Migration in south-west Lancashire (LPS 27)

Wyatt, G. (1989) Population change and stability in a Cheshire parish during the eighteenth century (LPS 43)

Yasumoto, M. (1981) Industrialisation and demographic change in a Yorkshire parish (LPS 27)

Yasumoto, M. (1985) How accurate is the Methley baptismal registration? (LPS 35)

Yates, E. M. (1982) The evolution of the English village (GJ 148)

Zell, M. (1984) Families and householders in Staplehurst, 1563–4 (LPS 33)

Index

(*Place names are indexed under the relevant county*)

Abbot, George, Archbishop of Canterbury, 63
abortifacients, 59
abortion, 39, 59
adultery, 51, 52
aggregative analysis, 113–31
agriculture, agricultural areas, 22–3, 27, 34, 42–4, 50–3, 63, 78
Agricultural Gangs Labour Act (1867), 51
Aiken, John, 43
apprentices, apprenticeship, 14, 28, 43, 48, 64, 76, 123, 126
Approaches to the history of the western family, 6
aristocrats, aristocracy, 13, 17, 29–31
Arkwright, Richard, 23
Association Oath, 94
Aubrey, John, 60–1

bachelors, 74
Ballot Act (1872), 111
banns, 121–3, *see also* marriage
baptism, 52, 61, 118; analysis of, 126–9
Bedfordshire, 170; Cardington, 96, 100, 102; Southill & Compton with Shefford, 198
Berkshire, Speenhamland, 46
betrothal, 67, *see also* common-law marriage
Bills of Mortality, 169
birth, *see* baptism.
birth control, 138
Bishop's Transcripts, 116–17
Blundell, Nicholas, 65
boarders, 90, 98
Booth, Charles, 79
bridal pregnancy, 31, 46, 128, 139–41, 161

Brookes, Revd. Joshua, 55
burgage tenure, 33
burial, 114; analysis of, 129–31, 168–70

Cambridgeshire, Cambridge, 104; March, 198; Melbourn, 108, 128; Willingham, 198
Cambridge Group for the History of Population and Social Structure (CAMPOP), 6–7, 132, 134–5, 147–8, 198–9
Carrington, Robert, 38
census, defined 85; analysis of, 102–12
Chartism, 27
Cheshire, 50, 55, 63, 92, 101, 170; Chester, 16; Congleton, 23; Disley, 75; Macclesfield, 23; Prestbury, 128; Stockport, 16, 56, 64, 71; Tintwistle, 87–92, 109–12, 173–5; Witton, 166
Child of the Jago, 73
childbirth, 52, 80; death in, 52, 130, 141
children, 26, 29, 37, 40–1, 60–73, 75, 76, 77; defined, 98, 129; working, 25, 44, 46, 48, 51, 72, *see also* baptism
Christian Israelites, 47
Church of England, 13–14, 17, 18, 31, 36, 45–7, 53, 66; courts, 40
civil registration, 132
Clark, Samuel, 38
Clegg, James, 38, 40, 61, 64, 66–7
coal industry, coal mining, 15, 16, 23, 45, 51, 53, 56, 58–9, 78
Cobbold, Richard, 78
Colquhoun, Patrick, 42
common-law marriage, 36–7, 46, 118, 120, 140, 161–2
community reconstitution, 104, 107–12

Compton census, 94
computerisation, 106–8, 112, 134, 142, 144
constables' accounts, 124
contraception, 39, 59
copyhold tenure, 33, 64, 155
Corn Laws, repeal (1846), 27
Cotchett, Thomas, 23
cottagers, 15, 22, 42, 137
Cotton Famine, 57, 69
cotton industry, see manufacture
crisis mortality, 130–1, 142
Crompton, Samuel, 23
Culpeper's Herbal, 59
Cumberland, 94, 170

Daniel, Alexander, 16, 42, 64
death, 20, 77; cause of, 129–31; see also burial
demography, 3, 83
depositions, 124–5
Derbyshire, Ashford, 17; Ashbourne, 107; Cromford, 23; Derby, 23; Glossop, 17, 58, 91; Peak Forest, 45
desertion, 52–3
Devonshire, Appledore, 97; Bridford, 198; Colyton, 125, 133, 138, 143–4, 198; Dawlish, 198; Hartland, 198; Ippleden, 198
Disraeli, Benjamin, 25–6
Dissent see Nonconformity
divorce, 36, 52
Dorset, 69; Puddletown, 104
dowries, 32–3, 35
drunkenness, 37, 70
Durham, 69; Stanhope, 124; Wickham, 198

Easter books, 194
education 63, 73, 76; Acts (1876, 1893, 1902, 1918), 73
electoral registers, 84, 111
emigration, 42
enclosure, 15, 22, 43
Engels, Friedrich, 25, 57
engineering, 23, 45
Essay on Population, 19
Essex, 16; Ealing, 95, 99, 100–1, 176–7;

Great Oakley, 142, 198; Terling, 126, 137–8, 140, 144, 198
estate records, 108
extended family, 93, 97, 99, 108, 154, 164–6, 168

Factory Acts (1833, 1844, 1845, 1847, 1850), 27, 44, 58, 72
Factory and Workshop Act (1891), 58
family history, defined, 1–9
family reconstitution, 132–44, 198–9
famine, 22
Federation of Family History Societies (FFHS), 1, 8, 171; News & Digest, 171
Ferriar, Dr J., 25
fertility, 20–1, 31, 42, 59, 67
Five hundred points of good husbandry, 34
flax-breaking, 65
Fox, Will, 40
friendly societies, 50
funerals, 77

Gaskell, Peter, 75–6
Gaynam, parson of the Fleet, 45
genealogy, defined, 1–3
gentry, 13, 17, 29–31, 48, 74, 137–8
Girls' Public Day Schools Company, 49
Glorious Revolution, 18
Gloucestershire, Forest of Dean, 16
Goddard, Thomas, 78
Godfrey's Cordial, 70
Gough, Richard, 17
governesses, 49
Greg, W. R., 59
guilds, 14, 76

Hampshire, 69; Odiham 198
hand-loom weavers, 54, 56, 167
Hardwick, Elizabeth, Countess of Shrewsbury, 17, 75
Hardwicke's Marriage Act (1753), 46–7, 120
harvest year, 118
Hearth Tax, 86–94, 137–8, 174–5
Herefordshire, 51
heriot, 77, 155
Hertfordshire, Aldenham, 89, 138, 198
Higson, John, 52–4

History of Myddle, 37
Hodgkins, Thomas, 37
honeymoon, 49, 55
Hopkinson, Katharine, 49
house dating, 109–10
house repopulation, see community
   reconstitution
households, defined, 98; size, 92–3
husbandry, husbandmen, 14, 15, 137

illegitimacy, 5–6, 46, 51, 56–7, 59, 67,
   70, 95, 112, 128–9, 139–41, 161–3,
   168
infanticide, 52, 130
infertility, 139
International Genealogical Index (IGI),
   102, 125, 135, 140–1, 162–3, 166,
   169
Interregnum, 18
Introduction to English historical demography,
   6
inventories, 89, 156
Irish, 69–70, 124
Italians, 70

Jackson v. Jackson (1891), 55
Jews, Jewish, 46, 70, 120, 169
jointure, 33, 75
Justices of the Peace, 14, 46, 51

Kent, Ash 198
Kilvert, Francis, 51–2, 71–2
King, Gregory, 15, 28–9, 42, 91, 94, 96,
   157, 180

Lancashire, 43, 50, 54–8, 63–4, 69, 92,
   138, 142; Ashton-in-Makerfield,
   65; Ashton-under-Lyne, 47;
   Billinge, 118, 122, 195–6;
   Blackburn, 58, 62, 71; Bolton, 47;
   Bury, 62; Cartmel, 115; Cheetham,
   Manchester, 70; Cockerham, 62;
   Croston, 103, 181–94; Culcheth,
   46; Denton, 55–6; Droylsden,
   52–4; Hawkshead, 115, 198;
   Heaton Norris, 129; Langho, near
   Blackburn, 56; Liverpool, 13, 70,
   73; Manchester, 13, 25, 44, 55, 64,

70, 169; Padiham, 62; Pendle, 64;
   Preston, 58, 71, 98–9, 104, 123, 155,
   164, 167; Prestwich, 62; Rivington,
   near Bolton, 56; Rossendale, 64; St
   Helens, 25–6, 58; Salford, 70;
   Trawden, 64; Ulverston, 115;
   Urswick, 121
landowners, landed, 15, 26, 43
Land Tax (1692), 84, 94
Langford, widow, 37
Latter-Day Saints, Church of, 147, 169
lay subsidies, 94
Lee, Ann, 47
Leicestershire, 69, 108; Bottesford, 126,
   198; Leicester, 70; Shepshed, 126,
   138, 198
Liberal Government (1906), 27
life expectancy, 21, 37, 133
Lincolnshire, Gainsborough, 198
list, defined 85; analysis of, 86–94
listing, defined 85; analysis of, 95–102
Local Historian, 172
local history, defined, 4–5
Local Population Studies, 7, 97, 148, 172
lodgers, 90, 98, 101, 115, 123
Lombe, John and Sir Thomas, 23
London, 6, 13, 16, 43, 45, 72, 92, 101,
   122–3, 129, 139, 158, 169;
   Finsbury, 69; St James
   Clerkenwell; 198; Quakers, 198
Lowe, Roger, 65–8
Luddism, 27

Malthus, T. R., 19–21, 47, 59
manorial courts, courts leet, 14
manufacture, domestic, 23–4, 50, 53–4,
   56, 78; factory, 23–6, 44–5, 53–4,
   57–9
Markham, Archbishop, 125, 166
marling, 65
marriage, 20–1, 26, 29, 30–59, 156–9;
   age of, 41–8, 102, 120–1, 128, 131,
   133, 137–9, 141–3, 151, 156–60;
   allegations 121, 124, 166; analysis
   of 119–24; clandestine, 45–6;
   horizons 122–4, 139; licences 119
Marriage Duty Acts (1696–1705), 74, 92,
   94, 118, 120

Married Women's Property Acts (1870, 1882), 55
Martindale, Adam, 61, 67
Methodists, Methodism, 53, 117
Middlesex, Hayes, 96
militia rolls, 138
Mines Act (1842), 56
mobility, 93, 102, 144, 154, 166–7; analysis of, 122–6
mortality, 20–1; infant 25, 61–2, 68–71; child 25, 61–2
mortuary, 77
Mothering Sunday, 72
multipliers, 91–2
Municipal Corporations Act (1835), 27
muster rolls, 94

National Insurance Act (1911), 80
National Register, 84
Newcome, Henry, 38, 62
Newman, Dr G., 69
newspapers, 108
new year ('New Year's Day'), 118, 133
Nightingale, Florence, 49
Nonconformists, Nonconformity, 47, 53, 117, 135–6, 140
Norfolk, 16, 50, 104
Northamptonshire, Cogenhoe, 18, 115, 126
Northumberland, Earsdon, 198
Nottinghamshire 90–1, 143; Clayworth, 83, 88, 96, 98–9, 126; Fledborough, 121; Gedling, 198; Hockerton, 101; Laxton, 90
nuclear family, 24, 97, 164

old age, 76–9
Old Age Pensions Act (1908), 79–80, 167–8
Owenites, 47
Oxfordshire, 46, 51, 71; Banbury, 199; Bletchington, 199; Chesterton, 199; Hamptongay, 199; Hamptonpyl, 199; Islip, 199; Kirtlington, 199; Liddington, 199; Lower Heyford, 199; Middleton Stoney, 199; Rousham, 199; Shipton, 199; Tackley, 199; Weston, 199

Paine, Thomas, 47
Paris, 6
parish registers, 56, 89, 113–44, 169–70; tests for suitability, 114–19, 134–6
Parliamentary franchise (1867, 1884, 1918), 27
paupers, pauperism, 15, 42, 68, 69
pedigree charts, 120–1, 130, 159–60
Pepys, Samuel, 34
police records, 108
poll books, 111
Poll Tax, 94, 98–9
Poor Law (1601, 1603), 14–15, 26, 32, 35, 36, 47–8, 52–3, 68, 76, 79; Amendment Act (1834), 27, 48; Guardians, 167–8
population growth, 14–15, 19–21, 24, 41–2
population pyramid, 95, 100, 177
Potter, Beatrix, 49
poverty cycle, 79
pre-nuptial pregnancy, 51
Presbyterians, 61, 94, 101
presentments, 141, 163
Price, Richard, 92, 133
probate records, 138, 152–6
projects, organisation of, 105–7, 114–19, 135–7, 141–2; publication of, 119, 170–2
property, 29–30
Protestation, 94, 101
Puritans, 33, 35

Quakers, 34, 46, 88, 117, 120, 198–9
Quarter Sessions Courts, 17

Reform Act (1832), 27
Reformation, 18, 76
Registrar-General, 133, 168
religious census (1851), 111
Restoration, 18, 43
Roman Catholics, 47, 117, 135–6
Rowntree, B. Seebohm, 79

Scots, 69–70, 124
seasonality, of baptisms, 127–8; of

burials, 129–31; of marriages, 120
servants, service, 28–9, 43, 45, 49, 51, 64,
    71, 90, 100–1, 104, 115, 123–4, 126,
    140, 165; taxes on (1777, 1785),
    74–5.
Settlement Act (1662), 14, 77
settlement certificates, 124
sexuality, 38–9
Shaking Quakers, 47
Shropshire, Myddle, 17, 37, 39–40;
    Wem, 62
silk industry, see manufacture
Skinner, John, 51–2, 71
smallholders, 15, 22, 64
Small Towns Project, 123, 167
solitaries, 74, 101–2, 144, 154, 167
Somerset, 16, 39, 50–1, 71
Southcott, Joanna, 47
spinsterhood, 49, 88, 99
spousals, see common-law marriage
Staffordshire, 69; Eccleshall, 199;
    Trentham, 130; Wolverhampton,
    70
stang riding, 55–6
starvation, 131
Suffolk, 16, 50; Lowestoft, 199;
    Thurleston, 199; Wortham, 78
Surrey, 69; Reigate, 199
Sussex, 50
swaddling, 60, 62

Talbot, George, Earl of Shrewsbury, 77
Thompson, Flora, 51, 71
tithe maps, schedules, 107–9
total reconstitution, 143–4
trade unionism, 27
transport, 22, 24
tuition bonds, 153
Turner, Thomas, 37
Tusser, Thomas, 34

Tyler, William, 40
Tyndale, Thomas, 76
Tyne valley, 16

under-registration, 104, 115–16, 130,
    136, 139

vagrants, vagrancy, 15–16, 18, 42
Vaughan, John, 39
Views of Frankpledge, 94

Wales, 105
Warwickshire, 69; Alcester, 199;
    Austrey, 199; Birmingham, 13, 124;
    Chilvers Coton, 78; Edgbaston, 108
weaning, 159
wet nursing, 62
weddings, 35–6, 45–6, 49–50, 55
Westmorland, 69, 170
widowhood, widows, 34–5, 53, 75, 77,
    88, 95, 99, 119, 121, 139, 153, 156,
    167–8; widowers 37, 74–5
wills, 33, 34, 76, 77, 89, 152–6
Wiltshire, 16, 50, 69
Window Tax (1696–1852), 94
wives, working, 25, 57–9; sale of, 52–3
women, working, 25, 44, 48, 57–9, 68–9
Wood, Alice, 40
Wood, Peter, 40
Worcestershire, Powick, 136, 138;
    Worcester, 123, 143
World we have lost, The, 6, 82, 83

yeomanry, yeomen, 13, 15, 17, 48, 74
Yorkshire, 121–2; East Riding, 69; West
    Riding, 16, 50; Birkstall, 199; Great
    Ayton, 199; Methley, 115, 138, 199;
    Middlesbrough, 105; Rothwell,
    115; Skipton, 125; York, 16